Embedded Systems
Programming
in C and Assembly

EMBEDDED SYSTEMS PROGRAMMING

in C and ASSEMBLY

John Forrest Brown

VNR VAN NOSTRAND REINHOLD
New York

Copyright © 1994 by Van Nostrand Reinhold

Library of Congress Catalog Card Number 93-33553
ISBN 0-442-01817-7

I(T)P Van Nostrand Reinhold is an International Thomson Publishing company.
       ITP logo is a trademark under license.

Printed in the United States of America.

Van Nostrand Reinhold
115 Fifth Avenue
New York, NY 10003

International Thomson Publishing Germany
Königswinterer Str. 418
53227 Bonn
Germany

International Thomson Publishing
Berkshire House,168-173
High Holborn, London WC1V 7AA
England

International Thomson Publishing Asia
221 Henderson Building #05–10
Singapore 0315

Thomas Nelson Australia
102 Dodds Street
South Melbourne 3205
Victoria, Australia

International Thomson Publishing Japan
Kyowa Building, 3F
2-2-1 Hirakawacho
Chiyoda-Ku, Tokyo 102
Japan

Nelson Canada
1120 Birchmount Road
Scarborough, Ontario
M1K 5G4, Canada

ARCFF 16 15 14 13 12 11 10 9 8 7 6 5 4 3 2

Library of Congress Cataloging in Publication Data

Brown, John Forrest, 1941-
    Embedded systems programming in C and assembly / John Forrest Brown.
    p. cm.
    Includes bibliographical references and index.
    ISBN 0-442-01817-7
    1. Embedded computer systems—Programming. 2. C (Computer program language) I. Title.
QA76.73.C15B764   1993
005.13'3—dc20   93-33553
                                                                        CIP

CONTENTS

PREFACE

This book is intended as a practical guide for people interested in embedded systems software development projects. Whether the reader is a hardware guru, a software professional, or an engineering manager, there should be something of value found in the following pages. The text presents concepts, basic knowledge, and common problems that apply across the board in developing embedded systems software in C language. In constructing such systems, the use of assembly language is a normally required tradition; and this book uses assembly as it is often implemented in the "real world."

A basic understanding of hardware function is required of embedded-systems programmers, but attempts have been made to keep transparent those things that are easily transparent from the programmer's perspective. Where feasible and considered useful, pertinent programming examples have been included. Most embedded systems software is device-specific and project-specific, but the source code contained in this text has been selected for its potential reusability as software templates. Because of the project-specific nature of each embedded system, the code examples contained herein are not intended as "plug and go" programs, but rather as "patterns" or "templates" that can be tailored to similar, but unique, situations.

There is no programming arena more professionally satisfying than the design and development of realtime embedded systems software; however, until now, information directly addressing embedded systems programming in C language has been scattered. In providing others with a single practical reference that might preclude learning a few lessons the hard way, this book contains experientially acquired information directly related to embedded systems software development. If this book helps an individual to construct embedded software differently, or helps to shortcut the embedded systems learning process, it has served its purpose. If it provides software templates pertinent to a given project, or provides someone with better insight into the embedded systems software development process, it has also served its purpose.

The process of creating a manuscript is an intensely individual effort, but it is doubtful that many have done it alone. I would like to thank Dr. Lu Penn, President of Penn-Point Computing, Athens, Georgia, for his input during the process, and Mr. Jim McDonald, President of JMT Technologies, Niceville, Florida, for the same reason.

Several friends at Eglin Air Force Base, Florida, contributed personal time and resources in assisting with uncompensated research for specific topics, and I thank them as well: Mr. Fred Davis, an unusually competent engineering manager for whom I have worked, and currently the technical adviser to the USAF Armament Test Laboratories, Flight Vehicles Branch; Mr. Clifford Boyce and Mr. Ralph Wade, outstanding engineers assigned to the USAF 3246th Test Wing.

A part-time Florida neighbor, Mr. Tom Prestwood, Sensors Program Manager, for the U.S. Army Defense Missile Command, contributed ideas for specific wording while reviewing initial versions of the text.

Mr. Neil Levine, the publisher's Senior Editor for Computer Science, saw merit in the initial concept and had faith in an unpublished author. I thank him for that, and for his assistance throughout the publishing process.

The manuscript was transformed into a book quickly, and in a pleasant fashion, thanks to the dedicated efforts of Chris Grisonich, the publisher's Production Editor. She coordinated major activities from editing, proofing, and typesetting, to diskette duplication—and in record time.

Rev. H.P. Hosey and his wife, Mindy, of Winnsboro, Texas, continue to contribute prayers and good wishes toward the book's commercial success (for acknowledgment by a much higher power).

Capt. Don Loren Hunter, USN, Supply Corps, Retired, of Lynden, Washington, who is a computer game freak, and who is the masterful military logistician who conceived, engineered, and implemented logistical concepts that ultimately proved highly successful in Operation Desert Storm, reviewed early versions of the book, and offered excellent suggestions that were incorporated into the text.

Finally and most of all, I thank my wife who tolerated my extremely long hours and sometimes ungodly temperament, and my son for his constructive criticism and creative editorial support.

1

Embedded Systems Concepts

WHAT *IS* AN EMBEDDED SYSTEM ANYWAY?

Typically, embedded systems are microcomputer systems with software self-contained in Read Only Memory (ROM) and without a readily-recognizable software operating system. In essence, the programmer has written a specialized operating system in the process of making the hardware function. Embedded systems are most often "dedicated" microprocessor environments with single functional utilization. Frequently, the systems are "black boxes" associated with manufacturing equipment, process control devices, or similar industrial hardware. These boxes generally provide the common benefits of directing, controlling, or monitoring specific functions of specific devices. They all contain microcomputer systems with software that is totally ROM-based, and they usually have programmable interfaces. The capabilities of individual systems, the devices attached, and the methods of gathering information from the operator and of disseminating information to the operator (operator/interface), are ostensibly unique, but have similar conceptual and technical characteristics.

With these common traits revealed, there is still no way to precisely define those systems that fall into the embedded category. A comprehensive and concise definition of embedded systems probably does not exist. Even the United States Department of Defense does not attempt definition within its series of "Military Standard" publications. If the operating system were removed from a typical personal computer (PC), and all the programs that were to be executed in a given environment were made to reside in ROM, then the modified PC might be considered an embedded system with processing dedicated to predetermined functions, but this is a stretch.

Better examples are found inside consumer products. Many American homes have microwave ovens, dishwashers, security systems, audiovisual entertainment centers, or communications equipment that use programmable embedded systems to monitor or control these units. The owner can "program" features of the device via touch panels, buttons, or hand-held remote controllers to accomplish a desired end, and the system does the rest. Some controlled operations are sequential, some are timed, and some are one-shot commands to the equipment.

Most new automobiles contain a computer "brain" which is an embedded system that has been encapsulated within a silicon or epoxy compound to provide a small electronic "brick." Using sensors within the gasoline metering system, this brick-brain can monitor and massage gasoline flow rates and provide an instantaneous display to the driver. The display can indicate the current consumption (miles per gallon to be anticipated) under the existing driving conditions. If the driver depresses or releases the accelerator, the display is updated instantly to the changed conditions. The brain can also provide other information such as the current state of door locks, seat belts, and leveling of the vehicle if the load shifts. This information can be displayed visually and/or audibly depending on how the system hardware is designed and programmed.

In the industrialized sector, modern plants have a number of electronic boxes controlling and monitoring many different types of machinery and equipment. Very often the controls are built as integral parts of specialized manufacturing devices or systems. Virtually all of these controlling units are embedded systems made by companies who are expert in specific manufacturing technologies.

WHY NOT USE A PC INSTEAD?

Obviously, a personal computer with an operating system can be configured to accomplish anything attributable to an embedded system. Ultimate cost, physical size, environmental life, anticipated quantities, and component availability are frequently overriding considerations. All design factors must be weighed by the product team at the highest level when committing to an embedded approach.

Some decisions are straightforward. It would hardly be practical or desirable or cost effective to use a "ruggedized" PC under the hood of an automobile. It would also be a tremendous waste of computer processing power. The functions currently addressed commercially by automobile brick-brains can be performed with less-powerful processors and inexpensive components. Very large quantities of the brick are distributed. The entire encapsulated unit (built to withstand relatively high under-the-hood temperatures and built even smaller than the average PC diskette drive) can be replaced at the retail level for several hundred dollars—roughly ten times less than the average PC cost on today's market.

On the other hand, well-respected American companies are making what may prove to be incredibly costly decisions while venturing into the microcomputer age for the sake of long-term survival. For example, one old-line manufacturer of production-line spray equipment has enjoyed a premier reputation for many years. They were relatively late entries into the micro age, but in 1988 unveiled their most complex microprocessor control ever. The "black box" is totally custom designed and is rather large at roughly 16 cubic feet. It has heated fluid routes including material hoppers, pumps, spray guns, and fluid lines. It has very fine controls and many additional features that include multilingual support, circuitry fault determination, interlocks, and other highly desirable bells and whistles. It is a well-designed, well-constructed, and currently viable system within their target markets.

However, in this new age of global competition, streamlining of corporations, and the need to eliminate waste and reinvention of the wheel, this apparent success should be carefully reviewed at the highest corporate level and with focus on the long-term. Astronomical resources are required to bring such a specialized and sophisticated product to market. Anticipated quantities to be sold are not massive. Eventually, some enterprising integrator may decide to design the necessary spray component modules to easily attach to a PC as the controlling unit. Off-the-shelf specialized boards could be used as adapter interfaces in many instances. The net result could be that the same spray-control benefits could be achieved at a substantially cheaper retail price with even greater features obtainable via prevalent operating systems and the evolving PC world. The upstarts with the PC-based spray controllers could knock the socks off the old-line boys touting their totally custom (and far less versatile) spray box.

In this case, it appears that minimal cost and optimum design could be achieved with a PC and a versatile, pre-emptive, multitasking operating system. In addition, the PC approach would provide the requisite interoperability and flexibility to accommodate the fast-paced evolution of computer technologies, as well as the slower, but ultimately ensuing, evolution of customer requirements. Considerations of this nature may prove to be a real concern for manufacturers of specialized equipment in many industrial areas.

A TYPICAL EMBEDDED SYSTEM

Embedded systems are used in a vast array of applications across many industries; however, most that will be encountered by consultants and others outside a specific market environment will be of a control nature for plant floor equipment or process control. Manufacturers of less complex, small systems seldom ask for help outside their organizations. Those who deal in larger and more complex systems frequently have other engineering focus, greater workloads, and a myriad of other reasons to ask for occasional outside help.

Technically, there are prevalent and common characteristics of embedded systems. From a programmer's perspective the following components are a minimum: Central Processing Unit (CPU), Random Access Memory (RAM), Programmable Read Only Memory (PROM) or Erasable PROM (EPROM), and Input/Output (I/O) space.

Since many embedded systems contain time-critical functions, another of ten-essential component is one or more system timers. Timer units are available in a variety of commercial forms. For boxes built around the VME or STD system bus architectures, timers are frequently included as features of CPU boards manufactured for these systems, or as separate specialized "timer boards." CPUs sometimes provide timers for programming purposes; Intel's 80186, for example, has three.

Device interaction is the sole reason for the system's existence, so application-specific devices are also ultimate system essentials. One or more devices will be used for operator interaction with the system (operator interface). All devices will be attached to the system via the I/O space. From the programmer's perspective, a baseline embedded system is shown in Figure 1-1.

Obviously, the devices above can vary drastically from environment to environment. For the spray equipment mentioned earlier, there might be multiple heaters, pumps, indicator lights, and interlocks as a minimum. A serial communications interface could allow remote configuration, and certainly a display and keypad would be required. Feedback from a conveyer could allow automatic adjustment of pump pressure for varying production-line speeds. For a carpet metering and cutting machine, there could be multiple photo eyes and conveyer motors. A measuring wheel, a cutting mechanism, a display, and a keypad would be desirable. Several serial communications interfaces could allow centralized reporting and/or bar-coded inputs for preprinted orders.

Operator interfaces are equally disparate devices. Control boxes for large plant floor machinery sometimes use serial interfaces to giant high-resolution color screens sporting Carroll infrared touch technology. The huge physical size allows a single individual in the plant to monitor several machines from a comfortable distance. Stand-alone embedded units typically have small keypads and small liquid crystal diode (LCD) displays that show only a few lines of text, or only a single text line of a few characters. This allows more economical construction when feasible. For further economy under the right circumstances, interfaces may even be digital switches for operator input with only indicator lights for problem determination.

Regardless of the devices used in the system, the programmer will be required

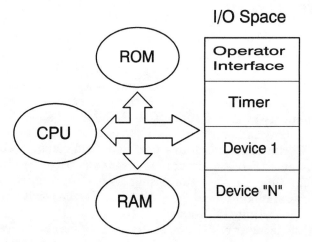

Figure 1-1. Baseline Embedded System

to write some level of driver for each device. The depth of knowledge required for a single device will depend entirely on its purchased capabilities and system-specific implementation details.

THE UP SIDE OF EMBEDDED PROGRAMMING

It is precisely the diversity of devices and the varying depth of knowledge required about each one, that makes embedded systems programming so attractive to those who choose the field. There is a constant learning process. Fun for the initiated includes the substantial timing challenges found in the "realtime" aspects of device coordination. In addition, since computer operating systems shield programmers from many low-level functions of hardware and peripheral I/O, the programming of embedded systems requires more in-depth knowledge of how platform components function and interact than does programming under an operating system. Embedded systems programming is much closer to the hardware.

In actual practice, restraints of economy can affect the quality and capability of selected components for a given system. When organizations must require that specific system board costs do not exceed a given figure, substantial programming challenges that translate to "drudgery" sometimes ensue. As with anything, there are good and bad projects.

The makeup of excellent programmers is still an elusive compound. Some are graduate musicians and airplane pilots rather than computer engineering majors. Whatever the ingredients, they share the common trait of project dedication born of genuine interest. All enjoy savoring the fruits of their labor when, for example, a control unit does exactly what it is supposed to do. A casual observer looking at computer-controlled machinery would see only moving parts; the programmer sees the coordinated execution of each code thread performing its function. Sometimes this is reward enough; but for those programmers with a less technical bent, embedded systems programming can be a real pain. Some things are better left unknown, and, to many, this includes device details and other aspects of the field.

SPECIALIZED MICROCHIPS

Intel and other chip manufacturers are currently making families of specialized chips for the embedded systems market. Intel's MCS-48 family, for example, consists of integrated microcomputer systems. A single integrated circuit contains the processor (CPU), RAM, PROM, a timer, and I/O space—basic essentials of an embedded system. Another Intel chip family, the MCS-96, has targeted the market of high-speed control functions. The family uses 16-bit processors with on-chip features that include a high-speed I/O subsystem, EPROM, a 10-bit A/D converter, five 8-bit I/O ports, and a 16-bit watchdog timer, among other things.

More recently Intel's 80960 32-bit chip family was developed from scratch for embedded control applications. It has been touted to eliminate architectural obstacles to state-of-the-art implementation techniques that allow parallel and out-of-order instruction execution. The Intel 80960KA, for example, uses Reduced Instruction Set Computer (RISC) technology in conjunction with a 32-bit processor, and is advertised by Intel as having a 512-byte instruction cache, a built-in interrupt controller, multiple parallel execution units, and an overall capability of execution rates in excess of 9.4 million instructions per second, and these are only a subset of the touted features.

Specialized chips like these, with such advanced and attractive features, simply did not exist until very recently. Such current and rapidly unfolding technological innovations indicate that the first full step of microcomputer evolution is not yet completed. With the proliferation of microcomputer systems in general and embedded systems in particular, newer technologies addressing the unique needs of embedded systems projects will constantly emerge; but, despite advances in hardware technology, the essential techniques of programming will remain unchanged.

Hardware evolution can reduce the quantitative code required of programmers. This is easily seen when hardware evolution is visualized as the evolution of board-level products containing state-of-the-art chip sets and sophisticated firmware. Regardless, hardware evolution is not likely to change the foundational methodologies of programming in the foreseeable future, and hardware still provides the "building blocks" that are ultimately utilized by the software.

EMBEDDED OPERATING SYSTEMS

Earlier it was stated that embedded systems typically do not utilize computer operating systems. This is essentially a true statement; however, there are a number of specialized embedded operating systems currently in use. Most of these software systems could be more precisely defined as "realtime executives"—not full-blown operating systems. Frequently they are task schedulers that allow timed, pre-emptive task scheduling of large embedded systems. Sometimes they are selected with the hopes of reducing the quantitative software development required for a particular system. Occasionally, they are highly necessary supervisors of specialized systems. The most common physical trait of these systems is that they require some interface convention of programmers. Typically, primitive descriptive tables are filled in by the programmer in order to identify task properties to the operating system. The operating system will include a library of task control interface routines that must be used by the programmer as specified by the system documentation. When the compiled software modules are linked together, operating system modules are included as a part of the final, executable module.

Most of these embedded operating systems will require specified areas of RAM for task control blocks and similar management functions. Some even duplicate the interrupt vector table. Regardless, these system-specific peculiarities are always well-documented and explained. It is the programmer's responsibility to ensure no memory contention under these circumstances, and it is the hardware designer's responsibility to provide for adequate RAM quantities.

CORPORATE EMBEDDED ENVIRONMENTS

Research and Development (R&D) environments typically build embedded systems. Frequently they are staffed with hardware designers and with those who profess to be both hardware and software professionals. Invariably, those who profess to be "both" have limited experience in software design and have a real penchant for hardware; however, they are extremely valuable in envisioning the proper division of function between hardware and software, and in designing the hardware system accordingly . Hardware engineers are normally proficient in writing test code to exercise low-level aspects of their creations and to ensure that circuitry is basically correct. Lack of dedication to software as a career precludes the skill development inherent in excellent programmers. Most hardware engineers have no desire to be software professionals. In many cases, exposure to outside software professionals will uncover significant software inadequacies within engineering organizations.

Inherent to R&D environments, there is a time crunch associated with embedded systems development. A perceived window of opportunity must be met. Ideally, the programmer would be presented with fully functioning and debugged hardware at the beginning of the software cycle (much like programming a PC). Unfortunately, this will never happen. Sometimes prototype hardware is functionally tested by the hardware engineer before releasing it to software; sometimes the burden of initial hardware testing is shared. In any case, at some point following project inception, hardware and software development proceeds in parallel—the more accomplished the software engineer, the greater the initial progress with sketchy and volatile information. Obviously, substantial synergy should exist between the chief hardware engineer and the chief software engineer. There is a constant dialogue and infusion of good ideas from both parties.

Normally, embedded systems projects do not require large staffs at the build level. Textbook design approaches frequently take a back seat to approaches developed over time and with experience. Productivity is usually of paramount importance with adequacy of documentation running a close second. Nevertheless, hardware and software issues require attention throughout the life cycle of the project and product. Whatever requirements, design, and specification methodologies are used, they should be founded in good technique, and should be readily understandable by others.

Regardless of the details of project and product evolution, the programmer typically thinks in terms of making "raw" hardware function within stated design goals and requisite time frames. The more productive programmers always have an eye on modularity, constructs, and future reusability of code. The hardware is designed to accommodate a single functional utilization and is not intended for use outside these conceptual confines; however, the maximum degree of software reusability should be realized from any project. Substantial commonality of code construction can exist between embedded projects, and software architecture can be of paramount importance for both life-cycle changes and cross-project utilization.

TECHNICAL EMBEDDED ENVIRONMENTS

From the focused perspective of the programmer in finalizing executable code, the primary difference between PC code and embedded systems code lies in absolute address resolution. When C code is compiled to execute on a PC, the source code and global data (whether initialized, uninitialized, or strings) are grouped into specifically identified address segments (or sections). At link time, these segments are located relative to the program load point which will be absolutely resolved by the operating system when the program is loaded. On the other hand, embedded systems are PROM-resident at permanent memory locations. The compilation process is the same, but additional link-and-locate capabilities are required. These capabilities allow programmers to assign specific addresses to specific code and data segments during the link-and-locate process. The appropriate parts of the final module will ultimately be loaded into PROM at the predesignated locations, using hardware and software designed for that purpose. (More about this in Chapter 6.)

Cross-compilers that allow software compilation on one platform into a format compatible with a different platform are excellent programming tools that allow, for example, an Intel-based PC user to compile code for a Motorola-based embedded system.

For years a number of companies have been supplying C software development environments for embedded projects. Typically these software systems include a compiler (or cross-compiler) with the ability to rename code segments, an assembler, a link-and-locate capability, and sometimes a debugger. These development environments ensure total compatibility of object module formats with the link-and-locate software that is provided. Other companies make generic link-and-locate software for use with various C compilers. The primary differences in embedded software development products are the compiler code-generation algorithms and the flexibility of link-and-locate capabilities. Like most competing software products, virtually all will ultimately achieve the desired end. Some prove less painful than others to use.

There are two embedded systems architectural schemes most likely to be encountered by consultants on an interim basis, or most likely to be built by integrators providing custom controls to clients—those built around a VME system bus chassis using the Motorola 68xxx family of CPUs, and those built around an STD system bus chassis using Intel 80xx CPUs. Both VME bus and STD bus invite the use of multiple processors on the system bus. Both schemes enjoy a rich set of reasonably priced and commercially available board-level products to accomplish almost any desired end. By designing systems to use these off-the-shelf products, development time can be substantially reduced. This approach is particularly attractive for proof of concept, for "one-shot" development cycles, and for development of low-volume products.

SOME GROUND RULES FOR C LANGUAGE

The C code encountered in this book will follow certain conventions that reflect the prejudices of the author. On several occasions, recognized C language authorities have stated that most C programmers do not write well-constructed code. In this context, quality is a highly subjective and frequently emotional issue. Regardless of a particular programmer's style or of the particular software development environment used, there are some things that can be done to increase a given programmer's lifespan. The author opts for those things that ease his own pain:

1. All typedefs will be in capital letters (CAPS).
2. Anything defined with a #define will be in CAPS.
3. All standard C data types will be redefined using typedefs.
4. All structure definitions will be typedefs.
5. Any typedefs of pointers will end in "PTR" or "PTRF" (far).
6. Only pointers, words, and double words are local variables (strings, structures, and arrays are never on the stack).
7. All constants will be manifest constants unless they are incorporated as one-time table insertions.
8. Any error message texts will be complete with x's reserving areas to be modified prior to display.
9. Header files will never require space.
10. All major source comments will include '$' when inclusion in automatically generated flow control charts is desired.
11. All source comments describing functions will include '&' when inclusion in automatically generated calling trees is desired.
12. Exceptions to the above may be encountered.

Some of the above conventions are de facto C standards. The comment conventions '$' and '&' are software-package-specific for documentation packages currently used by the author. The above conventions can be considered a part of the author's "software standards." (Every development environment needs at least some software standards. The overall tendency is to be too restrictive in their definition. The United States government's ongoing standardization scheme of using ADA language exclusively is an extreme case in point.)

The C code encountered herein will use both "new" and "old" conventions for specifying data types of C function arguments. This gives some variety, indicates more than one compiler-specific possibility, and hopefully placates those who prefer one style over the other.

Regarding data types that will be encountered, a header file, similar to the following header excerpts, is assumed to be included among the header files for C source code examples:

```
#ifdef XINTEL                       /* If compiling for Intel    */
typedef char CHAR;                  /* 1 byte signed             */
typedef unsigned char UCHAR;        /* 1 byte unsigned           */
typedef short SHORT;                /* 2 bytes signed            */
typedef unsigned short USHORT;      /* 2 bytes unsigned          */
typedef unsigned long ULONG;        /* 4 bytes unsigned          */
typedef long LONG;                  /* 4 bytes signed            */
typedef float SFLOAT;               /* 4 bytes Intel
                                       single-precision format   */
typedef double DFLOAT;              /* 8 bytes Intel double-
                                       precision format          */

#else                               /* Compiling for Motorola    */
typedef char CHAR;                  /* 1 byte signed             */
typedef unsigned char UCHAR;        /* 1 byte unsigned           */
typedef short SHORT;                /* 2 bytes signed            */
typedef unsigned short USHORT;      /* 2 bytes unsigned          */
typedef unsigned ULONG;             /* 4 bytes unsigned          */
typedef int LONG;                   /* 4 bytes signed            */
typedef float SFLOAT;               /* 4 bytes IEEE
                                       single-precision format   */
typedef double DFLOAT;              /* 8 bytes IEEE
                                       double-precision format   */

#endif

typedef void VOID;
```

Also, for purposes here, some example programs that use multiple modules will not have those modules compiled as stand-alone modules. A single module will contain #INCLUDEs for all source modules. This makes comparisons somewhat easier, and eases the overall task of consolidating examples, but it is not a style recommended in actual practice.

Finally, there are several basic C compiler concepts that should be completely understood by programmers writing embedded systems source code:

1. Uninitialized local variables (variables defined within C functions) are always placed on the RAM stack when the code is executed. When a C function is entered, the assembly-level code usually sets some CPU register equal to the stack pointer and then accesses the function arguments and local variables as offsets from that register.

2. Processing instructions, initialized data and initialized strings, uninitialized global data, and uninitialized global strings are each grouped together in separately specified addressable areas at link time. When the code is placed into a PROM chip, these individual groups will be specifically located by the programmer to coincide with actual hardware addresses (more in Chapter 6). In embedded systems work, default data is frequently defined as initial-

ized data and is placed into PROM by the programmer. During system initialization, a routine written by the programmer will copy appropriate parts of the PROM data into RAM where it can be modified by processing code.

3. Operating-system-dependent instructions for a given compiler cannot be used in embedded systems work, because there is no operating system available. Such instructions include those that are interrupt-dependent and/or ROM-BIOS-dependent, like console and disk access. Also included are memory allocation routines like MALLOC, CALLOC, and the rest. If any of these functions are necessary for a given system, specialized routines must be written by the programmer, but these routines are seldom required.

BUT WHAT ABOUT C++?

The use of C++ for software development is proliferating, and for good reason. C++ provides a number of desirable software characteristics in a transparent fashion. Such characteristics include the source code construction concepts of "modularity," "encapsulation," "information hiding," and "data abstraction." These traits are all obtainable with C, but C++ makes their realization easier.

C++ was created by Dr. Bjarne Stroustrup in attempting to provide a language with the following features as a minimum:

- A strong conceptual framework
- Classes and class hierarchies
- Strong type checking
- High performance in executing
- Minimal memory requirements
- Portability

Since C language already provided some of these features, it became the foundation of C++. C++ was created using C, and the traditional output of C++ compilers is C. The traditional C++ compiler will check syntax and semantics, build data structures, analyze functions, and ultimately translate the C++ source code into an internal representation of C. Because of this, C++ has been incorrectly classified by some as a "preprocessor." The C++ pioneered technology is more in using C as an intermediate language than in the technology of portable front-end compilers. Regardless, from a programmer's focused perspective, it is in up-front project design methodologies and source code construction techniques that C and C++ are truly set apart.

What all of this means is that the C language-specific and embedded-systems-specific information contained in this text is directly applicable to C++. Using the concepts presented, a programmer who can write custom C++ class libraries can also program embedded systems in C++ language. The executables are virtually identical in construction, and either C or C++ would require similar start-up code in a given embedded environment. The information presented earlier about the grouping of code and data by C compilers and the necessity of the link-and-locate process are also directly applicable, as are the comments about not using operating-system-dependent instructions. Some class libraries supplied with C++ compilers are system-independent and can be used in embedded systems work.

C++ embedded software development environments are currently scarce, and engineering environments are generally pleased with the use of C. Primarily out of curiosity, some engineers are beginning to explore C++ possibilities. Until more engineering organizations become enchanted with C++, C will dominate the embedded systems world. The coding examples in this text are all written in C, but the embedded concepts and information apply directly to C++.

AN OVERVIEW OF EMBEDDED SOFTWARE

Normally there is no mass storage device such as a disk drive attached to an embedded system. The programming code is not loaded from hard disk into RAM in order to be executed by the CPU. Typically, embedded systems code is stored internally in EPROM where it can be directly read by the CPU. Constant data items are also stored in EPROMs. Volatile data items are expected to be at specified RAM addresses, and data items to be retained for indefinite periods are normally kept in nonvolatile RAM (NVRAM). NVRAM is frequently battery-backed RAM.

At system power-up, Intel-based embedded systems typically execute a single assembly language software instruction which has been placed by the programmer at a designated CPU-specific address. This instruction normally causes a code "jump" to the program starting point. The starting point would be the EPROM location of the assembly language start-up module that is necessary to initialize volatile RAM and perform other desired hardware housekeeping functions before calling the MAIN() C language function.

Motorola CPUs typically require that the initial supervisor stack pointer and program starting address be located in the first eight bytes of the interrupt vector table (memory location 0). At system power-up the stack pointer and program counter are loaded from location 0 and execution commences at the specified program counter address, which would be the location of the start-up module.

Once the start-up module has called the MAIN() C function, embedded systems code frequently becomes realtime critical and interrupt intensive. In less encountered cases, embedded systems can even be on-line. Interrupts and timing issues are addressed later, but on-line issues are not presented in this text.

Of course, in order to write the start-up module, to address any RAM or ROM contained in the system, and to communicate with any peripheral equipment, the hardware must be defined in terms that the software can understand. One of the first project communications tasks of the hardware engineer is to provide descriptive hardware information to the software engineer. This is the essential subject matter of Chapter 2, "Defining the Hardware for Software."

2

Defining the Hardware for Software

MEMORY STRUCTURE ESSENTIALS

From a programmer's perspective, the essential embedded system hardware consists of a CPU for processing, ROM (or EPROM) for code and constant data, RAM for volatile data and stack, and I/O space for accessing peripherals. RAM and ROM are considered memory space. The memory and I/O space are collectively referred to as the *memory structure*. CPU chips sometimes supply memory structure components as chip-resident features.

I/O space can be provided by the CPU or it can reside in memory. Intel processors typically provide I/O space that is separate from memory. Motorola processors typically require the use of memory-mapped I/O, which is I/O space that resides in RAM. The differences in processor memory structure are shown in Figure 2-1.

With the appropriate hardware interface, Intel's CPU-provided I/O space can also be *memory-mapped* into RAM by the hardware engineer. Memory-mapping provides additional programming flexibility, but is slightly detrimental to performance. In a system with hardware-memory-mapped I/O space, the programmer can use any instruction that references memory in order to access a port, including string instructions. In non-hardware-memory-mapped I/O space, CPU-specific conventions must be followed in order to access the ports. The memory reference instructions take more time to execute and are less compact, but this will not be a significant consideration for most applications.

In laying out the memory structure for a given system, the hardware engineer will contend with CPU-specific reserved areas of memory and I/O space. Chip manufacturers sometimes reserve several ports and ROM locations for CPU-specific implementation considerations. Some of these considerations will be pertinent to an embedded system design, and some will not. Regardless, hardware engineers will

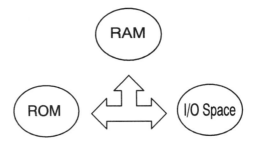

Intel 80XX Memory Structure

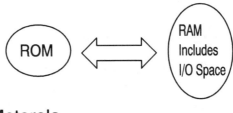

Motorola
68XXX Memory Structure

Figure 2-1. Motorola and Intel Memory Structures

usually map the memory structure with each area of RAM, PROM, and I/O space as contiguous (not necessarily contiguous with one another). There are, of course, exceptions to everything engineering-related. Valid reasons for splitting RAM address space do exist. This is noteworthy only in that split-RAM can give birth to minor problems in using the less-evolved software development systems.

The overall memory structure information required of hardware designers by programmers is a "map" of the pertinent areas as implemented. This would include the beginning and ending locations of ROM, RAM, and any memory-mapped I/O space. Specialized adapter boards used on a system bus can contain ROM or RAM or both. The starting and ending addresses for the memory space of each board should be included in the hardware map. If dual-ported RAM is used in the system, it will appear to reside at different addresses from different system perspectives, and complete information must be provided to the programmer. When memory structure components are supplied on-chip, there are normally special registers for use in indicating the starting address of each such component while hardware-mapping the system. An acceptable memory structure map is shown in Figure 2-2.

Code and data will always reside in the memory space, while peripheral devices will always reside in the I/O space. Any CPU-provided I/O space will be large. The Intel 80xx processor family provides a 64K I/O space that can accommodate up to 32,767 16-bit ports or 65,535 8-bit ports.

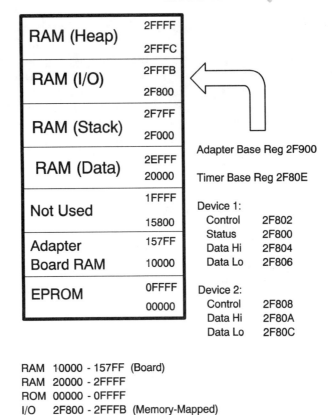

Figure 2-2. Typical System Memory Map

PORTS

Specific I/O space addresses constitute port addresses for accessing peripheral devices. Ports are the "portals" through which the CPU views the rest of the world. Peripheral devices attached via ports include timers and other system components such as displays, keypads, light-emitting diodes (LEDs), analog-to-digital (A/D) converters, and any other necessary system-specific devices. Port usage will fall into three major functional categories:

1. Control—for specifying device operational modes, or directing what the next port access will be expected to achieve
2. Status—for indicating current operational modes, port access conditions, or device error conditions
3. Data—for accepting data from, or giving data to, an attached device

Ports will be dedicated to one or more of the above functional usages, but a single port can be used for all three purposes. Further, devices attached to ports will always require at least one of the above usages, but not necessarily all three.

Port sizes are typically 8 bits or they are multiples of 16 bits. The maximum size of a port in CPU-provided I/O space is dependent on access conventions, addressing modes, and CPU register sizes. For the Intel 80xx family, such ports can vary in size from 8 to 16 bits. Memory-mapped I/O space provides greater flexibility, and port sizes are at the discretion of the hardware engineer.

Ports can be used to access more than one device, and devices can use more than one port. Ports can be either "read-only" or "write-only" ports, or they can be dual purpose. These options are generally dictated by device-specific and system-specific designs, limitations, and implementation techniques of hardware. What is important from a programming perspective is the bottom line:

1. Is the I/O space hardware-memory-mapped?
2. Which port(s) is each device using?
3. What is the function of each port?
4. What is the size of each port?
5. What is the function of each bit in each port?
6. What device-specific access criteria (if any) exist?

If the hardware engineer can accurately supply this information to the software engineer, or if the information is readily available in device-specific documentation, everyone involved with the project will live long and fruitful lives, with less of the time spent debugging, scratching for information, or screaming at one another.

ACCESSING THE DEVICE HARDWARE

In the digital computer world, all hardware access is via digital "reads" and "writes" to specific ports of the I/O space. Routines to accomplish port access are frequently supplied with C compilers. These routines are not ANSI C compliant, and some compiler-specific implementations of I/O functions are macros and some are not, and some can go either way depending on the inclusion of specific header files.

The bottom line with compiler-supplied port-access functions is that they can be considered architecture-specific. This includes INPORTB(), OUTPORTB(), INPORT(), OUTPORT(), INPW(), OUTPW(), and any other sometimes-supplied routine. All should perform satisfactorily within their normally anticipated environments, but embedded-systems programmers will occasionally be forced to write specialized routines for port access.

For example, when reading or writing to memory-mapped I/O space, custom routines would be necessary in addressing Intel-based hardware. Compiler-supplied library functions for a given Intel type compiler would typically anticipate non-memory-mapped I/O space. In this case, the custom routines required to access memory-mapped I/O would resemble the library functions normally supplied with a compiler for a Motorola-based platform:

```
/* MODULE PATH: \TEXT\PORTS1.C */
```

```
        /* --------------------------- */
        /* Routine to READ a 16-bit port */
        /* --------------------------- */
USHORT inport(USHORT *port_adr){return(*port_adr);}


        /* ---------------------------- */
        /* Routine to WRITE a 16-bit port */
        /* ---------------------------- */
VOID outport(USHORT *port_adr, USHORT value)
            {*port_adr = value; return;}


        /* ---------------------------- */
        /* Routine to READ an 8-bit port */
        /* ---------------------------- */
UCHAR inportb(UCHAR *port_adr) {return(*port_adr);}


        /* ----------------------------- */
        /* Routine to WRITE an 8-bit port */
        /* ----------------------------- */
VOID outportb(UCHAR *port_adr, UCHAR value)
            {*port_adr = value; return;}
```

Non-hardware-memory-mapped I/O space is accessed through CPU-specific conventions. The C library port-access functions supplied with a given compiler will make these conventions transparent to programmers. In rare cases, software engineers will be required to write their own port I/O C functions to follow CPU-specific conventions. In that case, intimate knowledge of the CPU chip architecture and a good knowledge of the assembly language is helpful.

Using Intel, for example, there are two I/O space access conventions dictated by two different addressing modes for the 80xx family. The size of the port being accessed is always taken from the size of the specified accumulator. At the assembly level, the first 256 ports (0–255) can be accessed directly by using an 8-bit immediate operand:

```
IN al,06h      ;Place a byte from port 6 hex into the lower
               ;8 bits of the ax accumulator register (al)

OUT 08h,ax     ;Output 16 bits from register ax to port 8 hex
```

Any of the 65,535 possible ports can be accessed by indirect port addressing:

```
IN al,dx       ;Place a byte from the port whose number is
               ;contained in register dx into the lower
               ;8 bits of accumulator register ax (al)

OUT dx,ax      ;Output the 16 bits contained in register ax to
               ;the port whose number is contained in register
               ;dx
```

These conventions must be incorporated into port access outines for this Intel family's CPU-supplied I/O space. Intel-specific I/O routines, written in C and using a compiler that allows in-line assembly instructions, might look like this:

```
/* MODULE PATH: \TEXT\PORTS2.C */
#include <\cp\newdat.h>

    /* ------------------------------------- */
    /* Routine to output a byte to an 8-bit port */
    /* ------------------------------------- */

VOID outportb(portaddr,value)

USHORT  portaddr;        /* absolute port address          */
UCHAR value;             /* 1 byte value to output         */
{
    asm push dx          /* save registers                 */
    asm push ax

    asm mov dx,portaddr /* port address to dx              */
    asm mov al,value     /* byte value to al               */
    asm out dx,al        /* output the value to the port */

    asm pop ax           /* restore the registers saved   */
    asm pop dx

    return;              /* return to calling function    */
}


    /* ------------------------------------- */
    /* Routine to input a byte from 8-bit port */
    /* ------------------------------------- */

UCHAR inportb(portaddr)
USHORT portaddr;         /* absolute port address          */
{
UCHAR value;
    asm push dx          /* save registers                 */
    asm push ax

    asm mov dx,portaddr /* port address to dx              */
    asm in al,dx         /* input byte from port           */
    asm mov value,al     /* move byte to local var         */

    asm pop ax           /* restore saved registers        */
    asm pop dx
```

```
            return(value); /* return the 8-bit value      */
    }


            /* ------------------------------- */
            /* Output routine for a 16-bit port */
            /* ------------------------------- */

    VOID outport(portaddr,value)
    USHORT portaddr;        /* absolute port address       */
    USHORT value;           /* 16-bit value to output      */
    {
        asm push dx         /* save registers              */
        asm push ax

        asm mov dx,portadd  /* port address to dx          */
        asm mov ax,value    /* 16-bit value to ax          */
        asm out dx,ax       /* output the value to the port */

        asm pop ax          /* restore the registers saved */
        asm pop dx

        return;             /* return to calling function  */
    }


        /* ------------------------------- */
        /* Input routine for a 16-bit port */
        /* ------------------------------- */

    USHORT inport(portaddr)
    USHORT portaddr;        /* absolute port address       */
    {
    USHORT value;
        asm push dx         /* save registers              */
        asm push ax

        asm mov dx,portaddr /* port address to dx          */
        asm in ax,dx        /* input 16 bits from port     */
        asm mov value,ax    /* move ax to local variable   */

        asm pop ax          /* restore saved registers     */
        asm pop dx

        return(value);      /* return the 16-bit value     */
    }
```

The format and methodology used to incorporate in-line assembly instructions is compiler-specific. The above examples would likely need modification for use with a given C compiler. For example, some compilers require semicolons at the end of each assembly instruction, some require brackets around a group of instructions, and some require both. Regardless, if programmers write C routines containing in-line assembly such as those shown above, an assembly-language listing of the module should be double-checked in order to ensure that the final code is doing exactly what is expected. The transparent use of registers by C language can produce results not anticipated by the programmer, and this includes any reference to C-defined variables by assembly language instructions.

Sometimes the magnitude of values required to or from a device can exceed the port size. In this case, multiple port accesses are used to grab the desired data. For example, if a 16-bit value were required to or from a device in a system with all ports defined as 8-bit, two accesses (one each to two consecutive ports) would be required in order to put or grab the 16-bit value. Using the lower-level I/O routines specified above, a special routine might be written to address the problem for all pertinent devices in a given system:

```
/* MODULE PATH: \TEXT\PORTS3.C */
#include <\cp\newdat.h>

                /* ------------------------------- */
                /* Get 16 data bits from device X */
                /* ------------------------------- */

USHORT Get_16bits_devicex(USHORT high_byte_port,
                          USHORT lo_byte_port)
{
USHORT value_in;
USHORT work_area;

   work_area = inportb(high_byte_port);   /*$ READ hi byte       */

   value_in = inportb(lo_byte_port);      /*$ READ lo byte       */

   value_in |= (work_area << 8);          /*$ OR the 2 together  */

   return(value_in);                      /*$ RETURN 16bit value */
}


                /* ------------------------------- */
                /* Write 16 data bits to device X */
                /* ------------------------------- */

VOID Put_16bits_devicex(USHORT high_byte_port,
                        USHORT lo_byte_port,
                        USHORT value_out)
{
```

```
UCHAR value8;

    value8 = (value_out >> 8);          /*$ ISOLATE hi byte    */

    outportb(high_byte_port, value8);   /*$ PUT hi byte         */

    value8 = (value_out << 8) >> 8;     /*$ ISOLATE lo byte     */

    outportb(lo_byte_port, value8);     /*$ PUT lo byte         */

    return;                             /*$ RETURN              */
}
```

A/D CONVERTERS

In the digital computer world, all CPU access to external devices is via digital "reads" and "writes" to specific ports of the I/O space. Analog devices are typically connected to ports via *A / D converters*. When reading an A/D converter, the analog value from the device is converted to a digital value that is available at the port as input from the CPU's perspective. When writing to an A/D converter, the digital output is written to the appropriate port, and is converted to analog device input from the device's perspective.

Device-specific access criteria are frequently encountered in accessing A/D converters, and multiple port operations can be required to obtain a single value. Using a hypothetical 16-bit A/D with a single read/write port for example, the high-order bit could be a "request" bit, the next highest bit could be a "conversion error" indicator, and the sign bit could have been moved to the third highest. This "example" A/D is designed to handle decimal values between 8,191 and –8,191 and negative values are expected. Using a "write port" function, the programmer might be required to "set" the high-order bit in order to indicate to the A/D that a value is desired. The setting of this bit would be the signal to the A/D to "latch" the analog value present on the analog device side, and to start converting the value to digital. Assuming a slow A/D, a delay of up to 30 milliseconds (ms) could be required in order to convert the maximum-sized number handled by the A/D. The length of time to pause before attempting to grab the value would be determined by the programmer within the context of the overall system timing requirements. After some pause, the value is read and the high-order bit's state is checked. If it is reset, then the conversion has been completed. If it is still set, then the conversion has not yet finished, and another pause is required prior to attempting to see the value again. Once a "good" read is obtained, the second-highest-order bit is checked. If it is set, then there was a conversion error. The value should not be used and the process must be repeated. If the error bit is reset, there was no error and the value can be used. The sign bit of the value read (the third-highest-order bit) could be extended through the highest order bit to get a signed 16-bit value.

The average case here is that the value grabbed would be roughly 20 to 40ms old, depending on the average magnitude of the values encountered. This hypothetical low-end A/D would not be used in highly time-critical or state-of-the-art hardware; however, the description accurately portrays access considerations that can be encountered by hardware-level programmers. The machinations shown in order to get a simple value are of typical complexity; the details will vary and are device-specific. Regardless, any device purchased will have very clear documentation regarding its use. Always, the bottom line for programmers is to determine how, and in what sequence and time frame, to "get" and "put" digital values from/to a port.

A flow diagram for accessing the above A/D, as described, is shown in Figure 2-3; however, it will been seen in Chapter 5 that an actual implementation would require the interaction and synchronization of several code threads. To preclude other processing for 20 to 40 milliseconds while waiting for a given value would not be acceptable in most environments.

SOFTWARE-MAPPING THE MEMORY STRUCTURE

Memory structure addresses are assigned by the hardware engineer in the design and build process. The physical locations of RAM and memory-mapped I/O space will be at the engineer's discretion within the limitations of the hardware

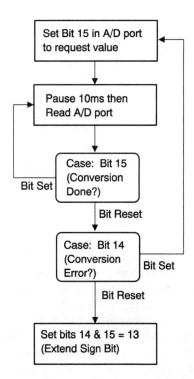

Figure 2-3. Flow Diagram for Hypothetical A/D Access

being used. The separate I/O space that is sometimes CPU-provided will start at location zero within that space. In all cases, the hardware engineer will assign specific I/O port addresses to specific devices.

A classic C language approach to defining the memory structure for software purposes is to map the structure in software using manifest constants contained in a header file. When using this approach in parallel-build efforts, memory-mapping with bogus address constants is still possible prior to actual address finalization. The correct addresses can be filled in at a single physical point in the header module when they are known. Code can be written and compiled error-free (even if no further testing can be done). Everyone knows that any testing with a bogus memory map structure is a sure way to make the entire system crash.

There is seldom any need to software-map the PROM area for programming purposes. This area is normally contiguous and extends from absolute location 0 to whatever size(s) of EPROMs are used. A single 64K EPROM would require that locations 0 to hexadecimal ffff be reserved for PROM-resident code and constant data. Adding a second 64K EPROM would extend the PROM area to hex address 1ffff. When the appropriate code and data items are loaded into PROMs at their predetermined locations, there is no further information required by the software; therefore, software-mapping would be superfluous.

Obviously, RAM must start outside the ROM area but can end at any point within the addressability limitations of the processor being used. For hardware upgrade purposes in environments that anticipate substantial future enhancements, there will always be large unused areas of space between ROM, RAM, and I/O space. If nonvolatile RAM (NVRAM) is used in the system, it is usually contiguous with RAM in that there are no realistic arguments for splitting the two. Hardware-memory-mapped I/O space is reserved contiguously in memory and extends as far as necessary. Non-hardware-memory-mapped I/O space is entirely separate from memory.

RAM is not fully software-mapped for programming purposes. As will be seen in Chapter 3, the "start-up" module will want to know the beginning and ending points of memory that it will initialize; but specific RAM locations are referenced logically by the code and do not normally require additional software-mapping. Allocation of existing RAM for software purposes, which would include an allocation for stack space, is the programmer's responsibility.

I/O space is typically software-mapped in great detail, whether or not it has been hardware-mapped to memory. Pertinent bit-specific information within each port is also mapped in detail, and these bit patterns are normally referred to as masks.

EXAMPLES OF SOFTWARE MEMORY-MAPPING

If the carpet metering-and-cutting machine mentioned earlier were reduced to a few devices, it might be software-mapped like this for a non-hardware-memory-mapped system using an Intel CPU:

```
/* -------------------------------------------------------- */
/* ROM Limits -- All code & constant data is in EPROM here */
/* -------------------------------------------------------- */

#define ROMSTART     0x0          /* ROM beginning address   */
#define ROMEND       0xffff       /* ROM final address (64K) */


/* ----------------------------------------------- */
/* RAM Limits -- All volatile data is in RAM here */
/* ----------------------------------------------- */

#define RAMSTART     0x100001     /* RAM start address       */
#define RAMEND       0x1ffffl     /* RAM final address (64k) */

/* ------------------------------------------------------- */
/* IO Space Map -- 8-bit ports, non-memory-mapped          */
/* ------------------------------------------------------- */

        /* LCD Display Device */
#define DISPCTRL    0x0    /* Control/status for display device  */
#define DISPDATA    0x1    /* Data port for display device       */

#define DLITEON     0x2    /* Bit for back light control, 1 = ON */
#define DNORESP     0x4    /* Bit for dislay responding,  1 = NO */

        /* Keyboard Device */
#define KYBDHI      0x2    /* Data port for 1st 8 bits           */
#define KYBDLO      0x3    /* Data port for 2nd 8 bits           */

        /* Motor Device */
#define MOTORCTRL   0x06   /* Control port for motor speed       */

#define MSLOW       0x01   /* Bit for motor speed,   0 = FAST    */
                           /* Bit for motor speed,   1 = SLOW    */
#define MSTOP       0x20   /* Bit for motor stop,    0 = GO      */
                           /* Bit for motor stop,    1 = STOP    */
#define MREVERSE    0x40   /* Bit for motor forward, 0 = FOR-
                              WARD                               */
                           /* Bit for motor forward, 1 = REVERSE
                                                               */

#define MFAST       0      /* Bit RESET definitions */
#define MGO         0
#define MFORWARD    0

        /* Photoeyes */
#define FOTOEYES    0x08   /* Data port for all 3 eyes           */

#define EYE1MSK     0x02   /* Bit for eye 1, 1 = Eye NOT clear   */
```

```
#define EYE2MSK    0x01  /* Bit for eye 2, 1 = Eye NOT clear   */
#define EYE3MSK    0x04  /* Bit for eye 3, 1 = Eye NOT clear   */
```

If the machine's I/O space were hardware-memory-mapped, additional RAM would be required, and the changes required to the above software map could look like this:

```
#define RAMSTART   0x100001 /* RAM start address                */
#define RAMEND     0x2fffff /* RAM final address 128k           */

#define IOSTART    0x200001 /* IO start address                 */
#define IOEND      0x2fffff /* IO final address (64k)           */

#define DISPCTRL   0x200001 /* Control/status display device    */
#define DISPDATA   0x200011 /* Data port for display device     */

#define KYBDHI     0x200021 /* Data port for 1st 8 bits         */
#define KYBDLO     0x200031 /* Data port for 2nd 8 bits         */

#define MOTORCTRL  0x200061 /* Control port for motor speed     */

#define FOTOEYES   0x200081 /* Data port for all 3 eyes         */
```

The main advantage to using these *manifest constant* definitions is that the numeric values are centrally located in one header file; not spread throughout the code with each numeric reference. Also, the code can become more self-documenting. For example, using the previously defined C I/O routines and the above memory map, a function call to direct a change in motor speed might look like this:

```
outportb(MOTORCTRL, (MGO | MFAST | MFORWARD));
           OR
outportb(MOTORCTRL, MSTOP);
           OR
outportb(MOTORCTRL, (MGO | MSLOW | MREVERSE));
```

The net result is that the code is easier to understand and all values are centralized for maintenance. During system evolution, it could become necessary to switch a device to a different port. In that case, only the port number in the header file need be changed. All usage instances throughout the code are changed automatically when the code is recompiled.

HARDWARE DEVICES REVIEWED

In the digital computer world, all devices are viewed as digital by the CPU. Analog devices are typically attached via A/D converters in order to present them as digital for processing. In every case, the programmer can access devices through ports contained in the I/O space. Via these ports, the devices can be controlled and directed, or can be monitored for data collection or status reporting, as appropriate. Access is straightforward within device-specific constraints. Eventually, timing becomes the ultimate programming concern.

Many devices will have characteristics that require specific I/O sequences, predetermined pauses between accesses, and multiple usages that will affect overall system timing considerations. These concerns are addressed in Chapters 4 and 5.

Operator interfaces encountered in embedded systems work will most often be small LCD displays, keypads, and LEDs for indicator lights on the front panel of stand-alone units. Higher-end interfaces may be large, high-resolution touch screens. In any case, the device(s) purchased should have very detailed instructions regarding their implementation.

The quantitative work required of programmers in addressing a specific device will depend entirely on the purchased capabilities and system-specific implementation. A "driver" for each piece of hardware is required of the programmer. The level of knowledge required about each device will vary. Some devices can be purchased with installed firmware that makes life easy for the programmer, but they are typically more expensive. Some devices are strictly "raw" hardware attached to a port, and may require the programmer to experiment in addressing the desired functionality.

In any case, code-construction techniques can maximize reusability aspects of software from project to disparate project. Remaining sections of this chapter address such techniques.

TABLE-DRIVING THE PORTS WITH BETTER MEMORY MAPS

The use of table-driven techniques will generally reduce the quantitative code required, increase overall software efficiency, facilitate easier "debugging," increase software reusability aspects, and substantially reduce the efforts required in long-term software maintenance. The larger the system, the more evident this becomes. Twenty percent more up-front effort can reduce the overall project effort by 40 percent. Even in the world of C++, table-driven techniques can be used to marvelous advantage in providing initializer data to class constructors under the right circumstances.

A good starting point for designing system tables can be in addressing the I/O ports. It is known that a port output image (image of the last bit pattern written to the port) and port address will frequently be needed in using the ports. In addition, if a single port can be accessed from more than one processing code thread in a multitasking environment, a flag to indicate whether or not the port is in use might be desirable. Where a single table contains all system ports, flags could also be used to indicate if the port is read-only or write-only or both. Another flag could indicate if the port has been initialized for usage.

For the previously used non-memory-mapped carpet machine example, the port table could take shape in six easy steps, as follows (structure definitions are contained in path \TEXT\PORT7.C on the accompanying diskette):

1. First, define the structure that will contain information about each port:

```
/* Port table structure (all system ports)  */

typedef struct port_table
{
UCHAR *port_addr;  /* Port address (8-bit ports)  */
UCHAR port_imag;   /* Last image written to port  */
UCHAR port_flgs;   /* Port flag bucket            */
} PORTBL, *PTPTR;  /* New port table data types   */
```

2. Next, define the usage of each bit in the "port_flgs" bucket:

```
/* Port Flag Bits (0 to 7) */

#define INUSEP 0x8 /* Bit for port in use, 0 = not in use   */
                   /* Bit for port in use, 1 = in use       */
#define READP  0x1 /* Bit for a read port, 0 = no read      */
                   /* Bit for a read port, 1 = read OK      */
#define WRITEP 0x2 /* Bit for a write port, 0 = no write    */
                   /* Bit for a write port, 1 = write OK    */
#define INITP 0x4  /* Bit for port init OK, 0 = not OK      */
                   /* Bit for port init OK, 1 = init DONE   */
```

3. Next, using each port in the system, create an array of "port_table" structures and fill-in the default data. The compiler will place this "initialized" data into a separate address area, which will be placed into EPROM by the programmer during the link-and-locate process.

```
/* System Port Table -- Default Data ROM */

PORTBL rom_system_ports[] = {

        0x00,0,READP | WRITEP,  /* Display CTRL/STATUS  */
        0x01,0,READP,           /* Display DATA         */
        0x02,0,READP,           /* Keyboard DATA hibyte */
        0x03,0,READP,           /* Keyboard DATA lobyte */
        0x06,0,READP | WRITEP,  /* Motor Control/Status */
        0x08,INITP,READP        /* Photoeyes Status     */
   };
```

4. Dynamically calculate the size of the system port table so that recounting is not necessary with table insertions and deletions:

```
#define MAXPORTS ((sizeof(rom_system_ports))/(sizeof(PORTBL)))
```

5. Assign "manifest constants" to each port offset within the system port array for future reference:

```
#define    DCTRLPORT      0        /* Display CTRL port        */
#define    DSTATUSPORT    0        /* Display STATUS port      */
#define    DDATAPORT      1        /* Display DATA port        */
#define    KDATAHIPORT    2        /* Kybd DATA hi port        */
#define    KDATALOPORT    3        /* Kybd DATA lo port        */
#define    MTRCTRLPORT    4        /* Motor CTRL port          */
#define    MTRSTATPORT    4        /* Motor STATUS port        */
#define    FOTOEYEPORT    5        /* Photoeye STATUS port     */
```

6. Now define the RAM-based port table that will be copied from ROM during system initialization. The "ram_system_ports" array size must be greater than or equal to the size of the "rom_system_ports." The dynamically calculated constant, MAXPORTS, ensures they are of equal size.

```
/* System Port Table (In RAM) */

PORTBL ram_system_ports[MAXPORTS];

/*
```

NOTE: The compiler will place code, initialized data, and uninitialized data into separate address areas. The initialized data and code will be placed into ROM at link-and-locate time. The uninitialized data will be expected to reside in RAM. During system initialization, the programmer will cause the ROM copy of the system port table to be copied to RAM.

```
*/
```

This "new" table-driven approach will have a minor effect on memory-mapping requirements, and will require a beneficial layer of port I/O software above the routines previously defined.

One of the primary purposes of mapping port addresses with "manifest constants" is to centralize values. With the existence of the port table, each address constant is used one time and is centralized within the table. There is no longer a need to "map" port addresses; however, this requirement is replaced with the mapping of table offsets, as shown in step 5 above. The memory map examples previously used would remain essentially unchanged, except that all references to port addresses would be deleted.

Combining the memory maps and tables defined up to now might result in splitting the information into two files—one header that requires no space, and one data file for RAM:

```
                       /* HEADER MODULE: */


/* ------------------------------------------------------ */
/* ROM Limits -- All code & constant data is in EPROM here */
/* ------------------------------------------------------ */
#define ROMSTART      0x0            /* ROM beginning address   */
#define ROMEND        0xffff         /* ROM final address (64K) */


/* -------------------------------------------------- */
/* RAM Limits -- All volatile data is in RAM here */
/* -------------------------------------------------- */
#define RAMSTART      0x100001       /* RAM start address       */
#define RAMEND        0x1ffff1       /* RAM final address (64k) */


/* ------------------------------------------------------- */
/* IO Space Map -- 8-bit ports, non-memory-mapped       */
/* ------------------------------------------------------- */

                    /* LCD Display Device */

#define DLITEON       0x2  /* Bit for back light control, 1 = ON */
#define DNORESP       0x4  /* Bit for dislay responding, 1 = NO  */

                    /* Motor Device    */

#define MSLOW         0x01 /* Bit for motor speed,   0 = FAST    */
                           /* Bit for motor speed,   1 = SLOW    */
#define MSTOP         0x20 /* Bit for motor stop,    0 = GO      */
                           /* Bit for motor stop,    1 = STOP    */
#define MREVERSE      0x40 /* Bit for motor forward, 0 = FORWARD */
                           /* Bit for motor forward, 1 = REVERSE */


#define MFAST         0    /* Bit RESET definitions */
#define MGO           0
#define MFORWARD      0



/* Photoeyes */

#define EYE1MSK       0x02 /* Bit for eye 1, 1 = Eye NOT clear */
#define EYE2MSK       0x01 /* Bit for eye 2, 1 = Eye NOT clear */
#define EYE3MSK       0x04 /* Bit for eye 3, 1 = Eye NOT clear */

          /* Port table structure (all system ports) */

typedef struct port_table
   {
   UCHAR *port_addr;  /* Port address (8-bit ports)   */
   UCHAR port_imag;   /* Last image written to port   */
```

```
            UCHAR port_flgs;   /* Port flag bucket            */
            } PORTBL, *PTPTR;  /* New port table data types   */

                /* Port Flag Bits (0 to 7) */

    #define INUSEP 0x8    /* Bit for port in use, 0 = not in use   */
                          /* Bit for port in use, 1 = in use       */
    #define READP 0x1     /* Bit for a read port, 0 = no read      */
                          /* Bit for a read port, 1 = read OK      */
    #define WRITEP 0x2    /* Bit for a write port, 0 = no write    */
                          /* Bit for a write port, 1 = write OK    */
    #define INITP 0x4     /* Bit for port init OK, 0 = not OK      */
                          /* Bit for port init OK, 1 = init DONE   */

            /* Port offsets in system port table */

    #define DCTRLPORT    0          /* Display CTRL port         */
    #define DSTATUSPORT  0          /* Display STATUS port       */
    #define DDATAPORT    1          /* Display DATA port         */
    #define KDATAHIPORT  2          /* Kybd DATA hi port         */
    #define KDATALOPORT  3          /* Kybd DATA lo port         */
    #define MTRCTRLPORT  4          /* Motor CTRL port           */
    #define MTRSTATPORT  4          /* Motor STATUS port         */
    #define FOTOEYEPORT  5          /* Photoeye STATUS port      */

                    /*    DATA MODULE    */

            /* System Port Table -- Default Data ROM */

    PORTBL rom_system_ports[] = {
                  0x00,0,READP | WRITEP,   /* Display CTRL/STATUS   */
                  0x01,0,READP,            /* Display DATA          */
                  0x02,0,READP,            /* Keyboard DATA hibyte  */

                  0x03,0,READP,            /* Keyboard DATA lobyte  */


                  0x06,0,READP | WRITEP,   /* Motor Control/Status  */
                  0x08,INITP,READP         /* Photoeyes Status      */
                  };

    #define MAXPORTS ((sizeof(rom_system_ports))/(sizeof(PORTBL)))

                /* System Port Table (In RAM) */

    PORTBL ram_system_ports[MAXPORTS];
```

When performing port I/O, now that all ports, images, and flags are contained in a table, it might be desirable to reference ports by their array offsets within the port table. To accomplish this, higher-level routines can be written to utilize the previously written I/O routines, as well as the "new" port table flags, as follows:

```
/* MODULE PATH: \TEXT\PORTS4.C */
        /* ----------------------------- */
        /* Table access - READ 8-bit port */
        /* ----------------------------- */

UCHAR read_portb(USHORT port_offset) /*& READ 8-bit port    */
{
UCHAR value_in;              /* value read from port       */
PTPTR ptptr;                 /* port table pointer         */

                             /*$ ASSIGN correct pointer     */

  ptptr = &ram_system_ports[port_offset];

                             /*$ WHILE port in use
                                (multitasking), PAUSE 1 millisec  */

  while (ptptr->port_flgs & INUSEP) pause(1);

                             /*$ INDICATE in use (multitasking) */

  ptptr->port_flgs |= INUSEP;

                             /*$ READ the port               */

  value_in = inportb(ptptr->port_addr);

                             /*$ RESET port flag (multitasking) */

  ptptr->port_imag ^= INUSEP;

  return(value_in);   /*$ RETURN the 8-bit value            */
}

        /* ----------------------------- */
        /* Table access - WRITE 8-bit port */
        /* ----------------------------- */

VOID write_portb(USHORT port_offset,
              UCHAR value_out) /*& WRITE 8-bit port          */
{
PTPTR ptptr;                 /* port table pointer          */

                             /*$ ASSIGN correct pointer      */

      ptptr = &ram_system_ports[port_offset];

                             /*$ WHILE port in use (multitasking),
                                    PAUSE 1 millisec   */

      while (ptptr->port_flgs & INUSEP) pause(1);
```

```
                                  /*$ INDICATE in use (multitasking)  */

               ptptr->port_flgs |= INUSEP;

                                  /*$ SAVE the last written value      */

               ptptr->port_imag = value_out;

                                  /*$ WRITE the port                   */

               outportb(ptptr->port_addr, ptptr->port_imag);

                                  /*$ RESET port flag (multitasking)  */

               ptptr->port_imag ^= INUSEP;

               return;            /*$ RETURN                            */
}
```

Using these techniques, this same level of routine can be written to accommodate application-specific timing, contention, and access scenarios. For example, there will be occasions when writing a given port will require inclusive ORing of the value to be output with the last value output (which is contained in the port table). A port-specific routine similar to the above could be written to handle any case.

The routine previously defined to get 16 bits from consecutive 8-bit ports could be incorporated into a special routine that might look like this in a multitasking environment:

```
/* MODULE PATH: \TEXT\PORTS5.C */

          /* --------------------------------------------- */
          /* Table access - READ 16 bits from 8-bit ports*/
          /* --------------------------------------------- */

USHORT read_16_portb(USHORT hi_port_offset,
                     USHORT lo_port_offset)/*& READ 2, 8-bit    */
{
USHORT value_in;               /* value read from port           */
PTPTR hiptptr;                 /* port table pointer             */
PTPTR loptptr;                 /* port table pointer             */

                               /*$ ASSIGN correct pointer         */

   hiptptr = &ram_system_ports[hi_port_offset];
   loptptr = &ram_system_ports[lo_port_offset];

                               /*$ WHILE port in use (multitasking),
                                   PAUSE 1 millisec                */
```

```
    while ((hiptptr->port_flgs & INUSEP)
       ||    (loptptr->port_flgs & INUSEP)) pause(1);

                              /*$ INDICATE in use (multitasking) */

    loptptr->port_flgs |= INUSEP;
    hiptptr->port_flgs |= INUSEP;

                              /*$ READ the port                  */

    value_in = Get_16bits_devicex(hiptptr,loptptr);

                              /*$ RESET port flag (multitasking) */

    loptptr->port_imag ^= INUSEP;
    hiptptr->port_imag ^= INUSEP;

    return(value_in);         /*$ RETURN the 16-bit value        */
}
```

A "call" to get 16 bits from the two keyboard ports would now be:

```
    value_in = read_16_portb(KDATAHIPORT, KDATALOPORT);
```

where the function arguments are port offsets within the array of port structures that is called the ram_system_ports table.

When developing untried hardware and while in the initial project stages, the programmer could elect to include slower routines that use the port table flags to validate port offsets and port status prior to accessing the port:

```
/* MODULE PATH: \TEXT\PORTS6.C */

            /* ----------------------------- */
            /* Table access - READ 8-bit port */
            /* ----------------------------- */

UCHAR read_portb(USHORT port_offset) /*& READ 8-bit port         */
{
UCHAR value_in;                       /* value read from port     */
PTPTR ptptr;                          /* port table pointer       */

                                      /*$ VALIDATE offset         */

    if ((port_offset > 0)
    && (port_offset < MAXPORTS))
    {

                                      /*$ ASSIGN correct pointer */

    ptptr = &ram_system_ports[port_offset];
```

```
                           /*$ IF port is a READ port
                                and has been initialized      */

    if ( (ptptr->port_flgs & (INITP | READP)) ==
                       (INITP | READP) )
          {
                              /*$ WHILE port in use (multitasking),

                                PAUSE 1 millisec */
          while (ptptr->port_flgs & INUSEP) pause(1);

                              /*$ READ the port                    */

          value_in = inportb(ptptr->port_addr);
          }
    else               /*$ IF port not a READ port or NOT init  */

          value_in = SOME_ERROR_INDICATOR;
    }
    else               /*$ INVALID offset into table            */

          value_in = SOME_ERROR_INDICATOR;

    return(value_in);   /*$ RETURN the 8-bit value or
                                SOME_ERROR_INDICATOR      */
}
```

The additional IF statements are time consuming, but can be a help in initial debugging. At some point in the project, the programmer might elect to remove all flag references from the above code with the exception of the INUSEP flag reference (if the system is multitasking and can access ports asynchronously from more than one code thread).

When incorporating these higher levels of I/O routines into a software design, the addresses of the I/O functions for a given port could be added to the port table structure previously defined. This would enable the use of an even higher-level routine to access any port. Such a function could use the port offset within the port table as an argument, and then simply call the function whose address is specified in the table for either input or output as appropriate.

There are many ways to design tables and to implement software designs, and some are better than others in a given environment. Personal preferences of individual programmers are unique. There are really no right and wrong ways to write functioning code, but there are better ways to obtain specific, desirable software characteristics and to increase productivity. Each programmer selects an approach based on personal experience and awareness. Potential requirements combinations are numerous when all aspects of systems, devices, and applications are considered together. The techniques outlined above can reduce the quantitative code required of programmers and can centralize future changes and modifications while increasing potential resusability, but only if a given programmer pursues the concept with enthusiasm. The essential, implied points are that:

- Designing tables forces the programmer to think in terms of placing like items together.
- Layered software, using tables as a foundation, facilitates "black-boxing" each layer as it is debugged. Future changes revolve around table definitions and are minimized. In some cases, the only changes required to a module will be changes to the table data contents (IE port addresses).

Once an entire system has been memory-mapped with well-defined tables, and the necessary I/O routines have been written, there will be a substantial amount of reusable header, code, and data items—no matter what the characteristics of the next system prove to be.

DIGITAL SWITCH COMMONALITY AND REUSABILITY

Many hardware devices require unique bits in a given port in order to switch the device among several device states. For example, LEDs beneath translucent templates are frequently used as lighted indicators on the front panels of embedded units. They have two elemental states—ON and OFF. The ON state of an LED can require that the appropriate port bit be SET or RESET, depending on how the LED is electrically grounded within a given system. BLINK is a commonly used sub-state of ON. A timed blink interval can be used to distinguish between several system indications that share a single LED. Blinking can best be accomplished via hardware (a separate port bit); however, blinking can also be accomplished in software by turning the LED ON and OFF at timed intervals.

An aircraft pilot's control panel for a given device could be somewhat similar. Relatively large translucent buttons can be back-lit to indicate that a given button has been pressed (or is currently active). If the pilot presses the button a second time, the button's light is turned OFF, and the pilot can see that the button function is no longer active. Blinking could be used to indicate various states of activity.

Using the term *digital switch* to refer to all system devices that use a single bit to flip between ON and OFF states, it can easily be seen that digital switches have inherent similarity. Software can be designed to accommodate several functions with one set of code. A case in point would be a multitasking unit that contained a single task to SET and RESET front-panel LEDs as well as system interlocks. Using system semaphores (bit flags, discussed in Chapter 5) SET by other tasks to indicate currently desired device states, the LED/interlock task could set the desired digital states when it gained processing control. There could be a few milliseconds delay between the need for state transition and the actual transition and its indication, but this would be acceptable in many embedded applications. Other digital switch devices in the system might even be handled with the same or slightly modified software.

PILOT CONTROL PANEL EXAMPLE

Appendix A contains an example of a "driver" for a fairly complex set of push-button switches which are incorporated into an aircraft pilot's control panel. Parts of Appendix A are used in Chapter 7, and the entire appendix becomes an integral part of the missile-to-aircraft example presented in Appendix D.

In Appendix A, memory is mapped, tables are designed, and a driver is written that interfaces to the control panel tables and performs port I/O. These actions incorporate the essence of Chapter 2.

3

Start-up Software Modules

START-UP CODE AND PORTABILITY IN GENERAL

Source code portability requires that differences in operating systems and differences in hardware architectures be addressed transparently for any given host system. In C language, compatibility insurance is provided in part by standardized compiler-supplied library functions such as those conforming to ANSI C standards. Criteria for function names, argument lists, and return values are specified in detail; consequently, programmers using these functions are assured that the code will work when compiled cross-platform, or with a different compiler on a similar platform. Programmers will not rewrite this code for new platforms because the rewritten code pre-exists in the form of the standardized, compiler-supplied functions. Some portability and environmental concerns are addressed by this scheme, but there are others that cannot be handled by standardized library functions. More compatibility insurance is realized by using *start-up* modules.

During the C object link process under any popular operating system, a compiler-supplied start-up module is bound together with the programmer's C object code. This module is called something strange like C0.OBJ or C01.OBJ, and is normally written in the assembly language of the host CPU. In order to save space in the executable module, compilers that support multiple languages, operating systems, and/or memory models will have a different start-up module for each such supported environment, and each supplied module will have a uniquely weird name. In any C program, only one of these modules will be used. In executing the program, this start-up module is always the first executable code encountered by the CPU and is processed prior to the MAIN() function. It accepts any command-line arguments passed to the C program by the operator, and performs environment-specific housekeeping duties. The duties vary (that's the whole point of having start-up modules), but they can include such things as setting up memory control blocks or predefined I/O streams used by the standard I/O functions, or setting up for floating point emulation, program overlays, or dynamic linking. In a C++ start-up module, some global classes may be provided with initializer data for class constructors. Regardless of the specifics, after a start-up module has done its preliminary housekeeping, it calls the MAIN() C function and gives it any command-line arguments that were entered by the operator. When MAIN() is exited, control is returned to the start-up module, and any necessary "reverse" housekeeping duties are performed before returning to the operating system.

The bad news is that embedded-systems programmers must write their own start-up modules in assembly language. The good news is that the start-up routines for embedded environments are not nearly as complex as those described above, and the programmer has complete control over the contents. If an embedded operating system is used, there will seldom be operating-system-specific issues for the programmer to address while writing the start-up code; if there are, they will be relatively minor. Certainly, there will be no command-line arguments passed by the operator. Embedded start-up modules are, however, hardware-specific and do require calling the C MAIN() function from assembly language. Before specific examples of embedded systems start-up code are given, additional hardware and compiler background is appropriate.

CPU DIFFERENCES

Typically, CPUs are comprised of three functional units:

1. Registers for temporary storage within the CPU
2. Arithmetic/Logic Unit (ALU) for binary operations
3. Control circuitry for the coordination of activity

How these units are designed and built varies substantially among chip manufacturers. Circuitry is quite different and hardware engineers use different implementation techniques in designing systems around either Intel or Motorola CPU products. From a programmer's perspective while writing embedded systems code, the primary impact lies in the differing assembly languages, register implementations (and register usage conventions), and memory addressing schemes.

Regardless of the CPU being used on the current project, embedded-systems programmers will always be required to gain at least some knowledge of the chip architecture and its associated assembly language; each CPU is unique. From a programmer's focused perspective (and excluding interrupt handling), the three most pertinent CPU differences can be typified by comparing two 16-bit processors from two different manufacturers, the Intel 8086 and the Motorola 68000. Both are frequently used in embedded systems, and they are competitive products. Currently, the more powerful processors are used less often in embedded projects due to increased costs and lack of any real need for the additional processing power. This will change in time; but, for now, the 16-bit processors still rule the embedded systems world.

Generally speaking, in addressing the two chips selected, all concepts and most detail presented will apply across the board to all related chip family members. For the Intel 8086, the information will generally apply to the 80186, 80286, and 8088 as well; however, there is less applicability to the 80386, 80486, and 80586 chips. For the Motorola 68000, the information will generally apply to the 68008 and 68010 as well, but there is less applicability to the 68012 and later family members.

Intel CPU registers will be discussed first and are depicted in Figure 3-1. The Intel chip provides fourteen 16-bit registers. As a group, the data, index, and pointer registers are sometimes called "general" registers. The special-purpose registers are sometimes known as "control" registers. The four data registers are referenced as AX, BX, CX, and DX, and can be addressed as 8-bit registers using AH, AL, BH, BL, CH, CL, DH, and DL, where "H" indicates high byte and "L" indicates low byte. At the assembly level, AX is typically used in returning C function values to the invoking routine.

BP and SP are pointer registers. SP is the stack pointer and BP is the base pointer. At the assembly level, C functions typically set BP equal to SP at function entry. This allows indexed referencing (off BP) of pertinent stack

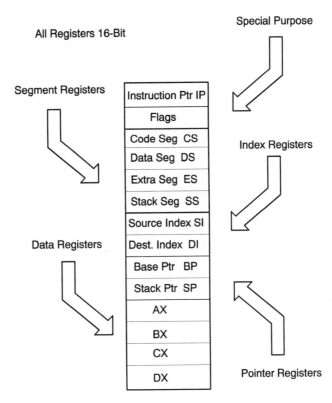

Figure 3-1. Intel 8086 Register Model

contents such as function arguments, the function return address, and local variables.

SI and DI are the source and destination index registers that are used primarily for string manipulation and additional addressing modes. Both can be automatically incremented or decremented. The two control registers are the FLAGS register, which provides the CPU status word, and the IP, which is the instruction pointer. The notorious segment registers are SS, CS, DS, and ES which contain segment addresses for stack, code, data, and the extra segment, respectively.

As shown in Figure 3-2, the Motorola 68000 provides 18 32-bit registers and a 16-bit status register A7 is normally counted as two registers because of the dual, dedicated usage mentioned later). The status register, SR, is similar to the Intel FLAGS register. One of the 32-bit registers is the Program Counter, PC, which utilizes only 24 bits of the 32, and which is the counterpart of the Intel IP register, although the two do not perform identically. (Intel's Bus Interface Unit instruction prefetch ultimately dictates that IP point to the next instruction to be fetched, while Motorola's PC points to the next instruction to be executed.)

Of the remaining registers seven are general-purpose address registers (AO

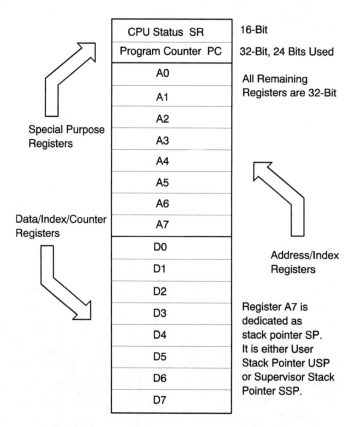

Figure 3-2. Motorola 68000 Register Model

through A6), which can also be used as index registers. When using A0 through A6 as assembly source operands of 16 bits, only the low-order 16 bits of the register are altered. In using these registers as destination operands, all 32 bits are altered regardless of the destination address length.

The eighth address register, A7, is dedicated as the stack pointer, SP. Register A7 is either the "supervisor" stack pointer (SSP) or the "user" stack pointer (USP) depending on the chip's current operational mode (only one stack can be accessed in each mode and both are referenced by SP). The two operating modes are switched by executing specified assembly instructions or actions that modify a single bit in the CPU status word; and there are certain privileged instructions that can only be executed while in supervisor mode. Once the CPU is in user mode, only an exception (interrupt) can return it to supervisor mode. Returning from an exception can return the CPU to user mode. A CPU reset returns the CPU to supervisor mode. The two modes exist mainly to separate systems software from user software in program-intensive environments. Frequently in embedded systems work, programmers can elect to maintain supervisor mode throughout processing.

There are eight 32-bit data registers (D0 through D7) that can be used to handle bytes, 16-bit words, or 32-bit words. They can double as index registers or data counters. When a data register is used as an assembly source or destination operand of less than 32 bits, only the least significant portion (8 or 16 bits) of the register is altered. At the assembly level, D0 is typically used to return C function values to the invoking routine.

Obviously, there are substantial differences between the two above chips in the implementation and use of registers. If the two could use identical assembly instructions, there would still be significant programming differences just in confronting the registers. The Intel chip has no operating modes equivalent to the Motorola "supervisor" and "user" modes. Equally significant programming differences are uncovered in looking at memory addressing schemes.

Motorola uses a flat addressing scheme to access memory. It is easy to understand in that physical addresses are available simply by the numbers. Restricted by the 68000's 24-bit address bus, potential address register values range from 0 to 16MB, as shown in Figure 3-3.

Intel uses the notorious segmented addressing scheme in which 20-bit physical addresses are constructed as combinations of segment + offset. Each of the four segment registers contain physical memory addresses divided by 16 (shifted right four bits), which is the segment address. The general registers are used as pointers to offsets within each segment. After multiplying the value in a segment register by 16 and adding the offset value, the desired physical address is obtained. Each 16-bit register has a maximum value of 64K, but when used in the above fashion, access to 1MB of memory is achieved as shown in Figure 3-4.

The Intel addressing scheme is sometimes ridiculed by Motorola chip proponents, but this may be lack of intimate familiarity. The segmented scheme, coupled with Intel's implicit register usages, can produce more concise code and reduce overall memory requirements. After typical compilers have had their impacts (which include boundary alignment and word size considerations),

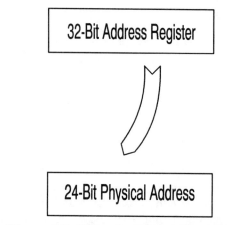

Figure 3-3. Motorola 68000 Address Model

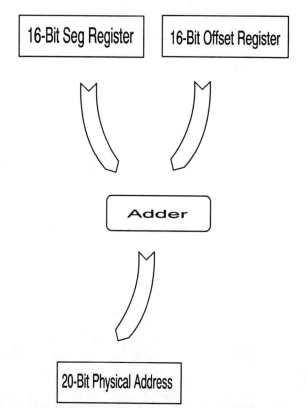

Figure 3-4. Intel 8086 Address Model

there can be a substantial difference in the amount of memory used by the chip-specific executable code.

At the C programming level, register differences and memory access differences are transparent; however, it is very important that programmers be familiar with project-specific CPUs, at least to the level described above. There will be assembly language programming on any project, and CPU knowledge will prove critical.

Having touched two of the three major impacts that varying CPU architectures have on programming, the focus might be directed to the third, the assembly language instructions. Examples of start-up code written in both Intel and Motorola assemblers will be given later, and syntax differences will be visibly obvious. Dissecting assembly languages is beyond the scope of this text, and many sources exist for learning specific assemblers. For now the CPUs can rest.

A point should be made to managers, human resources personnel, and other less technical types, who could have made it this far in reading. If you are seeking people for help in programming a given chip, anyone who can handle one of these architectures in depth can handle them all. As different as the hardware appears to the uninitiated, the successful professionals see a certain sameness throughout. Moving from one architecture to another is simply a matter of determining what the ground rules are, and then going forward. With the currently evolved state of documentation, and with a motivated player, this should not require excessive time—assembly languages included.

MIXED-LANGUAGE CONSIDERATIONS

Surprisingly enough, the process of invoking routines written in one language from routines written in another language is referred to as *mixed-language programming*.

In an embedded system, the Main() C function is always called from the start-up module, which is traditionally written in assembly language. Under the right circumstances, it is possible to write a start-up module in C, but in-line assembly would frequently be needed, and in any case, the gain seldom outweighs the pain. For this reason, the instance of mixed-language programming that calls the MAIN() C function form the assembly start-up code will normally exist in any C embedded system. Other instances will occur in the reverse direction—calling assembly routines from C. Severe system timing requirements can require the use of specialized routines, written totally in assembly language, to decrease processing time in a given module. Some embedded programmers are in the habit or always using assembly language simply to start system timers. For whatever reason, mixed-language programming is frequently encountered in the embedded systems world. Mixing C and assembly, in either direction, is the focus here. There are general considerations that will apply to mixing other languages with C, but other languages are not the immediate concern.

In mixing C and assembly, an assembly source module, such as the start-up code, is typically assembled into an object module which is ultimately linked with C object modules. The greatest single source of programmer frustration is in obtaining a good link between the two in a new software environment. The assembly modules must use naming conventions for code and data memory areas that are compatible with the project-specific C compiler's conventions, and the form of the variable and function names must be acceptable to both the C and assembly modules. By using a program that has been compiled and linked using the current project-specific tools, and by checking the link map output for that program, the programmer can get enough information about memory segments and naming conventions to proceed. Some experimentation with small, dummy routines is frequently required; it can be tedious, but not insurmountable. Once in a while, the answers to such questions are even contained in the software development environment's documentation.

A non-framework compatibility issue between different language modules is address lengths. In the Intel 80xx world, for example, the "near" and "far" keywords are used to distinguish between assembly procedures using 16-bit and 32-bit addresses. When a "near" routine is called, only the offset within the code segment is placed on the stack as a return address (16 bits). If the routine's keyword is "far," then both the segment and offset are placed on the stack (32 bits). Obviously, if the "large" model of the C compiler were unknowingly used with a "near" assembly routine (or vice versa), the entire system would crash when the two crossed paths. Programmers must ensure that all such characteristics are compatible between the two modules.

The actual coding of the two modules is a piece of cake. If an assembly routine invokes a C routine, it only has to place the C function arguments on the stack in the proper sequence and then issue the call. The C calling convention dictates that arguments be placed on the stack in reverse order. Argument n precedes argument $n-1$ which precedes argument $n-2$ and so on. The CALL instruction will place the return address on the stack. At the assembly level, the invoked C routine typically will set some CPU register equal to the stack pointer register and then access the pertinent stack items as offsets from the stack-pointer-at-entry address. When the assembly routine regains control, any value returned from the C function will be available via one or more CPU registers. In the Intel world, compilers most often return 16-bit values using register AX. In the Motorola world, D0 is frequently used for C return values. In any case, these conventions are compiler-specific. Sometimes embedded programmers must view existing code at the assembly level in order to determine what a specific compiler is doing; occasionally, the answers to such questions are documented.

The typical C compiler allows the declaration of assembly routines as C routines by using EXTERNs and C prototypes within the invoking C module. In this case, when the assembly routine is invoked from C, the C call treats it as just another C routine. In other words, the arguments would be placed on the stack in the proper order followed by the return address. The invoked assembly routine would be required to expect the arguments (parameters) to be at the appropriate offset from the stack-pointer-at-entry address. Likewise, the invoked assembly routine would be required to return values to the invoking C routine in accordance with the compiler-specific conventions for returning C function values. This is reasonably straightforward stuff; however, related examples will be set forth in the discussion of interrupts.

Traditional assembly routines accept arguments (parameters) via CPU registers. Before calling an assembly routine, the appropriate registers are set up with specified parameters, then the routine is invoked. Likewise, if values are returned from a traditional assembly routine, they are returned via CPU registers. If a programmer must interface to a pre-existing and traditional assembly routine from C, it is likely that in-line assembly would be necessary to set up the registers prior to invoking the assembly routine. When control is returned to the C function, in-line assembly would likely be needed to retrieve any values returned by the assembly routine. In this case, it is not likely that the returned values would be available in consonance with the project-compiler-specific conventions for C function return values. Fortunately for embedded-systems programmers, this interface requirement will seldom be encountered.

To recap, mixed-language framework issues are compiler-specific and project-specific, and are the greatest thorn in the mixed-language programmer's side. The actual invoking of mixed-language routines is straightforward within the confines of C calling conventions and assembly tradition. C compilers have compiler-specific register usage conventions and these must be considered when returning assembly values to invoking C routines. If a programmer is writing both the invoked and invoking routines, potential problems are minimized. If no arguments are passed and no values are returned, potential problems are further minimized. When mixed-language programming is required on a project, it is wise to experiment with small dummy routines in order to work out the framework issues; this is especially wise when acclimating to a new software environment.

EMBEDDED SYSTEMS START-UP CODE

Writing start-up code for an embedded system can be as simple or as complex as the programmer desires. There are programmers who write intentionally complex code, and there are old programmers; but there are no old programmers who write intentionally complex code. For now, the code will be kept as simple as possible.

The typical embedded systems start-up code is a *shell* to allow further execution. The programmer provides a way for the CPU to arrive at the entry point of the start-up module (either via Intel's "jump" or Motorola's vector table entry). Because there is no "regular" operating system, RAM is usually initialized to zeros by the start-up code. NVRAM is normally initialized once, the first time that the system is powered up. The CPU's interrupt vector table is defined, and so is the initial stack pointer. Additional CPU-specific details, such as the initial setup of Intel's segment registers, could be required. Outside of that, embedded systems start-up code is largely at the programmer's discretion. Some programmers opt to define exotic tables that define flags to indicate whether or not a specific interrupt has occurred at least once, and this is helpful in initial debugging.

Default RAM values, which are copied from ROM during system initialization, are normally copied from within the MAIN() C routine. The start-up code will initialize RAM to zeros, but the MAIN() C routine will insert RAM default data from ROM before falling into a repetitive processing loop.

If NVRAM is used in a system, it is normally zeroed the first time power is applied, and not thereafter. NVRAM will likely contain data that is to be retained for indefinite periods, and the programmer would not want to zero it after the system has been operating. The one-time initialization can be accomplished by checking an NVRAM word for a specific value such as hex 4ACE. If the value exists, NVRAM is skipped. If the value does not exist, NVRAM is set to zeros and the value is inserted.

As mentioned earlier, development-software-specific framework issues will be a concern for start-up code. Names of sections or segments of code, variables, and routines must be in forms acceptable to both the assembler and the C development environment. Because of this, the example code shown later could require minor modification in order to be linkable and locatable with differing software products.

Example start-up modules follow for both an Intel-based 8086 system and a Motorola-based 68000 system. They are dissected in great detail for those familiar with one language, but not the other. The CPU's interrupt vector table and interrupts in general are discussed in Chapter 4; therefore, the vector tables will not be shown with the start-up code examples.

INTEL EXAMPLE START-UP CODE

At system power-on time, the Intel 8086 executes the instruction at absolute location hex FFFF0. Sixteen bytes are reserved at that location for reset. The programmer normally places an unconditional jump instruction at hex FFFF0, which would jump to the entry point of the start-up routine. The specific Intel 8086 transparent reset process is to load register CS with hex FFFF, load IP with 0, clear the FLAGS register, and put zeros into CS, DS, SS, and ES; therefore, the programmer needs to set up the segment registers as part of the start-up code. When the start-up code takes control, CS will already have been changed to point to the segment containing the initialization code.

The specific segments that follow will be located by the programmer to correspond to actual hardware addresses at link-and-locate time.

```
; MODULE PATH: \TEXT\INTELSU.ASM

_TEXT           segment public 'CODE'
                assume cs:_TEXT
public          _enabli, _disabli, _INITCPU
extrn           _main
INITSP          equ 0fffeh
INITSS          equ 02000h
INITDS          equ 01000h
RAMSTRT         equ 010000h
RAMEND          equ 02ffffh
```

```
HALFRAM        equ 0ffffh
;
_INITCPU       proc far
               cli                     ;disable interrupts
               mov ax, INITSS          ;set up intial SS & SP
               mov ss,ax
               mov ax, INITSP
               mov sp,ax
               mov ax,INITDS           ;set up initial DS, ES
               push ax
               pop ds
               push ax
               pop es                  ;set up initial ES
               xor ax,ax               ;put zeros in di
               push ax
               pop di
INITRAM:
               mov cx,HALFRAM            ;set word count
               rep stos word ptr [di]   ;move words of 0s to RAM
MAIN:
               sti                     ;enable interrupts
               call _main              ;call MAIN
               cli                     ;disable interrupts
STOPBOX:
               hlt                     ;HALT processor
               js STOPBOX              ;insurance for HALT
_INITCPU       endp                    ;end of procedure
_enabli        proc far                ;routine to enable interrupts
               sti
_enabli        endp
_disabli       proc far                ;routine to disable interrupts
               cli
_disabli       endp
_TEXT          ends
_RTXT          segment public          ;seg to locate for CPU reset
               jmp _INITCPU
_RTXT          ends
               end
```

Dissection of the above start-up module:

1. Define the segment for this code.

```
_TEXT          segment public 'CODE'
               assume cs:_TEXT
```

2. Define the routines in this module as being available to other modules, define MAIN as available to this module from another, and define needed equates. The equates would be specified in accordance with actual hardware mapping.

```
public         _enabli, _disabli, _INITCPU
extrn          _main
```

```
INITSP     equ 0fffeh
INITSS     equ 02000h
INITDS     equ 01000h
RAMSTRT    equ 010000h
RAMEND     equ 02ffffh
HALFRAM    equ 0ffffh
```

3. Define the initialization procedure and disable external interrupts ("cli" clears the interrupt flag for Intel CPUs).

```
_INITCPU   proc far
           cli
```

4 . Set up the stack segment and initial stack pointer.

```
        mov    ax, INITSS
        mov    ss,ax
        mov    ax, INITSP
        mov    sp,ax
```

5. Set up the data segment and extra segment registers.

```
        mov    ax,INITDS
        push   ax
        pop    ds
        push   ax
        pop    es
```

6. Zero ax and use it to place zeros in register di.

```
        xor    ax,ax
        push   ax
        pop    di
```

7. Initialize RAM to zeros. Move words of zeros to the contents pointed to by registers es:di (es is implicit), increment di to next word, and decrement register cx until cx = 0. When cx is zero, go to next instruction.

```
INITRAM:
        mov cx,HALFRAM
        rep stos word ptr [di]
```

8. Enable interupts and call the MAIN() C routine. Sometimes it is better to enable interrupts from inside the MAIN() C routine after additional initialization. In that case, the "sti" instruction would be deleted here, and "_enabli" could be called from C. ("sti" sets the interrupt flag for Intel CPUs.)

```
MAIN:
    sti
    call _main
```

9. After returning from MAIN, disable interrupts and halt processing.

```
        cli
STOPBOX:
        hlt
        js STOPBOX
```

10. Define the end of the initialization procedure.

```
_INITCPU    endp
```

11. Define a procedure for enabling interrupts that can be called from C.

```
_enabli     proc far
            sti
_enabli     endp
```

12. Define a procedure for disabling interrupts that can be called from C.

```
_disabli    proc far
            cli
_disabli    endp
```

13. Define end of the current code segment.

```
_TEXT       ends
```

14. Define a segment to contain the initial JUMP instruction and incorporate the actual jump. This code will be located by the programmer at hex FFFF0 at link-and-locate time.

```
_RTXT       segment public
            jmp _INITCPU
_RTXT       ends
            end
```

MOTOROLA EXAMPLE START-UP CODE

At system power-on time, the Motorola 68000 loads the Supervisor Stack Pointer from the first four bytes of the interrupt vector table, which is not shown here. The Program Counter, PC, is loaded from the second four bytes and must point to the entry point of this start-up routine, INITCPU. Execution begins at the address contained in PC.

The following sample start-up code for a Motorola 68000 should work well with Microtec Research's development environment. Some of the conventions herein may vary slightly with other products. The "names" for Microtec Research code sections are numbers, which gives incredible flexibility in the fashion that it is implemented. The specific numbered sections will be located by the programmer to correspond to actual hardware addresses at link-and-locate time. In this sample code, the 68000's "supervisor" operating mode is being maintained throughout processing.

```
* MODULE PATH: \TEXT\MOTOSU.ASM


            OPT    CASE
INITCPU     IDNT
RAMSTRT     EQU    $20000
```

```
RAMEND          EQU  $27FFF
*
        SECTION      14
        XREF         ????STACKTOP
        SECTION      15
        XDEF         ????HEAP
????HEAP DC.L    1
        SECTION 9
        XREF         .main
        XDEF         INITCPU,INITRAM,STOPBOX,ENABLI,DISABLI
INITCPU:
        MOVE.W       #$2700,SR          * DISABLE INTERRUPTS
        MOVE.L       #????STACKTOP,SP   * INITIAL STACK POINTER
INITRAM:
        MOVE.L       #(RAMEND-RAMSTRT)/2,D0   * CALCULATE WORDS
        LEA          RAMSTRT,A0              * ADDR to A0
INITRAM1:
        CLR.W        (A0)+         * CLEAR A WORD, INCR A0 ADDR
        DBF          D0,INITRAM1   * COUNT EXHAUSTED? CONTINUE
        MOVE.W       #$2000,SR     * ENABLE INTERRUPTS
        JSR          .main         * CALL MAIN() 'C'
STOPBOX:
        STOP         #$2700        * HALT EXECUTION
        BRA.S        STOPBOX       * INSURANCE FOR HALT
ENABLI:
        MOVE.W       #$2000,SR     * ENABLE INTERRUPTS
        RTS
DISABLI:
        MOVE.W       #$2700,SR     * DISABLE INTERRUPTS
        RTS
        END          INITCPU
```

Dissection of the above start-up module:

1. Specify upper case typestyle for source code:

   ```
   OPT    CASE
   ```

2. Identify the start-up module:

   ```
   INITCPU    IDNT
   ```

3. Specify starting and ending points of RAM (whatever they are):

   ```
   RAMSTRT    EQU    $20000
   RAMEND     EQU    $27FFF
   ```

4. Section 14 is selected by the programmer for stack. The ????STACKTOP allows specifying the initial stack pointer at link time using the Microtec Research system.

   ```
   SECTION      14
   XREF         ????STACKTOP
   ```

5. Section 15 is selected by the programmer for heap. The ????HEAP allows

specifying the initial heap address at link time using the Microtec Research system. Heap is not really required in this system, so it is defined as a word length.

```
SECTION 15
XDEF        ????HEAP
????HEAP DC.L    1
```

6. Section 9 is selected by the programmer for code. The main routine is specified as external, then the code labels contained in the start-up code are defined for external use.

```
SECTION 9
XREF        .main
XDEF        INITCPU,INITRAM,STOPBOX,ENABLI,DISABLI
```

7. Still in Section 9 and at the entry point of the start-up code, hex 2700 is moved to the Status Register in order to maintain supervisor mode and ensure that the external interrupts are disabled (CPU-specific). If the $2700 were $0700, the CPU would be placed in user mode and the initial user stack pointer would be moved into the SP register. As shown, supervisor mode will be maintained throughout.

```
INITCPU:
MOVE.W    #$2700,SR
MOVE.L    #????STACKTOP,SP
```

8. Using the predefined start and end addresses for RAM, RAM is cleared to zeros. At INITRAM, the number of words to clear is calculated an put in D0, the address of RAM start is put into A0. At INITRAM1, the contents specified by A0 are cleared for a word length and then AO is incremented to the next word, and the loop continues for the count specified in D0.

```
INITRAM:
        MOVE.L        #(RAMEND-RAMSTRT)/2,D0
        LEA           RAMSTRT,A0
INITRAM1:
        CLR.W         (A0)+
        DBF           D0,INITRAM1
```

9. Enable interrupts and calls the MAIN() C routine. Sometimes it is better to enable interrupts form inside the MAIN() C routine after additional initialization. In that case, the MOVE.W instruction would be deleted here, and ENABLI could be called from C.

```
        MOVE.W #      $2000,SR
        JSR           .main
```

10. After returning from the MAIN() C routine, disable interrupts and halt execution.

```
STOPBOX:
        STOP          #$2700
        BRA.S         STOPBOX
```

11. Define a routine that can be called from C to enable interrupts.

```
ENABLI:
     MOVE.W#          $2000,SR
     RTS
```

12. Define a routine that can be called from C to disable interrupts.

```
DISABLI:
     MOVE.W#          $2700,SR
     RTS
```

13. Specify END of module.

```
     END             INITCPU
```

4

Handling Realtime Interrupts

INTERRUPT ESSENTIALS AND VECTOR TABLES

It has been shown that external devices are connected to the CPU via ports in order to exchange data with the program that the CPU is currently executing. Sometimes, in addition, they are connected via Interrupt Request lines (IRQs). When a device wants the CPUs attention, it can assert an interrupt signal on its IRQ to let the CPU know that it feels ignored. When that happens, the CPU is interrupted in its current processing, and is vectored to a predetermined location in response to the IRQ signal. The code that it begins executing is called an Interrupt Service Routine (ISR). When the ISR is finished, the CPU begins execution where it was interrupted as if nothing had happened. This is the essence of an "external" interrupt.

The CPU itself may want to interrupt current processing in order to provide some type of exception service, such as giving an indication that it has encountered a "divide by zero" while processing the current code. Again, it is vectored to a predetermined location, but this time in response to its own signal. When the ISR is finished, the CPU begins execution where it was interrupted, as if nothing had happened. This is the essence of an "internal" interrupt.

Obviously, there are two classifications of interrupt request sources, those requests external to the CPU and those generated internally by the CPU. All interrupts generated from software, such as interrupts generated via the Intel assembly INT instruction, or the Motorola assembly TRAP instruction, are internal interrupts. Both Motorola and Intel use the *internal* and *external* terms, but Motorola refers to *exceptions* rather than *interrupts*. Motorola literature refers to *exception processing* rather than *interrupt processing*. However, in this book Motorola *exceptions* will be referred to as *interrupts*.

When an interrupt request is detected by the CPU, whether internal or external, processing must be vectored to a specific ISR for that interrupt. This is accomplished by assigning type numbers to interrupts, and correlating those numbers to a table of vectors to ISRs. For the chip families previously discussed, the vectors are 32-bit addresses of ISR entry points, and the vector table always begins at absolute location 0. The location of the desired ISR address within the vector table is the interrupt type number multiplied by 4 (since there are 4 bytes per address). The ISR address for Interrupt type 1 would be at memory location 4, preceded by the 4 bytes constituting the ISR address for interrupt type 0. For example, when the CPU detects interrupt 6, it would grab the ISR address from memory location 24 and then begin execution at the grabbed ISR address, which would be the entry point of the ISR that services interrupt type 6.

The vector table, for both the Motorola 68000 and the Intel 8086, consumes the first 1K of memory, allowing for 256 32-bit ISR addresses. In the desktop PC world, many vectors are reserved for specific purposes, but, in the embedded systems world, vector assignment is largely at the programmer's discretion.

Embedded-systems programmers must write all ISRs used in the system. This includes ISRs for both internal and external interrupts. Most embedded systems will contain only a half-dozen or so "active" ISRs, and it is frequently a good idea to write a "dummy" ISR that simply increments a RAM-based counter. This dummy ISR can be inserted at every vector table location not used by the system. In case of a spurious or unexpected interrupt during hardware debug stages, the counter will indicate the number of such occurrences. For the PC world in general, unused vector types will typically point to a "return from interrupt" instruction; if an interrupt request is issued against a valid, but not implemented, type number, the "interrupt return" instruction will properly relieve the stack.

Remembering from Chapter 3 that the first two vectors are reserved by Motorola for chip reset, an interrupt vector table, written as a stand-alone module to be linked with the Motorola 68000 sample start-up code previously shown, could look like this using Microtec Research development software:

```
             OPT         CASE
IVECTORS     IDNT

             SECTION     9
             XREF        .isr001      * ISR EXTERNS
             XREF        .isr002
             XREF        .isr003
             XREF        .isr004
             XREF        .i_dmmy

*

             SECTION     14
             XREF        ????STACKTOP
*
             SECTION  0

             ORG    $0    * RESET VECTOR
```

```
        DC.L    ????STACKTOP * SP ADDRESS
        DC.L    INITCPU      * PC ADDRESS
*
        ORG     $08          * DUMMIES
* VECTOR 2
        DC.L    .i_dmmy
        DC.L    .i_dmmy
        DC.L    .i_dmmy
                 .
                 .
                 .

* VECTOR 64
        ORG     $100         * DEVICE 1 ISR
        DC.L    .isr001
        DC.L    .i_dmmy
* VECTOR 66
        ORG     $108         * DEVICE 2 ISR
        DC.L    .isr004
        DC.L    .i_dmmy
* VECTOR 68
        ORG     $110         * DEVICE 3 ISR
        DC.L    .isr003
        DC.L    .i_dmmy
        DC.L    .i_dmmy
        DC.L    .i_dmmy
* VECTOR 72
        ORG     $120         * DEVICE 4 ISR
        DC.L    .isr002
        DC.L    .i_dmmy
        DC.L    .i_dmmy
                 .
                 .
                 .

* VECTOR 250
        DC.L    .i_dmmy
        DC.L    .i_dmmy
        DC.L    .i_dmmy
        DC.L    .i_dmmy
        DC.L    .i_dmmy
        DC.L    .i_dmmy
*
        END
```

A vector table can be written in C; however, the project's software development environment must allow the programmer to locate this initialized data at EPROM location zero. (Sometimes this can be achieved by arranging the sequence of modules linked during the link-and-locate process.) Such a C vector table could look like this:

```
extern VOID far isr_001(VOID);
```

```
extern VOID far isr_002(VOID);
extern VOID far isr_003(VOID);
extern VOID far isr_004(VOID);
extern VOID far isr_dmmy(VOID);

typedef struct isr_addr {

        VOID (far *israddr) ();

        } ISRADR;

ISRADR vector_table[] = {
                                /* Vector 0   */
                isr_dmmy,
                isr_dmmy,
                    .
                    .
                    .
                isr_dmmy,
                                /* Vector 64 */
                isr_001,
                isr_dmmy,
                                /* Vector 66 */
                isr_002,
                isr_dmmy,
                                /* Vector 68 */
                isr_003,
                isr_dmmy,
                isr_dmmy,
                isr_dmmy,
                                /* Vector 72 */
                isr_004,
                isr_dmmy,
                    .
                    .
                    .
                                /* Vector 255*/
                isr_dmmy
                };
```

If the above code were for a 68000 processor, the first two dummy vectors would be replaced with the initial stack pointer and the initial IP values, like the preceding Motorola example.

When a CPU begins interrupt processing in response to a request for interrupt, there are CPU-specific actions that occur transparently to programmers. For instance, Intel 8086 CPUs will push the FLAGS (CPU status word) onto the stack, and then perform the equivalent of an intersegment indirect CALL. The CS and IP registers are pushed onto the stack to save the address of the next instruction, which is where the CPU will resume execution after the ISR is done;

then the CS and IP registers are loaded with the ISR address which is contained in the vector table at the appropriate table offset. When the ISR is done, the FLAGS are restored, and control is transferred back to the interrupted program at the saved address.

Motorola 68000 processors provide an analogous scheme, but also place the processor into the supervisor mode while ISRs are executing; the status word is saved in an internal register at the beginning of interrupt processing. The assembly instruction RTE, which is executed in returning from an interrupt, can return the 68000 to the user mode. Motorola chips typically have some additional interrupt twists that will not be discussed here, but are reasons for selection of the term *exception processing*. Also, there are some differences in the way that Motorola chips respond to specific interrupts.

LEVELS, PRIORITIES, MASKING, AND NESTING

Normally, external interrupts are prioritized by interrupt signal levels. Devices can be chained within priority levels so that a large number of peripherals can assert interrupt requests. During a typical interrupt request, a device would encode its assigned level on the interrupt request lines. The ensuing CPU acknowledgment of that request would fetch the vector type (number) from the interrupting device, and the vector type is used to locate the associated ISR.

If two devices attempt to interrupt the CPU simultaneously, the one with the higher priority will be serviced first. Interrupt masks, which work in conjunction with the levels, are located in the CPU status word (SR for Motorola, FLAGS for Intel). Using the Motorola 68000 for example, setting three specified interrupt mask bits in the SR will disable all external interrupts except level 7, which is Motorola's non-maskable interrupt (NMI) level, and highest priority. Setting subsets of the same three bits will enable lower levels, and disable those below the lowest enabled level. Level 1 is Motorola's lowest interrupt priority. The NMI level is normally reserved for catastrophic or very urgent interrupts.

For the Intel 8086, a separate NMI line exists, and the priority levels of external interrupts are reversed with level 0 being the highest. The Intel NMI interrupts are predefined as type 2. The Intel status-word's interrupt mask is a single bit and the assembly instructions CLI and STI either "clear" or "set" it respectively. When it is set, external interrupts are enabled. The greatest difference here, from a programmer's perspective, is in the reversal of priority levels between the two families. All interrupt handling details are CPU-specific, but are very similar between chip manufacturers and CPU families, and are dissected in depth by the manufacturer-supplied documentation.

As a rule, internally generated interrupts cannot be disabled and have a higher priority than external interrupts. This proves to be an entirely satisfactory scheme in that the programmer has more control over both the contents of the ISRs, and the requests for internal interrupt service. In contrast, the programmer has no control over occurrences of external requests, other than to completely disable them. On both the Motorola 68000 and the Intel 8086, when interrupts are disabled via the appropriate CPU status word mask, only external interrupts are disabled. Internal interrupts and catastrophic interrupts (non-maskable) are not.

When two or more interrupt requests reach the CPU simultaneously the highest priority interrupt is serviced as soon as the CPU completes the current instruction. Two signal-sensing mechanisms are used by processors in obtaining interrupt requests. They are *level-sensitive* and *edge-triggered*. External interrupt requests are usually level-sensitive. Catastrophic and/or NMI requests are frequently edge-triggered. Typically, level-sensitive interrupt request signals are not *latched*, so they must be held active until serviced or they will be lost. Edge-triggered requests are frequently latched in order not to be lost, but subsequent requests could be lost. The point here is that simultaneous interrupts sometimes result in lost interrupt requests, and systems must be designed to handle project-specific impacts.

The Motorola 68000 has three Interrupt Request lines (INTRs) for externally generated interrupts, plus provision for bus error, address error, and reset interrupts. The Intel 8086 has only one INTR plus the separate NMI. The Intel chip's INTR is typically connected through Intel's 8259 Programmable Interrupt Controller (PIC) which arbitrates IRQs from the attached devices, including control of interrupt priorities.

Typically, when an ISR is entered by the CPU, external interrupts have been either totally disabled or they have been disabled below the current interrupt's priority level. (The former is true for Intel, the latter for Motorola.) This prevents another device (of a lower priority) from interrupting the executing ISR before it is done. Sometimes this is absolutely necessary; but more often, robust applications will allow an ISR to re-enable all external interrupts in order to prevent the loss of subsequent interrupt requests, regardless of priority. This can mean that more ISRs will interrupt other ISRs, and could give birth to more "nested" interrupts. If the execution times were such that nesting levels increased with system operating time, the stack would eventually overflow, and the entire system would crash. Of course, a properly designed system would allow nesting, but would ensure its occasional use with total recovery in each instance. In dealing with intense interrupt-driven communications environments, it is very important that external interrupts be enabled constantly in order to ensure robust communications and to minimize the loss of communicated data. Multiport, asynchronous, interrupt-driven, character I/O is an incontestable case in point.

CONSIDERATIONS WHEN WRITING ISRs

As a rule, ISRs can commence following any given assembly language instruction; there is no "warning" to the code under execution that an ISR is about to be processed. For example, an ISR could gain control right after a C routine (at the assembly level) has moved a value into a register in preparation to return that value to the invoking function. If the ISR changes the contents of that particular register, when the C routine regained control, it would return an incorrect value to its invoking function. Saving all pertinent registers at ISR entry, and subsequently restoring them just prior to ISR return, is an unavoidable necessity in writing ISRs and is critical to re-entrancy.

As a habit, programmers should write all ISRs as totally re-entrant. This means that any ISR should be able to interrupt itself without detrimentally affecting anything in the system. Re-entrancy is an inherent concept of well-written C. Local variables, for example, are stack-resident for each iteration of a given C routine. Several instances of the routine can be in process simultaneously within a given system, and each instance contains its own unique data area; there is no danger of local data collision. Global variables give re-entrancy a slightly different spin, and these issues are addressed while discussing shared RAM in Chapter 5.

Assembly language instructions for a given CPU will always have a "special" return-from-interrupt instruction for returning control from an ISR to the interrupted code. This instruction will anticipate a "far" return address regardless of the code's address-model size. Since any processing module can be interrupted at any location, "far" addresses are always used in invoking ISRs and in returning from ISRs (in consonance with the vector table scheme). The interrupt return instruction will also typically cause the CPU's status word to be restored before relinquishing control to the interrupted routine. In Intel assembly, the interrupt return instruction is IRET (interrupt return), for Motorola assembly it is RTE (return from exception). For the 8086 and 68000 families, the return addresses are always 32-bit.

As mentioned in the preceding section, ISRs will most often re-enable external interrupts when the ISR is entered. This is to avoid loss of subsequent external interrupt requests that may occur while the current ISR is underway. CPUs typically disable external interrupts between receiving an interrupt request and commencing the ISR. Sometimes it is desirable not to enable external interrupts until an ISR has completed; in this case, if ISRs were enabled in the interrupted code, they will typically be enabled when that code regains control. This is due to the transparent saving and restoring of the CPU status word during interrupt processing.

Not too long ago, if the use of C language were desired in an ISR, embedded-systems programmers had to write an ISR shell in assembly language in order to invoke the necessary C routines. Typically, the shell would enable external interrupts, save all pertinent CPU registers, and invoke the appropriate C routine to perform the details required of the ISR. After regaining control from the invoked function, the shell would restore CPU registers and return from the interrupt.

The ISR shell is still a frequently useful programming approach, and an example of such a routine is given later; however, many of the more evolved C compilers now permit the writing of ISRs in C language. Typically, these compilers use a PRAGMA scheme or similar compiler directive to indicate that a given routine or module is an ISR. By using the compiler directives to generate "special" routine entry and exit code, the better compilers will adequately take care of all ISR register saving, restoring, and interrupt return considerations; but they seldom have the capability to enable external interrupts at ISR entry. For example, Microtec Research uses a compiler switch to indicate that the ensuing code is to be compiled as an ISR. This switch is set by defining $INTERRUPT:

```
#define $INTERRUPT

ISR code goes here.

#undef $INTERRUPT
```

ISRs written in C must not return values in the fashion that C functions do. Also, these ISRs must not accept arguments. The programmer has no control over the transparent aspects of the CPU-specific interrupt handling process, and the process is not identical to the invocation of C functions or subroutines.

It is a good idea to place all ISRs written in C into a separate source module(s). During the ISR compile process, stack checking must be disabled and, generally speaking, compiler optimization of any kind should be avoided—but these are compiler-specific determinations.

ISRs written in C should always be declared as VOID routines. If the current code's address-model requires the FAR keyword to achieve a 32-bit address, the ISR should be declared as VOID FAR. Sometimes compilers that allow writing ISRs in C will provide the compiler-specific data type of INTERRUPT and require its use in the ISR function declaration. In that case, VOID FAR will be implied with the use of the INTERRUPT data type.

Parameters can be passed to ISRs via CPU registers in much the same fashion that traditional assembly language routines receive parameters. The prevalent use of parameter-passing to ISRs is in software interrupt requests issued by the programmer. To facilitate this, Intel-based C compilers usually have a compiler-specific INTxx instruction available for issuing software interrupts; this instruction typically makes the full set of CPU registers available both before and after the interrupt. However, if an ISR invoked from software needs to pass something back to the invoking program, it is usually best that the far address of the destination area be passed to the ISR, and that the ISR directly deliver the information before issuing the interrupt return instruction.

Examples have been given of how 8086 and 68000 processors generally handle interrupt processing. For any given CPU, in-depth knowledge of the interrupt handling process is a requirement for embedded-systems programmers; this information is readily available from documentation supplied by chip manufacturers.

The next two sections are examples of the previously mentioned ISR assembly shell written in Intel assembly language, and an ISR written using Microtec Research's software development environment for Motorola processors. The framework issues that were discussed in Chapter 3 under "Mixed-Language Considerations" apply to the Intel shell example. Compiler-specific framework issues apply to the C example, and minor changes would be required for specific embedded software environments.

EXAMPLE ASSEMBLY SHELL FOR ISRs (INTEL)

Before looking at the actual Intel ISR shell code, further explanation of Intel addressing is in order. The data segment register, DS, always points to the segment address of the current data area in use. Data buckets are accessed by general-register-contained offsets within that data segment, and some Intel general register usages are implicit. For example, [BX] implies DS:[BX]. Should DS not point where expected, the wrong bucket would be accessed.

This can be particularly troublesome to programmers working in multitasking environments. Generally speaking, if any global data is to be referenced in such environments, the data segment of the C function that will be called to perform the detail service of an ISR should be saved during the system initialization process, and should be restored from the ISR shell prior to calling that C function. This ensures that DS points where the C routine expects it to point while it executes the code that will perform ISR service. Hybrids of this scheme will work in all Intel-based environments, including operating system environments.

In order to save the data segment at system initialization time, a routine called _SAVEDS is included in the shell's assembly module. This routine can be called from a C program, and it will save the DS and ES register contents known to the C program at the time the routine is called. For most stand-alone C programs, simply calling this routine shortly after the program is loaded will accomplish the desired end. In multitasking environments, this routine can be called when the task containing the desired ISR C functions is loaded. Embedded-systems programmers can frequently bypass this routine by simply inserting the correct, and previously known, data segment value into DS from within the assembly shell before calling the C routine.

In order to restore the previously saved registers, a routine called GETDS is used internally by the ISR shell prior to calling the C function whose registers were saved. After calling GETDS, the data segment and extra segment will always point to the desired data areas of the C routine being called, if_SAVEDS were used properly. Again, this routine could be bypassed by embedded-systems programmers.

```
; MODULE PATH: \TEXT\ISRSHLL.ASM
;
;
; In order to save and restore the machine state at entry, this
; assembly language is required in order to call C processing
; for ISRs.
;
;
    name ISRSHLL              ; module name
;
```

```
      public _isrshell          ; ISR name
      public _saveds            ; routine to save DS
  ;
      extrn _c_fcn:far          ; C routine to call
  ;
  ;
  _TEXT    segment public 'CODE'
     assume cs:_TEXT
  ;
  ; DATA AREA TO STORE SAVED VALUES OF ES & DS
  ;
  savds dw ?
  saves dw ?
  ;
  ; --------------------------------
  ; ROUTINE TO SAVE DS & ES FROM  C
  ; --------------------------------
  ;
  _saveds proc far
     push ax                    ;save registers
     push bx
     push dx
  ;
     push ds                    ;save current ds
     push cs                    ;ds = cs
     pop ds                     ;ds = cs
  ;
     mov bx,offset savds        ;get bucket offsets
     mov dx,offset saves        ;get bucket offsets
     pop ds                     ;restore current ds
  ;
     mov ax,ds                  ;put current ds into ax
     mov cs:[bx], ax            ;save current ds
  ;
     mov bx,dx
     mov ax,es
     mov cs:[bx],ax             ;save current es
  ;
     pop dx                     ;restore registers
     pop bx
     pop ax
  ;
     ret
  _saveds endp
  ;
  ; ----------------------------------
  ; ROUTINE TO RESTORE DS & ES FROM ISR
  ; ----------------------------------
  ;
  getds proc far
     push ax                 ;save registers
```

```
    push bx
    push dx
;
    push cs              ;data seg = code seg
    pop ds
;
    mov dx,offset savds
    mov bx,offset saves
;
    mov ax,cs:[bx]       ;saved value of ds to ax
    push ax
    pop ds               ;restore ds
;
    mov bx,dx
    mov ax,cs:[bx]       ;saved value of es to ax
    push ax
    pop es               ;restore es
;
    pop dx               ;restore registers
    pop bx
    pop ax
;
    ret
getds endp
;
; --------------------------------------------
; ASSEMBLY SHELL ISR TO CALL C FOR PROCESSING
; --------------------------------------------
;
_isrshell proc far
;
    sti                  ;enable external interrupts
    push ax              ;save registers
    push bx
    push cx
    push dx
    push ds
    push es
    push bp
    push si
    push di
;
    call getds           ;get saved values of ds and es
;
                         ;If any parameters were passed to
                         ;the isr via registers, they could
                         ;be pushed onto the stack here in
                         ;order to pass them on to the C function.
;
    call _c_fcn          ;call desired function
;
```

```
        pop di
        pop si
        pop bp
        pop es
        pop ds
        pop dx
        pop cx
        pop bx
        pop ax
;
    iret
;
_isrshell      endp
_TEXT          ends
        end
;
```

A similar shell could be created in Motorola assembly language; but there would be no need for any code corresponding to the _SAVEDS and GETDS subroutines shown above.

EXAMPLE ISR WRITTEN IN C (MOTOROLA)

A number of C ISRs for a Motorola-based system are presented later. At this point, the form is more important than the processing code, so this example is very brief. The dummy ISR mentioned earlier is presented here using Microtec Research's conventions:

```
/* MODULE PATH: \TEXT\IDMMY.C */

USHORT dmmy_cnt;       /* RAM Counter for dummy interrupts    */

#define $INTERRUPT    /* Following code = ISR                */

/*
   -------------------------------------------------------------
   Dummy ISR to increment a global bucket with each iteration.
   -------------------------------------------------------------
 */

VOID i_dmmy(VOID)
{
   ++(dmmy_cnt);       /*$ INCRMNT global bucket */
}

undef $INTERRUPT       /* No more ISR code in this module */
```

TIMING CONSIDERATIONS

In general, ISRs should be as efficient as possible. It is not desirable to keep a CPU in the interrupted state for undue periods. Also, levels of nesting are decreased with ISR efficiency. When execution time is marginally critical, it is sometimes better to write C ISRs as point-to-point code rather than invoking functions at lower levels. This is particularly true if systems require that external interrupts be disabled during ISR execution. Sometimes ISRs must be written totally in assembly language for maximum execution efficiency.

While an ISR is executing, nothing else can be processed except another ISR. Whether or not another ISR is allowed to interrupt the currently executing ISR is somewhat CPU-specific as previously presented; however, the final resolution typically depends on the condition of the interrupt mask in the CPU status word and the interrupt priorities of the interrupts in question. The programmer has considerable control over these conditions by re-enabling external interrupts at ISR entry, or otherwise affecting the interrupt mask.

When ISRs are written for interrupt-intensive embedded systems, the execution time of each ISR should be determined. Today, there are a number of software products that allow such analysis of typical C programs; however, in embedded systems work, this will usually be done with an in-circuit emulator (ICE) unit. ICE units will be covered in Chapter 7. For now, the fact that a method exists to determine ISR execution times is all that is needed. In practice, the maximum frequency of interrupt occurrence is absolutely limited by the length of the interrupt execution time.

The frequency of interrupt occurrences, execution times of ISRs, desired intervals for obtaining device data, time required for servicing devices, and the time required for processing the sum total of main code threads, all work together in determining overall system timing requirements. It is important that all these things be reasonably estimated and that enough CPU time be available to accomplish design goals. Knowing how long it takes to execute each system ISR, for example, can head off stack-overflow problems.

If the system has been well analyzed in the design process, all hardware will have been selected properly at the beginning of the project; but if not, timing considerations can lead to the use of a more powerful CPU and/or faster and more expensive components. Many embedded systems have an RS232 communications capability, and the capability is frequently interrupt-driven character I/O. This is especially true in plant-floor environments. For an immediate example of component selection considerations, a hypothetical RS232 communications environment will be used. The purpose here is to show how component capability and some interrupt timing issues can affect the component selection process in realizing system design goals.

Assume the following: a system is utilizing Intel's 80186 processor at a clock speed and implementation that can handle 14,400 interrupts per second, plus or minus 100; the 80186 CPU is a coprocessor on an STD system bus; it is used in conjunction with four Zilog 8530 Serial Communications Controllers (SCCs), which control a total of eight RS232 ports. For purposes of this example, all communications are interrupt-driven character I/O, although the Zilog SCCs have additional communications capabilities. The receiving of each character causes an interrupt, indicating to the CPU that the character is available for pickup in the SCC's receiver; the transmitting of each character causes a transmit-buffer-empty interrupt when the SCC's transmitter is empty. This part of the total embedded system is strictly dedicated to serial I/O, and passes the communicated information to other system areas via a dual-ported RAM window. (Such a dual-ported RAM window appears to reside at different addresses from different system perspectives. Specifically, the coprocessor board's processor accesses this RAM using an address within its purview, but the same window of RAM is mapped differently within the host system.) As described, the example environment is interrupt-intensive, and is realtime critical in preventing the loss of characters at any given port.

In order to determine the maximum baud rates that can be used within the system, more information is required about the strings being communicated:

- Is full-duplex operation required?
- What is the frame size of each character?

Assuming a requirement for 7 data bits, 1 start bit, 1 stop bit, and 1 parity bit, the frame size is 10 bits. Assuming asynchronous bidirectional communications, full duplex is required. A single port's maximum quantitative interrupt requirements could be closely approximated as follows:

$$(BAUD\ RATE * 2) / FRAMESIZE = number\ of\ interrupts.$$

Using 9600 baud, full duplex, 10-bit frame, the answer is 1,920 interrupts per second per port, if all ports are operating identically. Multiplying this figure by 8 gives 15,360 total interrupts per second for 8 ports; therefore, the implementation as described would not handle all 8 ports simultaneously in full duplex at 9600 baud using 10-bit character frames. Fewer ports and/or slower baud rates and/or half-duplex and/or larger frame sizes could allow their simultaneous use, or another CPU might be considered. Increasing the character frame size by a single bit will reduce the total interrupt requirements to less than 14,000. In actual practice, many applications would use different communications parameters for different ports; however, the above formula could be used to calculate interrupt requirements for each port.

Along similar lines, overall I/O timing issues can be analyzed by using the "1ms per character at 9600 baud" rule-of-thumb. At 9600 baud, 10-bit character frames require about 1.04ms for transmission; 13-bit frames require about 1.25ms. If the mean system message size is 30 characters, programmers would probably want to check receiving buffers at about 32–38ms intervals. But, again, these considerations are entirely project-specific.

EXAMPLE 8530 SCC RS232 ISRS (INTEL)

When dealing with communications issues such as those outlined in the preceding section, ISRs for transmit and receive should be kept as small as possible. For example, a hardware ISR for receiving character I/O, as in the above example, should only grab the incoming character from the 8530 SCC's receiver and place it into a hardware receive buffer contained in software. Some overhead is necessary in buffer management, but this is unavoidable in creating a flexible and robust system.

In the 8530 world, what happens is that a character's availability in the SCC receiver causes the SCC to externally interrupt the CPU. The CPU processing is vectored to the SCC's receiver hardware ISR which should simply grab the character, stuff it into a buffer, manage the buffer, and return to the interrupted program. Hardware-level receiving essentially operates in the background, transparent to other processing. A following section will show how an application program would typically interface to the hardware ISR's buffer in order to get the data it needs; for now, the typical hardware receiver ISR is addressed, as shown in Figure 4-1.

Using the Intel assembly shell for ISRs that was previously presented, the following C routine could be called to accept asynchronous character input into the software receive buffer at the hardware level:

```
#define RXBUFFSIZ 256      /* size of receiving buffer       */
#define BUFFOVRN  0x08      /* flag to indicate buffer overrun */
#define IUSRESET  0x38      /* mask for 8530 SCC IUS reset    */

UCHAR inportb(UCHAR *portadr);
VOID  outportb(UCHAR *portadr, UCHAR value);

/* Sample Port Control Block (for receiving only) */

typedef struct xxpcb {

UCHAR *datareg;       /* SCC data register addr          */
UCHAR *ctrlreg;       /* SCC control register addr       */
USHORT rx_remcnt;     /* buff byte cnt not in use        */
USHORT rx_curcnt;     /* buff byte cnt in use            */
UCHAR *rx_usrptr;     /* addr next user access in rx buffer */
UCHAR *rx_comptr;     /* nxt hdwr receive addr           */
UCHAR rx_errstat;     /* receive error status            */
```

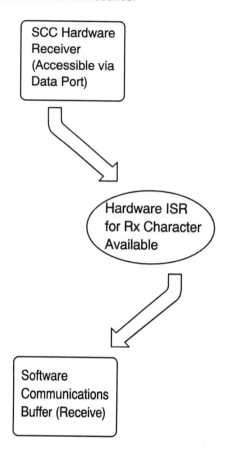

Figure 4-1. Typical Hardware ISR for Receive

```
UCHAR rx_numerr;       /* num characters in error in buffer  */
UCHAR *rxbstart;       /* rx buffer starting addr            */

} XPCB, *XPCBPTR, far *XPCBPTRF;

#define NMBRPORTS 8   /* number of ports in system          */
#define THISPORT  0   /* this port's offset in PCB array    */

                      /* array of PCBs, one per system port */
extern XPCB pcb_array[NMBRPORTS];

/*
  -------------------------------------------------------------
  Routine to receive one character from 8530 SCC receiver and
  place it into the ISR's software receiving buffer.
  -------------------------------------------------------------
*/
```

```
VOID rx_char(VOID)/*& Receive char & manage rx buffer */
{
XPCBPTR pcbx;
    pcbx = &pcb_array[THISPORT];
    if (pcbx->rx_remcnt > 0)    /*$ ENSURE room in buffer    */
    {
                          /*$ PUT char into next buff position  */

    *(pcbx->rx_comptr) = (UCHAR) inportb(pcbx->datareg);

    ++(pcbx->rx_comptr);        /*$ INCREMENT buff position  */
    ++(pcbx->rx_curcnt);        /*$ INCREMENT received count */
    --(pcbx->rx_remcnt);        /*$ DECREMENT count available */

                /*$ CHK for buffer wrap (circular buffer)    */

    if ((ULONG) pcbx->rx_comptr
        == ((ULONG) pcbx->rxbstart + RXBUFFSIZ))
                              pcbx->rx_comptr = pcbx->rxbstart;
    }
else                                /*$ NO ROOM in buffer  */
    {
    pcbx->rx_errstat |= BUFFOVRN;    /*$ SET buffer overrun */
    ++(pcbx->rx_numerr);             /*$ INCREMENT err cnt  */
    }

        /*$ RESET SCC highest Interrupt Under Service (IUS)  */

    outportb(pcbx->ctrlreg,IUSRESET);
}
```

By duplicating the ISR shell for each port in the system and by modifying the above routine to accept the XPCBPTR as an argument from each shell (and of course, by adjusting the shell accordingly), this routine could be shared by all system ports. A table of Port Control Blocks would be needed—one PCB per port. Also, a PCB would normally contain all necessary data buckets for both transmitting and receiving; the above is a sample for receiving only.

In a similar fashion the 8530 SCC's hardware ISR for transmit should be kept as small as possible. Again in the 8530 world, each time the hardware transmitter becomes empty, an SCC transmitter-empty interrupt occurs. The CPU is vectored to the SCC's transmitter hardware ISR which should simply transmit one character, manage the transmit buffer, and check the buffer count to see if all characters have been transmitted. If all the characters have been transmitted, the routine should reset the 8530's transmit-interrupt-pending bit to cease transmit activity. This scheme causes hardware-level transmitting to operate in the background, transparent to other processing.

The programmer must place the first character into the SCC's hardware transmitter (via a port) in order to start the transmit process and to subsequently get the transmitter-empty interrupt. This is normally accomplished via software ISR at the same time that strings are moved from the application program to the ISR's software buffer for transmission. A following section will show how an application program would interface to the hardware transmit ISR; but for now, the typical hardware transmitter ISR is addressed as shown in Figure 4-2.

Again using the Intel assembly shell for ISRs, the following C routines could be used to perform asynchronous, hardware-level character transmission:

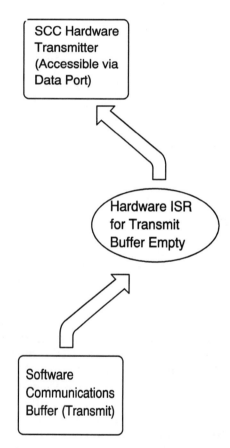

Figure 4-2. Typical Hardware ISR for Transmit

```
#define NMBRPORTS  8        /* Number of system ports  */
#define  TXBUFFSIZ 256      /* Size of transmit buffer */

#define IUSRESET 0x38       /* msk to reset highest IUS          */
#define TXPRESET 0x28       /* msk to reset tx interrupt pending */
#define TXURESET 0xc0       /* msk to reset transmit underrun    */
#define TXBUFMTY 0x04       /* msk for tx empty (read reg 0)     */

#define NOBUFSPACE TXBUFFSIZ+10  /* Error return */
```

```c
typedef struct xxpcb {
UCHAR *datareg;        /* SCC data register addr             */
UCHAR *ctrlreg;        /* SCC control register addr          */
USHORT tx_remcnt;      /* byte cnt to transmit               */
USHORT tx_curcnt;      /* byte cnt actually transmitted      */
UCHAR *tx_usrptr;      /* addr next user access in tx buffer */
UCHAR *tx_comptr;      /* addr next char to transmit buffer  */
UCHAR tx_errstat;      /* transmit error status              */
UCHAR tx_numerr;       /* number transmit errors             */
UCHAR *txbstart;       /* tx buffer starting addr            */
} XPCB, *XPCBPTR, far *XPCBPTRF;

UCHAR inportb(UCHAR *portadr);
VOID  outportb(UCHAR * portadr, UCHAR value);

extern XPCB pcb_array[NMBRPORTS];

/*
  ----------------------------------------------------------
  This routine is SHARED by hardware & software tx ISRs
  ----------------------------------------------------------
  Routine to PUT 1 character from the tx buffer into
  the SCC transmitter & manage tx buffer
  ----------------------------------------------------------
*/

VOID tx_1_char(XPCBPTRF pcbx)
              /*& Transmit 1 char & manage tx buffer  */
{
USHORT sendata;
                                  /*$ SAVE char to send */
   sendata = *(pcbx->tx_comptr);

   if (pcbx->tx_remcnt > 0)       /*$ CHK # char to tx   */
        {
        ++(pcbx->tx_comptr);      /*$ INCR to next addr */
        --(pcbx->tx_remcnt);      /*$ DECR cnt to send  */
        ++(pcbx->tx_curcnt);      /*$ INCR sent count   */

             /*$ CHECK buffer wrap (circular buffer)   */
        if    ((ULONG) pcbx->tx_comptr ==
               ((ULONG) pcbx->txbstart + TXBUFFSIZ))
                   pcbx->tx_comptr = pcbx->txbstart;

        outportb(pcbx->datareg,sendata);/*$ OUTPUTchar*/
        }
   return;                                /*$ RETURN       */
}

/*
```

```
-----------------------------------------------------
    Routine to transmit characters from the tx buffer
    and check if transmission done.
-----------------------------------------------------
*/
VOID tx_char(XPCBPTR pcbx)
                        /*& Transmit char & manage tx buffer    */
    {
                        /*$ OUTPUT 1 char & manage tx buffer     */
    tx_1_char((XPCBPTRF) pcbx);

                        /*$ CHECK for tx DONE                    */
                        /*$ IF done, reset tx intrpt pending     */
                        /*$ IF done, reset cnt sent              */
    if (pcbx->tx_remcnt == 0)
            {
            outportb(pcbx->ctrlreg,TXPRESET);
            pcbx->tx_curcnt = 0;
            }
                        /*$ RESET SCC highest IUS                */
    outportb(pcbx->ctrlreg,IUSRESET);
    }
```

As before, the ISR shell could be duplicated for each port, and this routine could be modified to accept the XPCBPTR as an argument from each shell; then, this routine could be shared by all system ports. Also, this PCB is only a sample—for transmitting.

INTERRUPT LATENCY

There is a time lag between a device's request for service and the actual servicing of that request. The time required for the CPU to recognize an interrupt request and begin executing the associated ISR is called *interrupt latency*. For both Intel and Motorola processors, interrupts are not processed until the current assembly-level instruction has completely finished execution, excluding internal interrupts that occur under catastrophic conditions.

This implies that maximum interrupt latency will be experienced if the current instruction requires a high number of CPU clock cycles for execution. Maximum interrupt latency should be expected during multiplication, division, variable bit shift and rotate, and similar instructions. In isolated cases, worst-case latency can span two processing instructions due to CPU-specific instruction sequences that are precluded from interruption.

Internal interrupts that occur under catastrophic conditions are sometimes permitted to preempt the currently executing assembly-level instruction. In this case there is no latency involved. When interrupts with such a high degree of privilege are used, typically they are allocated by chip manufacturers for urgent conditions like imminent loss of power.

Interrupt latency is mentioned as a separate topic since it is an important concept in dealing with highly time-critical and/or state-of-the-art embedded systems. For most applications that will be encountered, interrupt latency will not be a critical design issue; however, latency will be mentioned again in the discussion of timer interrupts.

TIMER INTERRUPTS

No discussion of embedded systems interrupts would be complete without mention of timer interrupts. Timers are used in a multitude of ways, but one of the most common uses within embedded systems is to provide for interrupt requests at precisely timed intervals. For example, a device could require "adjustment" 32 times per second (every 31.25ms), and in order to adjust that device, input from another device might be sampled at the same interval. Timers can request interrupts at specified intervals, and the associated ISRs can perform most any service.

Timers are normally fed by some type of high-frequency pulse source, such as an oscillator. The frequency of the pulsed input is the "speed" of the timer. Typically, an onboard "counter" can be set in accordance with timer-specific documentation, and this counter is decremented proportionally to timer speed in order to provide a precise time interval with each instance that the count reaches zero.

Some timers provide for requesting an external interrupt when the count reaches zero. In this case, the associated ISR will normally reset the counter at ISR entry, so that another interrupt request will be generated at the desired interval. The implication here is that sequential timer interrupts at specified intervals are more accurate with less interrupt latency; this is certainly true. Some programmers are in the habit of writing timer initialization routines in assembly, and this has some effect on interrupt latency. But normally, a few CPU clock cycles will not have great impact on an application.

For the Intel-based PC world in general, the CPU clock speed typically is fed by an oscillator that varies from 6MHz to 50MHz. In order to keep hardware and peripherals happy while dealing with different CPU speeds, a system timer-tick interrupt is requested at a constant interval (about 18.2 times per second), regardless of CPU speed. This timer-tick interrupt provides the requisite timer baseline for compatibility of operation between a multitude of PC products hosting popular operating systems. Of course, this timer-tick interrupt is not required of embedded systems in that popular operating systems and cross-platform compatibility are not design issues.

In order to use a timer, it must be initialized and set up for whatever counts are desired. Some timers allow programmer selection of speed, and virtually all will require some up-front calculations on the part of the programmer. The calculations are in accordance with timer-specific documentation, and generally entail determining the appropriate "counts" to use in a given system. Timer initializations are highly device-specific in detail, but a typical timer initialization routine could look like this in Motorola assembly language using Microtec Research development software and a hypothetical timer with odd-byte-boundary register addressing (this is an 8-bit device on a 16-bit data bus):

```
* MODULE PATH: \TEXT\TIMR.ASM

   OPT    CASE
INITMR          IDNT
                XDEF RECNT32,HLTMR,INITMR
*
* Offsets from base address
*   $21         Timer Control Register
*   $23         Timer Interrupt Vector Register
*   $25         Counter Register HI
*   $27         Counter Register LO
*

BA  EQU  $02F80E      * TIMR BASE ADDR

INITMR:
  MOVE.L AO,-(SP)     * SAVE AO
  MOVE.L DO,-(SP)     * SAVE DO
*
  LEA          BA,AO                 * SET BASE ADDRESS
  MOVE.B       #$00,$21(AO)          * RESET TIMER - HALT
  MOVE.B       #$60,$23(AO)          * SET INTRRUPT VECTOR TYPE $60
  MOVE.L       #$1E84,DO             * SET COUNTER TO 31.25MS
  MOVEP.L      DO,$25(AO)            * OUTPUT COUNTER BYTES
  MOVE.B       #$88,$21(AO)          * RESET TIMER - START
*
  MOVE.L       (SP)+,DO              * RESTORE DO
  MOVE.L       (SP)+,AO              * RESTORE AO
  RTS                                * RETURN FM SUBROUTINE
*
RECNT32:
  MOVE.L       DO,-(SP)              * SAVE DO
  MOVE.L       AO,-(SP)              * SAVE AO
  LEA          BA,AO                 * SET BASE ADDRESS
  MOVE.L       #$1E84,DO             * SET COUNTER TO 31.25MS
  MOVEP.L      DO,$25(AO)            * OUTPUT COUNTER BYTES
  MOVE.B       #$88,$21(AO)          * RESET TIMER - START
  MOVE.L       (SP)+,AO              * RESTORE AO
  MOVE.L       (SP)+,DO              * RESTORE DO
  RTS
*
HLTMR:
  MOVE.L       AO,-(SP)              * SAVE AO
```

```
    LEA         BA,A0                * SET BASE ADDRESS
    MOVE.B      #$00,$21(A0)         * RESET TIMER - HALT
    MOVE.L      (SP)+,A0             * RESTORE A0
    RTS
*
    END                             * MODULE END
```

In the above example, the base register location would be project-implementation-specific, as would the ISR vector type and the desired time interval. The values written and the sequence in which the values are written would be device-specific, and the values would depend on timer clock speed. However, this example shows what is entailed typically in setting a timer to interrupt at a specified interval. The associated ISR might have to move the counter value into the appropriate register in order to reset the counter, and then restart the timer. This would provide for the next interrupt. The routine RECNT32 could accomplish this in spite of the odd-byte addressing. The example is hypothetical because timers are intensely device-specific and implementation-specific, but the programming of timers can be this simple. This timer example is similar to an actual Signetics 68230 parallel interface timer implementation on a Mizar Digital Systems, Inc., (Carrolton, Texas) board with a Motorola 68000 CPU. The timer is set to interrupt at 31.25ms intervals (32Hz) using these calculations for a .125usec clock period:

8MHz clock speed (CPU input)
8,000,000 tics = 1 second
1 clock count = 32 tics
250,000 counts = 1 second
62,500 counts = .25 seconds
32Hz = 7812.5 counts = 1/32 seconds = 0x1e84

Such a timer could be used in a missile-to-aircraft interface box. The current aircraft pressure-altitude reading from a synchro-to-digital altimeter interface could be required in order to service an Inertial Navigation System (INS) at 32Hz. The above timer has been set to request an external interrupt every 31.25ms (32Hz). The resulting timer-caused interrupt could acquire the desired pressure altitude reading if its associated ISR would restart the timer for the next interrupt, read the current synchro position, massage the reading to an altitude value, place that value into a bucket ultimately destined for the INS, and return to the interrupted code:

```
USHORT curr_altitude;        /* desired final value    */
UCHAR  intrrpt_flg;

/* 16-bit ports used by this ISR */
#define SYNCCTRL ((USHORT *) 0x02FA081)
#define SYNCOARS ((USHORT *) 0x02FA0A1)
#define SYNCFINE ((USHORT *) 0x02FA0C1)
```

```
/* Mask indicating synchros locked (in control port)  */
#define SYNLKD 0xe000

/* Assembly routine to reset timer for next interrupt */
extern VOID RECNT32(VOID);

/* C fcn to convert synchro input to altitude (feet)*/
extern USHORT massage_data(SFLOAT coarse_read, SFLOAT fine_read);

#define $INTERRUPT

VOID far int_hz32(VOID)
{
USHORT PActrlIN;
SFLOAT coarse;
SFLOAT fine;

   RECNT32();                  /*$ RESET timer (assembly)*/
   PActrlIN = *SYNCCTRL;       /*$ LOCK synchro reading  */
   intrrpt_flg = 1;            /*$ SET interrupt flag    */

                               /*$ CHECK synchros LOCKED */
   if ((PActrlIN & SYNLKD) == SYNLKD)
   {
                               /*$ READ coarse then fine */
   coarse = *SYNCOARS;
   fine   = *SYNCFINE;
                               /*$ MASSAGE values input  */
                               /*$ SAVE desired altitude  */
   curr_altitude = massage_data(coarse, fine);
   }
   *SYNCCTRL = 0;              /*$ RELEASE synchros      */
}
#undef $INTERRUPT
```

The above MASSAGE_DATA() function would be highly device-specific. Typical machinations for the function might require scaling the synchro input and making other adjustments with calculated device-specific constants, ensuring that the calculated degrees were not greater than 360, and ultimately converting the degrees to feet in accordance with device documentation.

Regarding the interrupt-occurred flag, it is set primarily for initial debugging purposes. After the system is operating properly, such flag settings for active ISRs are normally removed in the interest of ISR efficiency.

INVOKING ISRs FROM SOFTWARE

Both the Motorola 68000 and the Intel 8086 allow software to generate interrupts. The address of a software ISR would have been placed into the vector table just like any other ISR. When ISR services are needed, the programmer can issue an interrupt request to the previously assigned "type" number for that ISR. At the assembly level, Intel provides the INT instruction and Motorola provides the TRAP instruction. The Motorola 68000 dedicates vectors 32 through 47 for the TRAP instruction. The Intel INT instructions has no such restriction. Invoking vector 32 at the assembly level could look like this:

INT 32 for Intel or TRAP 32 for Motorola

Intel-based C compilers usually provide a compiler-specific INTxx function for issuing software interrupts. Typically it allows CPU register setup prior to executing the function, and allows checking the registers "as returned" from the ISR. This function normally saves and restores all CPU registers transparently before and after allowing programmer access:

```
INTxx(interrupt number,  pointer to registers in,
                         pointer to registers out)
```

The ISRs that are executed as a result of software interrupt requests can be used to answer a multitude of challenges, but one of the most effective uses is in interfacing application programs to "background" communications buffers in environments like the one that dominates earlier sections of this chapter. In that example environment, the hardware ISRs take care of the "background" communications, and they load and unload the ISRs receive and transmit buffers transparently to other processing. When an application program is ready to receive a message or part of a message, it can generate a software interrupt that immediately grabs the available data from the hardware ISR's receiving buffer.

In an earlier section, a hardware ISR was presented for receiving serially communicated characters in the background. The software ISR to satisfactorily interface to that hardware ISR's receiving buffer could also use a modified ISR shell and invoke a C routine for detail processing within the ISR. An ISR for "receiving" character I/O into an application program is shown in Figure 4-3. The following code is a C routine that would provide for the depicted function, if called from an ISR shell:

```
#define NMBRPORTS 8        /* number of ports in system  */
#define RXBUFFSIZ 256      /* size of receiving buffer    */

/* Sample Port Control Block (for receiving only)   */

typedef struct xxpcb {

UCHAR *datareg;     /* SCC data register addr       */
UCHAR *ctrlreg;     /* SCC control register addr    */
USHORT rx_remcnt;   /* buff byte cnt not in use      */
USHORT rx_curcnt;   /* buff byte cnt in use          */
```

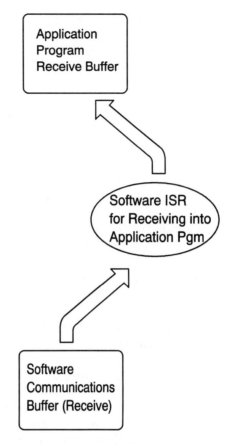

Figure 4-3. Typical Software ISR for Receive

```
UCHAR *rx_usrptr;      /* addr next user access in rx buffer */
UCHAR *rx_comptr;      /* nxt hdwr receive addr               */
UCHAR rx_errstat;      /* receive error status                */
UCHAR rx_numerr;       /* num characters in error in buffer   */
UCHAR *rxbstart;       /* rx buffer starting addr             */

} XPCB, *XPCBPTR, far *XPCBPTRF;

                       /* array of PCBs, one per system port */
extern XPCB pcb_array[NMBRPORTS];

/*
   -----------------------------------------------------------------
   Routine to grab all available characters from hardware
   receiving buffer and move them to application program buffer.
   -----------------------------------------------------------------
 */

int recv_it(USHORT portno, USHORT offset, USHORT segment)
```

```
              /*& Place all received data into program buffer */
{
USHORT i;
XPCBPTRF pcbxptr;
USHORT retcnt;
UCHAR far *destination;

   pcbxptr = &pcb_array[portno];/*$ GET PCB addr        */
   retcnt = pcbxptr->rx_curcnt; /*$ SET return char cnt */

                              /*$ MAKE a far DEST PTR */

   destination = (UCHAR *) ((ULONG) ((offset << 16) | segment));

                              /*$ FOR each avail char   */

   for (i = 0; i < retcnt; i++)
    {
                              /*$ MOVE char to app pgm  */

   *destination = *(pcbxptr->rx_usrptr);

   ++(pcbxptr->rx_remcnt);   /*$ INCR cnt not in use  */
   --(pcbxptr->rx_curcnt);   /*$ DECR cnt available   */
   ++destination;            /*$ INCR destination addr */
   ++(pcbxptr->rx_usrptr);   /*$ INCR source addr     */

                              /*$ CHK for buffer wrap -- circular
                                               buffer */

   if ((ULONG) pcbxptr->rx_usrptr ==
      (ULONG) ( pcbxptr->rxbstart + RXBUFFSIZ))
             pcbxptr->rx_usrptr = pcbxptr->rxbstart;
    }
   return;
}
```

To use this C routine, the programmer would invoke INTxx() against whatever vector type pointed to the correct ISR shell for this desired ISR. The programmer might have placed the segment address of the application program's destination buffer into register ES, the offset into BX, and the port number whose data is being acquired into register AX before using INTxx().

The ISR assembly shell would receive the application program's destination buffer address as a segment and offset in ES and BX respectively. The port number arrives in AX.

The assembly shell would have to push ES, BX, and AX onto the stack in that order prior to calling the C function RECV_IT(). This would provide the arguments needed by RECV_IT() in the order that RECV_IT() expects them. RECV_IT() assembles the segment and offset into a far pointer recognizable to C, which is where it stores each character and subsequently increments this destination address.

When the ISR has ended, the hardware receive buffer has been relieved and the application program's buffer contains all characters that were available from the requested port when the ISR was entered. It follows that the application's buffer must be at least as large as the hardware ISR's buffer.

A similar software ISR could be written to fill the software transmit buffer from an application program. This ISR would also use an ISR shell and would be invoked just like the receive ISR, but, of course, it would not be the same vector type or shell. Also, another parameter, the "count" of characters to be moved, would be required from the application program. After moving the "count" number of characters from the application program to the ISR's transmit buffer, this ISR could use the same TX_1_CHAR() routine used by the hardware ISR in order to start the transmit process if transmission is not already underway after the "new" characters have been moved. If transmission is already underway, TX_1_CHAR() is skipped, but transmission will continue thanks to the SCC's transmitter-empty interrupt. In either case, the characters that this routine places into the buffer will be transmitted. An ISR for "transmitting" from an application program is shown in Figure 4-4. The following code is a C routine that would provide for the depicted function, if called from an ISR shell:

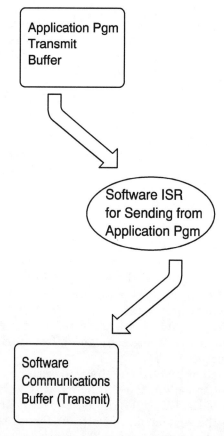

Figure 4-4. Typical Software ISR for Transmit

```
#define NMBRPORTS  8        /* Number of system ports    */
#define TXBUFFSIZ 256        /* Size of transmit buffer    */
#define TXBUFMTY 0x04        /* Msk for tx empty (Read Reg 0)*/
#define NOBUFSPACE 0x8       /* Error mask                 */

typedef struct xxpcb {
UCHAR *datareg;      /* SCC data register addr            */
UCHAR *ctrlreg;      /* SCC control register addr         */
USHORT tx_remcnt;    /* byte cnt to transmit              */
USHORT tx_curcnt;    /* byte cnt actually transmitted     */
UCHAR *tx_usrptr;    /* addr next user access in tx buffer */
UCHAR *tx_comptr;    /* addr next char to transmit buffer  */
UCHAR tx_errstat;    /* transmit error status             */
UCHAR tx_numerr;     /* number transmit errors            */
UCHAR *txbstart;     /* tx buffer starting addr           */
} XPCB, *XPCBPTR, far *XPCBPTRF;

UCHAR inportb(UCHAR *portadr);
VOID  outportb(UCHAR * portadr, UCHAR value);

extern XPCB pcb_array[NMBRPORTS];

/*
 ----------------------------------------------------
  Routine to transmit characters from application
  program to tx buffer and start transmission if
  transmission is not underway.
 ----------------------------------------------------
*/

VOID tx_async(USHORT portno,USHORT offset,USHORT segment,
        USHORT count)/*& Place data in buff & begin tx */
{
SHORT i;
XPCBPTRF pcbxptr;
UCHAR far *source;

  pcbxptr = &pcb_array[portno]; /*$ GET PCB address   */

                              /*$ MAKE a FAR source PTR */
  source = (UCHAR *) ((ULONG) ((offset << 16) | segment));

                              /*$ CHECK buffer space    */
  if ((TXBUFFSIZ - (SHORT) pcbxptr->tx_remcnt) < count)
        {
        pcbxptr->tx_errstat |= NOBUFSPACE;
        ++(pcbxptr->tx_numerr);
        }
  else
        {
```

```
            /*$ MOVE data from application into tx buffer */
            for (i = 0; i < count; i++)
                    {
                    *(pcbxptr->tx_usrptr) = *source;
                    ++(pcbxptr->tx_remcnt);
                    ++source;
                    ++(pcbxptr->tx_usrptr);

                        /*$ CHECK for circular buffer wrap */
                    if ((ULONG) pcbxptr->tx_usrptr ==
                        (ULONG)(pcbxptr->txbstart + TXBUFFSIZ))
                            pcbxptr->tx_usrptr = pcbxptr->txbstart;

                    } /* FOR end */

                /*$ CHECK if tx in progress, start it if not    */
            i = inportb(pcbxptr->ctrlreg);  /* 8530 specific    */
            if (i & TXBUFMTY)               /* 8530 specific    */
                    tx_1_char(pcbxptr);/* start tx if necessary */
            }

        return; /*$ RETURN */
    }
```

In actual practice, the buffer addresses passed in the above examples would likely be the address of some type of application program control structure. In a fashion similar to the implementation of the PCB on the ISR end, application programs frequently have communications control buffers for greater flexibility in conversing with the ISR. The structure could contain the needed buffer addresses, as well as counts, error codes, and other desirable buckets. Normally, such control structures are implemented within Application Programmer Interfaces (APIs) that interface to board-level communications products, and such products typically are written by embedded-systems programmers. A communications interface scheme using an application control structure is shown in Figure 4-5.

FULL-BLOWN RS232 COMMUNICATIONS

RS232 communications protocols prevail in many embedded systems areas. For example, it has been estimated that about 60 percent of American plant-floor manufacturing systems have RS232 implementations, and that another 20 percent have the capability as a not-implemented option. Most embedded-systems programmers will encounter these protocols more than once.

Appendix F contains an example of full-blown multiport, interrupt-driven, asynchronous, RS232, character I/O for Zilog 8530 SCCs. The example is written in C language for IBM's Multiport or Multiport/2 ARTIC board (Asynchronous Realtime Interface Coprocessor). The example executes under IBM's RCM (Realtime Control Microcode) multitasking system that is available for the ARTIC board. The example is board-specific, chip-specific, and RCM-specific, but

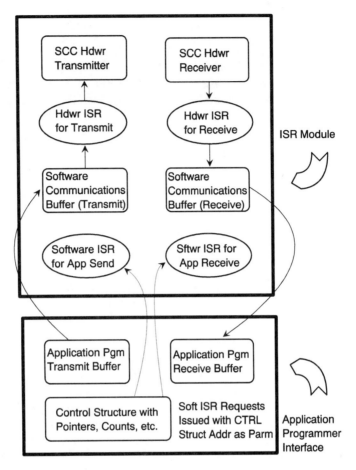

Figure 4-5. Baseline RS232 Communications Software Design

subsets of the code with relatively minor modification will allow its use in a variety of RS232 environments, especially those utilizing Zilog 8530 SCCs. An API is included, as is the RCM task that loads and "owns" all of the hardware ISRs.

Along similar lines, an Intel assembly language example of interrupt-driven RS232 character I/O for Zilog 8530 SCCs is contained in Appendix G. This example was written to provide background communications for several embedded systems that used Pro-Log Corporation's (Monterey, CA) 7863 Multimaster CPU/Communications board. As indicated in Appendix G, software ISRs issued by the process which desires interface to the communications buffers are reasonably compatible with IBM BIOS conventions.

Both of the above RS232 examples are readily adaptable to other communications environments, and are particularly adaptable to environments that use Zilog 8530 SCCs. A number of companies (including Sealevel Systems of Liberty, SC) are currently manufacturing communications board product lines that make heavy use of Zilog 8530 SCCs. The code of either Appendix F or Appendix G is adaptable to such products with a relatively small amount of work.

5

Putting It Together

In general, software has always been a major determining factor in sales of computer systems. In the past, corporate giants like IBM have provided large-scale, total solutions throughout corporate enterprises, and the ultimate measure of success was heavily software-dependent. With the current prevalence of distributed processing, many companies compete to provide solutions for relatively small computing problems, and software seems to play an even greater role in contract awards. When individuals buy PCs for home use, the general availability of software for a given platform is a major consideration.

If two vendors build commercial embedded systems for the same application, software capabilities will set them apart irrespective of hardware foundations, and the software will always be a primary factor in system comparisons. Developing full-featured software is not a "seat-of-the-pants" or "trial-and-error" operation. All desired features must be well-planned and completely analyzed at project inception. The process of changing embedded systems software often creates special technical challenges, as well as customer service challenges, and this is particularly true if the modifications are done in the field. The quality assurance, control, distribution, and installation of modified EPROMs are not small tasks when a system is widely distributed. Embedded-systems vendors generally attempt to provide high-quality embedded units and to limit software modifications to occasional major enhancements. In order to determine the desired, competitive software capabilities for commercial units, and to minimize short-term software modifications, special attention is paid to embedded software requirements during the initial project stages.

In determining the requirements for one-shot noncommercial embedded applications, engineers frequently conduct the entire process. A missile-to-aircraft interface project will be presented later, and is a reasonably good example of requirements determination by engineers. In this case, both "ends" of the system are predefined in that the missile and the aircraft are both pre-existing. The problem of interface is a relatively straightforward engineering problem of allowing the pilot to command a missile from an aircraft switch panel. The missile computer has predefined expectations of messages, and the problem is simply to provide correct message traffic as requested by each switch. However, in determining the requirements for a "new" commercial embedded application, input will probably be required from all organizational areas. Marketing, production, engineering, and top management are likely to be involved, at a minimum. At this level, the most valuable input will be from those with practical experience within a given industry. Once the desired benefits and features have been determined for a new product (or for the strategic enhancement of an existing product), and after the overall system requirements document has been produced, the engineering staff can create technical requirements documents that provide for the desired results. During this process, special attention should be paid to software requirements and life-cycle issues—particularly to considerations of future software maintenance and expandability.

The more difficult software issues to resolve are those surrounding specific target markets, and in particular, trying to predict future market needs and meet them. Budgetary issues will sometimes affect the final outcome. Using a stand-alone embedded unit with a small LCD display and keypad for operator interface as an example, assume that the unit will be used in several countries and must support multiple languages. The best software solution would be to design the software in a fashion that would allow all operator "prompt" texts to be stored in a single EPROM. Ultimately, this could allow using different EPROMs for different languages. A large EPROM might hold texts for several languages, but a smaller EPROM might have space for only one set of operator prompts. In any case, if the unit's target cost and overall design permit only a small EPROM, or if the unit's cost and design permit no separate EPROM for languages, the engineering staff will have to find another route, or justify higher wholesale costs to marketing, within the context of increased final unit costs. Obviously, determinations of this nature should be made before the unit is under construction. The EPROM example is a bit simplistic, but the point here is that optimum system and software design can be preempted by budgetary issues, and that early project stages sometimes include questions of whether or not optimum design is a viable approach within a given market. Sometimes flexibility of design must be approached within sub-optimum boundaries, and many of these instances will represent false economy on the part of the vendor.

The bottom line here is that an embedded unit is generally judged by users according to the capabilities of its software, and marketing and upper management will be most concerned with ultimate unit capability. The vendor's engineering staff is likely to be less concerned with relatively cut-and-dried application implementation issues, and to spend more time in ensuring that the unit construction and software construction easily facilitate future enhancements and planned configurations. The application capabilities of the software are designed within the context of goals expressed by the overall system requirements documents. The software flexibility and maintainability issues are totally software design and software construction issues, but these are addressed within the context of overall system requirements and final hardware construction. Overall project and product success is entirely dependent on a thorough requirements analysis, and this sometimes involves teamwork from individuals with varying points of view, experience, and expertise.

THE SOFTWARE DEVELOPMENT PLAN AND DOD-STD-2167A

In putting together any system, planning is critical, and good results are frequently proportional to the quality of up-front planning. Irrespective of degrees of formality, software development plans are necessities in providing a common route through the software development process for all project personnel. The degree of formality of the development plan is generally related to the size of the project, and informal plans will frequently suffice for embedded systems development.

The software development plan typically addresses the major activities of the development process, which in its simplest form, can be represented as consisting of five major activities: requirements gathering, design, coding, testing, and implementation. In-depth representations of the process are further breakdowns of these five activities, and there are many good sources that address the software development process as it might be conducted within varying sizes of organizations. For example, the United States Government publishes a document called DOD-STD-2167A that is approved for use by all departments and agencies of the Department of Defense (DOD). It is entitled *Defense System Software Development* and is the "bible" for developing software for defense purposes. Among other things, the document specifies what the government, as a customer, expects from software developers in the way of deliverable products, reviews, audits, and baselines.

In the process of specifying these expectations, an excellent road map for a full blown software development project cycle is presented. From software requirements analysis through final testing, it steps through the development process in a detailed breakdown, and is a good reference addition to any software professional's library. DOD-STD-2167A decomposes software systems into three major categories of code that are tantamount to building blocks:

1. Computer Software Units (CSU), a separately testable element of a Computer Software Component
2. Computer Software Component (CSC), a distinct part of a Computer Software Configuration Item (CSCI) composed of one or more CSCs and CSUs
3. Computer Software Configuration Item, a configuration item for computer software

Also within the document, the five essential activities of the software development process are further divided into eight major activities:

1. System Requirements Analysis/Design
2. Software Requirements Analysis
3. Preliminary Design
4. Detailed Design
5. Coding and CSU Testing
6. CSC Integration and Testing
7. CSCI Testing
8. System Integration and Testing

In the process of conducting these activities under a DOD contract, formal plans are created and documented in an overall software development plan. Within the development plan, formal reviews and audits can be required, and provisions are made for risk management, security, subcontractor management, and interfacing with Independent Verification and Validation (IV&V) agents. The intent and validity of approach are rock-solid, and identical concepts are used by all successful developers, but in a much less formal fashion. Formality and detailed procedure can become very expensive very quickly.

Some government contractors contend that the documentation and reporting requirements of DOD-STD-2176A can raise software costs by an order of magnitude, and worse yet, relatively minor omissions within deliverable documents can create payment delays to contractors. From these complaints, it would appear that inflexible adherence to the document's comprehensive requirements for documentation, reporting, review, and audit, can constitute a contractual minefield and drastically increase project costs. DOD-STD-2167A does give some leeway to government program managers for tailoring its comprehensive requirements to particular situations and specific contracts, and tailoring is typically accomplished by deleting nonapplicable requirements of the document. Nevertheless, companies winning federal contracts have invested considerable resources in the bid and proposal effort, and contract negotiation is often restricted by confines implied in the bid solicitation documents. Documentation requirements may not be an item open to negotiation, and program managers may not be sensitive to the needs of contractors trying to make a buck. Apparently DOD-STD-2167A is sometimes a cruel taskmaster.

Assuming that documentation overkill and procedural rigidity are the underlying beefs of the complaining contractors, and assuming that such complaints are legitimate, the point to be made here is that somewhere between the ideal and the unacceptable lies "adequate." Procedure-driven organizations tend to overlook "adequate" in making documentation a goal rather than a tool. Smaller organizations are more likely to accomplish project goals with far less formal development plans, but with very good results. The degree of formality for a given software development plan can vary considerably from environment to environment, but software development projects undertaken without adequate planning, whether or not the plans are formal in the corporate sense, will result in drastically increased use of resources or failure, or both.

DESIGN PHILOSOPHY

Embedded systems design does not differ in concept from the design of other computer systems, and the software development plan should provide for adequate design documentation. There are no perfect requirements and specifications documents, and there are no perfect design documents. Ultimately, design adjustments will be required on most projects, and corporate mechanisms to facilitate such adjustments should be efficient. Generally speaking, the more freedom that software professionals have in solving software problems, the better the final project results. Fortunately, most computer professionals are both competent and dedicated, and need minimal guidelines for success. Computer programs and operating systems, often initially designed in part on fast-food carry out bags while software developers shared hamburgers, have been highly successful and are distributed throughout the world.

The purpose of a software design document is twofold. First it provides a common route for project personnel to take in getting from point 'A' to point 'B,' and second it provides enough information for professional newcomers to the project to learn the system in a reasonable time frame. Newcomers can arrive during the project proportionally to personnel turnovers, or can arrive months later for the purpose of system maintenance or enhancement. In accomplishing both goals, economical design documentation is written for other computer professionals with credentials pertinent to the project at hand, and not for administrators with marginal technical interest. Attempting to document a design for non-hardware/software professionals is ludicrous and expensive, no matter what the final outcome; however, effective software design documentation is readily understandable by other professionals, irrespective of the documentation format used.

In putting together any system, familiarity with formal methodologies of design is helpful, but not an ultimate solution. Some popular methodologies generate mounds of paper in formalizing the simplest of designs, and seem to be somewhat wasteful. The wise and cost-effective software developer will not rigidly follow any specific documentation or design methodology unless it is a nonnegotiable requirement of the current corporate environment, or a current client requirement. In pleasing the boss or the customer, common sense sometimes takes a back seat. Some administrators worship specific design methodologies, and giant procedure-driven bureaucracies use highly formalized, rigid, and costly design procedures. Procedural flexibility is the key to cost-effectiveness, reduced timeframes, and overall success at any project stage, including design.

Assuming that an effective system with proper and understandable documentation is the ultimate destination, many different paths can lead there. Designs can be very detailed or can be cut short at relatively higher levels. They can be highly formalized or can be initially set down on lunch table napkins. In every case "adequacy" of design is the ultimate issue. The criteria for adequacy vary with specific systems, development environments, and overall system complexity. On the other hand, blind adherence to formalized procedure is inflexible. Applying inflexible procedure to varying situations can result in undesirable effects, particularly in the areas of economy.

DOCUMENTATION ISSUES

Software documentation is a tool for information exchange among professionals of like credentials. Results, and the documentation of those results for future use, are ultimate goals of any software project. When project results are being produced on schedule, documentation issues draw less attention, but when results are suffering, lack of adequate documentation sometimes becomes the scapegoat for other causes. Poor software documentation is seldom encountered these days since most professionals give it the attention that it deserves. Today's software corps is conscious of documentation issues, and there are a number of commercially available software tools that ease the documentation burden.

Formal methodologies are espoused in virtually every area of systems development, and some of these methodologies have spawned cults; however, all such formal techniques are better utilized as tools for the intellect, not as dogmas. There is no systems methodology that solves problems in the real world, although methodologies can provide standardization within procedure-driven organizations that perceive inflexible constraints as having positive impact. There is no design methodology that teaches "how" to design a project. Design methodologies recommend specific methods of approaching and documenting designs. The skill of software design is not content-specific and cannot be satisfactorily taught; specific individuals have innate design skills that can be developed if there is appropriate interest. Knowing how to pass a football doesn't make an individual NFL material—innate athletic skills are required. Regardless, in any discussion of documentation, age-old issues of form versus substance get revived. In actual practice, using specific techniques and methodologies is less important than obtaining clear, meaningful content generated by an economical process.

In earlier sections, "adequacy" of documentation was stressed over "formality" of documentation. The point to be made is that many companies sometimes expend considerable resources in "over-documenting" software. Documentation standards are necessary in most environments, and they can be a pleasure to accommodate when they are flexible enough to allow common sense to prevail in varying situations. For example, in developing specifications for large companies, as many as twenty pages can be required for in-house specification requirements with only two pages needed for the actual specification. If the in-house requirements were used as a guideline, rather than incorporated into every specification, considerable time, as well as space and paper, would be saved in its creation and use. As a rule, documentation in the 1990s should be computer-based, and documentation standards should address form as it relates to interoperability and overall content criteria, rather than detailed content.

Embedded systems software projects are typically small, but relatively complex, and they are often conducted under severe time constraints. The unending arguments over "when" to document software are usually precluded by reality, and "working" documentation is maintained during development with final documentation polished at the end of the project.

The least complex breakdown of the development cycle consists of five major activities: requirements gathering, design, coding, testing, and implementation. Picking up at the design phase, the embedded project documentation is likely to proceed as follows, when correlated with programmer activities:

1. Analyze the requirements and get a handle on the problem at hand. Using engineering input, create a system overview drawing and a system memory map.

2. Consider how the system will be tested and begin the functional decomposition process. Create a software system overview drawing of appropriate high-level modules. Continue with drawings of intermediate levels of software modules as the design and functional decomposition begin to crystallize.

3. Augment all drawings with combinations of text files, flow diagrams, and pseudocode, as appropriate.

4. Lay out all data structures to be used and document the use of each structure and structure element.

5. Provide a road map for the coding process by making rough primitives of C functions to be used.

6. Create a rough but reasonably complete test plan, including the module test sequence and equipment needed. Use diagrams and text as appropriate for the magnitude of the problem. Constantly update this plan as the project unfolds.

7. Begin coding. While coding the primitive routines previously outlined, keep documentation updated with markups and notes as anomalies are uncovered and rectified.

8. Follow through with the test plan, keeping all notes and documentation updated as changes are made and problems are overcome. After preliminary testing and before systems integration testing, there is often time to update all computer-based documentation using the notes and markups previously generated.

9. Continue with systems integration, and maintain documentation as before. When systems integration is completed, finalize, polish, and computer-base all documentation.

These steps are not particularly formal, but are entirely adequate for most embedded projects, and seem to enhance productivity. More importantly, this is typical of the way that documentation unfolds during an embedded project. There are many PC-based documentation-enhancing packages on the market, including inexpensive CAD packages, formal design tools, and flow-charting tools. Most of the above design and documentation can be accomplished using such tools, but in many cases, hand sketches in a notebook will be used until the project has unfolded to the test stages. In all cases, the final documentation should be polished and computer-based before the project is considered completed.

During the coding phase, certain vendor-specific conventions can be followed in commenting and documenting software modules; and these conventions will allow automatic generation of calling trees, flow diagrams, C function proto-types, and/or module cross-reference indexes of C functions. If such tools are used and the conventions followed, end-of-project documentation can be quite accurate and economical. This form of reverse-engineering for documentation creates current documentation taken directly from source code, so that the two always match. Formal documentation is seldom kept current throughout the development process except in large procedure-driven organizations operating under "cost plus fixed fee" contracts in which economy bows to other consider-ations.

MISSILE-TO-AIRCRAFT INTERFACE EXAMPLE

Appendix D draws on information presented in Appendices A and C, and builds an embedded-system interface box for a hypothetical missile-to-aircraft inter-face. The example uses a predetermined requirements specification in present-ing the software design and software code construction of the box.

The intent of the Appendix D documentation is a combination of brevity and adequacy in presenting an introduction to a simplified military application that is analogous to those that can be encountered in proof-of-concept practical demonstrations found in the early stages of some DOD development programs.

In Appendix D, a system overview is presented with higher-level components specified in enough detail for professionals to grasp the system intent and design goals. This is accomplished with some text and several line drawings. First there is a look at the overall system, then a system memory map, and finally, a breakdown of the major software components. Software components are norm-ally and progressively broken down into smaller and smaller pieces.

The example of Appendix D is single-tasking and is simplified enough that some shortcuts were taken in the presentation of the smaller software pieces. If the reader is an experienced software professional and can grasp Appendix D easily, the design documentation of Appendix D has served its purpose and is adequate, despite the brevity. Nitty-gritty details are presented via documented source code.

SINGLE-TASKING OR MULTITASKING?

An embedded application environment can require parallel processing in order to achieve proper execution balance in controlling the attached devices, and in this case, a system bus hosting multiple processors might be used. Multiple processor implementations are sometimes found in embedded applications with massive processing requirements, such as the control of very complex machinery. In actual practice, the majority of embedded-systems programmers will not encounter these configurations; if more than one processor must be used within a system, the requirement will have become apparent long before the programmer begins a software design. Regardless of the number of processors on the system bus, at some point the programmer must determine whether or not to use an embedded multitasking system with a given processor.

The determination of whether or not to use an embedded multitasking system is normally made in the up-front design process; but it is not always a straightforward decision and experience on the part of the software engineer will be the deciding factor. Overall system complexity, system timing requirements, design goals, and hardware implementations will always affect such decisions.

Some professionals working in the embedded-systems arena believe that an embedded multitasking system must be used if a given project entails any significant degree of complexity. Occasionally, multitasking systems are absolutely necessary, but in spite of perceptions to the contrary, many complex problems can be solved with single-tasking designs. The effect of multitasking can be achieved via ISRs that provide coordinated augmentation of the main code thread; the resulting illusion can appear as either synchronous or asynchronous processing.

For example, in both single-tasking and multitasking environments, interrupts occur in an asynchronous fashion. Random interrupt requests, external from devices attached via the I/O space or internal from software, indicate the need for ISRs. The perception of randomness on the part of the CPU includes timer interrupts that occur at regular intervals. The requesting entity has determined that servicing is required, and has asserted an interrupt request that appears at random to the CPU. The ISR associated with that interrupt request can perform most any desired function, or can trigger either future or immediate additional action.

Despite the CPU's perception of randomness, interrupts occurring at precise time intervals are synchronous in the literal sense, and can trigger other events in the same fashion. At a specified interval, control can be passed to an ISR execution thread that may require action of a second code thread. The second thread can be synchronized with the occurrence of some event or manipulated semaphore from within the first execution thread. In this case, both synchronization of events and synchronization in the literal sense has occurred. In a single-tasking environment and depending on overall system timing requirements and design goals, the second thread might be the main processing thread or a software ISR.

Nevertheless, when multitasking operating systems are necessary and properly selected, they can substantially relieve programming burdens on a given project. Unfortunately, there is no surefire formula or rule of thumb for determining whether or not to invest in an embedded operating system. This is at least a part of the reason that up-front software design is still in vogue.

INTER-PROCESS COMMUNICATION AND SYNCHRONIZATION

Software implementations for embedded systems are frequently single-tasking designs used with single-processor systems as depicted in Figure 5-1. In this case, inter-process interface considerations are limited to those considerations that apply between a main code thread and the system's *Interrupt Service Routines (ISRs)*. In Chapter 4, the use of software ISRs was effective in transporting data between a distant code thread and RS232 buffers used for background communications in the same system. The concepts presented in discussing the use of ISRs in communications buffer interfaces can be applied to answer other inter-process interface challenges as well. ISRs can be an effective tool for inter-process communication within embedded systems.

Bit flags, located in RAM and accessible by multiple code threads, are frequently used in embedded systems to route or coordinate processing threads by signaling the occurrence of events and/or for observing specific resource states. Flags used in this fashion are referred to as *semaphores*, and semaphores are a primary means of inter-process communication and synchronization within embedded systems.

In Chapter 2, for example, bit flags were used to coordinate port access between two code threads in a multitasking environment, and as state indicators for control panel switches. In the case of port access, the flags were used by one process to exclude another process from an output port in order to prevent data collision. They were also used to prevent another task from grabbing port data while the data was being updated. In the case of state indication, the flags were used to route processing in accordance with current switch states.

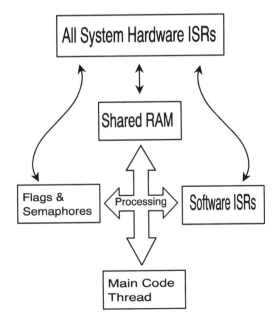

Figure 5-1. Single-Tasking Software Overview

Shared memory is a third prevalent method of inter-process communication used by embedded systems. The concept implies *shared data resource*. For example, a single code thread may be required to update a specific global bucket in memory, and another code thread may be responsible for emptying that bucket and for using the current value for display or calculation purposes or for communicating the current value to another external system or device.

Shared memory involving shared data resources sometimes requires mutually exclusive access-semaphores and precludes re-entrancy. Such code areas are sometimes referred to as *critical sections*. However, the RS232 example code of Appendix F drives eight communications ports and is re-entrant. A number of transmit and receive routines are shared by all eight hardware ISRs; but none of that code shares data resources. Each port in the example system has an associated port control block for unique data resource.

When mutually exclusive access-semaphores are required for shared data resources, the implementation is simplified if priorities are not involved. One thread can wait to update a data resource while another thread has a particular flag set. After the first thread resets the flag, the second thread can set it, thereby gaining exclusive control of the resource; however, if the updates are asynchronous and prioritized, the problem becomes more complex.

Situations involving asynchronous, prioritized resource contention can require semaphore and/or resource control blocks. The problem is that a low-priority thread could be updating a data resource when a higher priority thread comes along with a better idea. The control block(s) used must contain enough information for the dominant thread to preempt control of the resource from the servile thread, allow the dominant thread to "do its thing," and then signal the servile thread either to terminate unfulfilled or to continue processing, depending on project specifics.

Issues of similar conceptual nature are a matter of course in building operating systems, but less complex requirements generally prevail in the world of embedded systems. They are mentioned as possibilities rather than probabilities for embedded-systems programmers. If such challenges are encountered, their solution is project-specific rather than generic; the programmer has substantial control over both the design and the implementation approaches, and alternative approaches will exist on a given project.

Shared memory is the primary method of communication between multiple processors on the same system bus. Each processor board lives in a unique world and communicates to other worlds via shared RAM. Of course, the shared RAM area might also contain semaphores for areas accessed by more than one processor. A baseline multiprocessor environment is shown in Figure 5-2.

Multitasking environments for embedded systems, as shown in Figure 5-3, use the same methods of inter-process communication and synchronization that are used by single-tasking environments. The programmer must deal with the same basic issues of resource contention and device coordination in either case. Of course, the multitasking system will hide low-level details of its own inter-task communication and synchronization from the programer.

In summary, three predominant methods of inter-process communication and

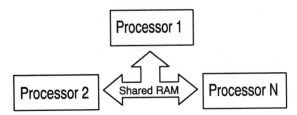

Figure 5-2. Baseline Multiprocessor System

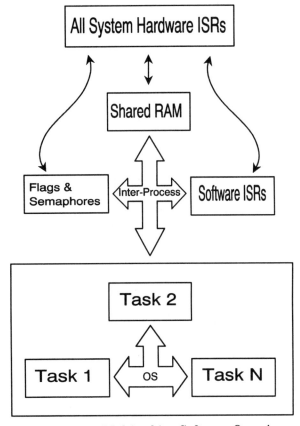

Figure 5-3. Multitasking Software Overview

synchronization are used in embedded systems projects: semaphores, shared memory, and software ISRs. The methods are used for both single-tasking and multitasking environments, regardless of whether are not there are multiple processors on the system bus. Each method of inter-process communication and synchronization is presented with some unique characteristic(s), but demarcation lines are not always distinct dividing the three presented. For programmers, definitive distinction is less important than effective implementation, and effective implementation usually entails some hybrid combination of these concepts.

In Chapter 2 accessing a hypothetical A/D device from a single routine was presented with the understanding that multiple code threads would be required for actual use in a given system. The next section looks at how that device might be accessed in either a single-tasking or multitasking environment.

A/D CONVERTER REVISITED

In Chapter 2, a single code thread for accessing a hypothetical A/D converter was depicted in Figure 2-3. Assuming that a requirement exists to read a value from the hypothetical A/D every 300ms, some modification to the sample routine would be required for use in either a single-tasking or a multitasking environment.

In a multitasking environment, it might be desirable to increase the pause between read attempts from 10ms to 30ms. This would ensure a good read with every attempt, because the A/D's specification indicates that a maximum delay of 30ms is required to convert the higher-magnitude numbers recognizable by the A/D. Each time a value is grabbed, the task might place the value into a shared RAM bucket for use by another task. In addition, the entire routine might be contained in an infinite processing loop, preceded by operating-system-specific hooks into a task scheduler. At the bottom of the loop, a 270ms pause could be inserted to give a total "pause" time of 300ms within the task. The desired 300ms delay between readings would be in error by the execution time of the remaining code, but that would likely be acceptable within the context of the overall system. (For the uninitiated, multitasking control is normally passed to other system tasks when the currently executing task enters a "paused" state.)

For use in a single-tasking system, more change would be needed. First, the 300ms interval could be achieved with a timer interrupt. The associated ISR could set the latch bit in the A/D port to indicate that conversion should begin on the current value. The ISR could also set a semaphore for the main code thread and thereby signal the main thread to check for conversion "done" with each iteration of the thread's processing loop. Once the main thread detects conversion "done," it could read and properly dispose of the value.

QUEUES AND BUFFERS

In putting any system together, processing bottlenecks require that data be *buffered* or *queued* until the system can handle the throughput. In actual practice, the distinction between a buffer and a queue is virtually nonexistent, and the two terms are used almost interchangeably by programmers.

In the literal sense *queue* is both a noun and a verb. The noun is defined by Webster's as "A waiting line, as of persons before a window." The verb is defined "to arrange in, or form a queue." (Word has it that Webster was visiting the local post office when these definitions were formalized.)

Using a portion of the RS232 code of Appendices F and G in the literal sense for an example, characters are queued for transmitting, but are placed into a buffer in order to queue them. Frequently programmers refer to "queuing messages" and "buffering characters." In some circles, queues contain only addresses and buffers contain data; in others, buffers are for convenience and queues are of necessity. Regardless of formal definitions, the bottom line is that they both are forms of "holding tanks" for information that is awaiting further processing.

Circular buffers are used in the examples in Appendices F and G for holding characters that have been moved from the application program to await transmission, and for storing received characters until the application program needs them. Both instances are classic examples of advantageous buffer usage. Bulk character strings can be moved quickly between the application program and the buffers, and the buffers can be serviced at far greater intervals than the 1ms arrival and departure rates of characters at 9600 baud.

Messages in need of transmission at the application level can be queued if the transmit buffer is filled. If communications are at 9600 baud, the application might check the transmit buffer at about 100ms intervals and discover that roughly 100 characters could now be moved from the application message queue into the transmit buffer.

In the above cases, the buffers and queues are presumed to be FIFO implementations. Most computer professionals are familiar with LIFO, FIFO, and GIGO buffering schemes: Last In, First Out; First In, First Out; Garbage In, Garbage Out.

DESIGN ESSENCE

Assuming that the requirements gathering has been completed and well documented, regardless of the level of formality, initial software planning can be undertaken. The overall problem at hand is to create a logical and physical software design, to construct the software, and then to evaluate what has been built. In initially using the requirements documents and starting the software design process, ultimate system function can be analyzed within the context of processing requirements, data manipulation requirements (including I/O and storage), and data transport (communications) requirements.

From this point forward any formal design methodology preferred by the designer can be used or discarded. Structured methodologies for C and object-oriented methodologies for C++ still seem to prevail in design efforts, and CASE tools are used by some developers. Many good sources exist that address these documentation concepts.

Analyzing data and device relationships, timing issues, and functional relationships, the programmer should try to create a design that is modular, correct, reliable, and maintainable, as a minimum. "Efficient," "flexible," and "portable" are frequently less urgent adjectives in the world of embedded systems, but the more productive programmers strive for these features as a matter of habit. During analysis, special attention should be paid to time-critical, I/O-intensive, and processing-intensive areas as they are uncovered. Functional decomposition of the overall problem is a classic design approach, as is the creation of data structures and tables when the design begins to crystallize. If modularity by device is feasible and desirable, data structure creation and the separation of "like" device characteristics to be processed can ultimately lead to the appropriate functional decomposition.

SEPARATING FUNCTIONALITY

The ideal embedded-system design would contain "drivers" for each hardware device in the system. System software would be modularized and encapsulated in order to service each system component in an independent and secretive fashion. In a single-tasking system, the individual modules dedicated to specific hardware components would be tied together in the main code thread, as shown in Figure 5-4; and for a multitasking system they would be coordinated by the operating system software, as shown in Figure 5-5. The manner in which function is isolated in an embedded system can have a major impact during the test phase. When initially designing a system, considerable thought should be given to how the final unit might be tested. Generally speaking, if the code construction ideal of independent drivers is approached reasonably well, testing will be simplified. The more complex the overall system, the more apparent this becomes.

The concepts of modularity and encapsulation are realized to some extent in Appendix D. The control panel software is highly modularized and somewhat encapsulated. Other modules interface to the control panel software by calling

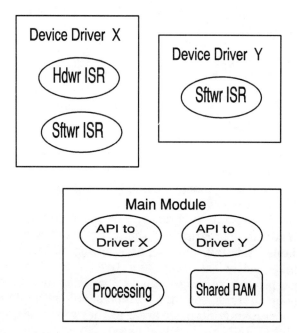

Figure 5-4. Ideal Construction Model for Single-Tasking Software

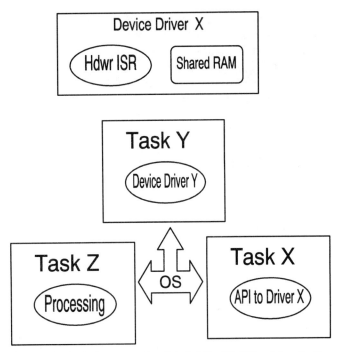

Figure 5-5. Ideal Construction Model for Multitasking Software

SW_DONE() or SW_ERRO() to set specific switch states to DONE or IN ERROR respectively. Encapsulation is incomplete because other modules can also directly check the CP and/or switch table flags to determine the current state of a given switch, and the CP data is not "static" in the C context.

In the example in Appendix D, the 1553 bus adapter board software is less modular. The board's initialization and self-test routines must be included in the MAIN() code prior to its falling into the repetitive processing loop. Message transfers on the 1553 bus must be accomplished by interrupt service routines, and two are required—one for outgoing traffic and one for incoming. The pressure-altitude interface must be included in the outgoing message routine in order to ensure currency of data at the time of transfer. Still, the software is reasonably modular, and cross-project utilization is maximized.

Virtually all of the switch panel code can be used in other projects provided that the switch table data is modified to fit new requirements. The concept breaks down only when hardware engineers make random port and bit assignments to specific switches. (The algorithms of the control panel code assume that port bit assignments will be as logical as those of the example.)

With very minor modification, the 1553 bus adapter code is certainly reusable in many 1553 projects. The synchro-to-digital code is also reusable after extraction from the 32Hz ISR; but this assumes that the same custom interface card will be used. The timer code is always usable with the same CPU board and/or timer implementation; only the magnitude of the timer constants will change with differing time interval requirements.

The Appendix D separation of functionality is not absolute, but it is substantially adequate. Absolute division of device functionality and total encapsulation, complete with application programmer interfaces (APIs) to each device's software services, would be ideal.

The ability to interchange device types in a fashion transparent to the processing code might also be desirable for cross-project utilization purposes; but such generic code construction concepts begin to infringe on preemptive, object-oriented operating system concepts, and require orders-of-magnitude-greater effort on the programmer's part. This is, in part, the reason that a number of companies are currently marketing embedded-systems operating systems.

PROBLEMS PRECLUDING THE IDEAL

Appendices C and D show that strict software modularity for the 1553 bus adapter card is precluded by adapter function. Two ISRs are needed for 1553 bus message transfers, and initialization routines for the adapter must be contained within the main code thread. Similar constraints on software modularity will be encountered with other devices.

Also, in actual practice, restraints of economy sometimes produce less-than-desirable hardware component selection and hardware designs. System performance constraints ensue, and ultimately produce additional challenges for the embedded-systems programmer. It is not always possible to isolate functionality, or more precisely, functionality may have to be isolated in a less-than-desirable fashion. Most often, overall system timing requirements are the driving force of software construction in these cases.

For example, Current Transformers (CTs) are sometimes used in embedded systems to monitor electrical current flow, or to sense the absence or presence of current in specific circuitry. Such implementations can allow software to determine if specific circuits are open or shorted or overloaded while the system is operating. (Each time that specific CT circuits are checked, control ports could allow turning devices associated with that circuit ON or OFF in order to check for opened or shorted circuits.) In a system with multiple CTs, it would not be economically feasible to dedicate an A/D converter to each CT. Multiple CTs could be multiplexed off a single A/D device, as shown in Figure 5-6. Certain bits in a mux control port could allow selecting a specific channel in order to read a specific CT. As electrical current flow through the monitored circuit would likely be controlled primarily from another code thread, circuitry might need time to "settle" each time that a "new" channel were selected, before the channel's reading were actually taken.

For even further economy, the CTs could be multiplexed and connected via the "slow" hypothetical A/D converter of Chapter 2. Assuming that a minimum circuitry "settle" time of 240ms is desirable between CT readings, and that the maximum time of 30ms for A/D conversions must be allowed, there would be a minimum time between CT readings of roughly 270ms. If there were eight such

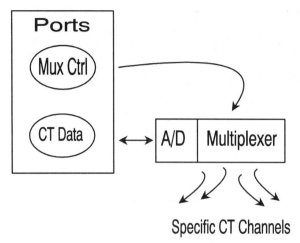

Figure 5-6. Multiplexed Current Transformers

CTs in a given system, the minimum time interval for checking each specific circuit would be about 2.16 seconds. Assuming that having a circuit open or shorted for 2.16 seconds would not be a problem in a given system, and assuming an implementation within a multitasking environment, a single task might be dedicated to circuitry fault determination.

To complicate the problem a bit more, assume that the CTs are used to monitor heater circuits, and that temperature values must be read via Resistive Thermal Devices (RTD) that are also multiplexed and connected via the same A/D device. Using these devices, temperature is determined by measuring current flow through either a standard grade of nickel or platinum at a known voltage (the resistance of these metals varies with temperature in a predictable fashion). A single bit in the mux control port might allow selection between the two multiplexers, while other bits allow selecting specific mux channels for reading specific RTDs or CTs. Although the RTD currents are also measured via current transformers, the RTDs will not require circuitry "settle" time when "new" channels are selected, but will still require the 30ms A/D conversion time. This more complex multiplexer configuration is shown in Figure 5-7.

Also assume that the temperature values must be read at precise intervals, no matter what those intervals prove to be, and that the circuits must be monitored with each pass, regardless of effects on the system. In this case, dedicating two tasks (one to fault determination and one to monitoring temperature) would not likely prove satisfactory. Now that the A/D is shared by two functions under time constraints, the more time-critical of the two must become the driving force of A/D use. Assume also that each CT monitors a heater circuit that hosts four heaters. There is a system total of 8 CTs and 32 heaters to coordinate, and each heater is dedicated to only one temperature monitoring point. There are 32 RTDs used to monitor temperature.

The design goal is to check each CT circuit, and to read each RTD, as quickly as possible under the constraints imposed by the multiplexing scheme and the slow A/D. The software solution might be to select the CT mux and a specific CT

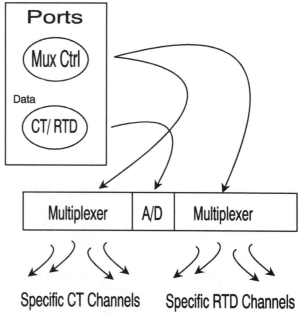

Figure 5-7. Multiplexed CTs and RTDs

channel, and then, while the circuitry is settling, switch to the RTD mux and read eight separate RTD channels. Reading the eight RTDs would require 240ms, which is the required settling time of the CT circuitry. Switching back to the CT mux and reading the previously selected channel would now produce a good CT value. This process could be repeated for each CT, using eight different RTDs each time. The net result is that the CTs are being accessed as quickly as possible under the constraints of hardware, and each temperature value is being accessed at twice the frequency of the CT accesses. The total software solution is depicted in Figure 5-8.

The solution has created what is tantamount to an A/D driver that keeps the A/D working as much as possible within the specific design constraints. Processing is totally dedicated to setting up for, then reading, the A/D device. Shared RAM could be used to store all values obtained, and other tasks could access the shared RAM in order to utilize the data acquired from the A/D.

With each iteration of the A/D processing loop, 8 CT accesses and 64 RTD accesses occur, and the total time for loop execution is about 2.16 seconds, plus a few microseconds of execution time. Each CT is accessed at intervals of 2.16+ seconds, and each RTD's raw temperature value is acquired at intervals of 1.08+ seconds. Each unique access includes a 30ms pause where other tasks can grab control of processing and "do their thing." Within each processing-loop iteration of 2.16+ seconds as described, a total of 2.16 seconds is available to other tasks. The example task uses only a few microseconds of actual processing time.

Device implementation timing constraints such as these can be encountered in specific manufacturing environments where ultimate economy of unit con-

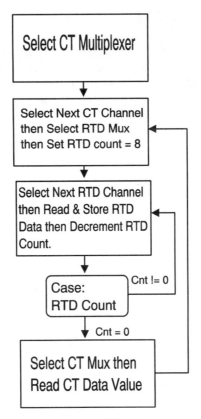

Figure 5-8. Multiplexed CT/RTD Software Solution

struction takes design precedence over unit performance, or more precisely, where the goal is minimum component cost to provide adequacy of performance for a given purpose. In all such cases, product flexibility suffers.

ERROR DETECTION AND CORRECTION

Error-detection and correction algorithms within software are important for any system, and embedded systems are no exception. These issues are normally emphasized during the software design phase, and then made a part of the overall software development plan. Error detection and correction is highly device-specific and project-specific but can be discussed via precept and example.

In discussing errors, the more prevalent distinctions between types of errors are whether they are *hard* or *soft*. *Hard errors* typically fall into the category of "show-stoppers," which are errors detectable by the system, but which cannot be corrected without operator assistance. A good example of such an error is found in looking at the CT circuits of preceding section. If the CT processing located either an open or shorted circuit within the system, there is nothing that the system could do to correct the problem. The system could only notify the operator that a problem exists.

In notifying the operator that a problem exists, the system might display an error message, set off an audible alarm, or flash a front panel LED. If the error were serious enough to provide danger on the plant floor, for example, some combination and exaggeration of these methods might be used. A siren could blast and a warning light similar to K-Mart's blue-light-special signal might be activated. Simultaneously, all power to the offending circuit might be shut off by emergency relays.

Those errors falling into the soft category can generally be corrected within software and without operator intervention. In building communications systems, for example, lost characters or lost messages or confused buffer pointers can be corrected "automatically" by software by either discarding a series of characters, or by discarding the entire communications buffer contents, and then re-synchronizing communications within the context of the specific application's requirements.

Also, semaphore accesses that include timeout errors are frequently considered as soft errors until some number of retries are exhausted. Once the maximum allowable retries have been exhausted, the error may be reclassified as "hard" within the context of a specific embedded system. In any case, the specific applicability of recovery techniques, as well as the specific recovery techniques themselves, are entirely device-specific and system-specific, and consequently, project-specific. They must be addressed within the context of individual system design goals.

A common error-detection problem among embedded systems involves those systems that utilize NVRAM. To verify that NVRAM has not been corrupted due to loss of battery power or other problems, a checksum scheme might be implemented at power-on time; however, practical implementations of checksum algorithms for NVRAM are virtually nonexistent for systems that use NVRAM in mainstream processing. If NVRAM is used in routine processing, sudden loss of power at various CPU processing points would preclude maintaining an ongoing checksum value with any degree of reliability. If NVRAM is modified only by successful shutdown algorithms, the software problem is simplified, but the burden of exercising such algorithms is placed on the operator, and the software must be properly exited by the operator before removing power.

A non-foolproof alternative scheme might be to check several permanently stored NVRAM patterns—one at the beginning of NVRAM and one at the end. If the patterns are other than anticipated, the unit could be assumed to be nonfunctional. This raises the problem of when to initialize NVRAM from within software. Normally, a specific pattern is expected to reside at a specific location if NVRAM has been initialized once. This prevents NVRAM from being initialized more than once. However, if NVRAM is corrupted for whatever reason, it will likely be re-initialized, and all "permanent" patterns are placed into NVRAM at that time.

The typical real-world solution is to signal the operator if NVRAM is initialized. The algorithm that initializes NVRAM based on the absence of a particular pattern(s) is used. It is assumed that a corrupted NVRAM will result in pattern corruption, and NVRAM will be re-initialized. If the operator is informed that NVRAM has been re-initialized, the operator can take whatever action is appropriate.

In any event, error-detection and correction routines of the nature described above are normally known as either *self-tests* or *diagnostics*. Demarcation lines are fuzzy, and colloquially they are given little distinction. Self-tests are typically the unit's self-diagnostics which are conducted at power-up. Diagnostics are typically conducted while the entire system is in full operation. In either case, any corrective action that might be taken can be less-than-desirable. Using the automobile brick-brain of Chapter 1 as an example, it is easily seen that error-correction routines have a downside. There have been isolated cases of vehicle subsystems (such as air-conditioning systems) being erroneously shut down because the brain momentarily believed that a problem existed. In some cases, the halted system cannot be restarted by turning the ignition OFF and ON. Power must be removed from the microcomputer by disconnecting the negative terminal of the vehicle's battery for at least 30 seconds, and then reconnecting. Similar results have been realized after a car with fuel consumption displays runs completely out of gasoline.

The brick-brain problems appear to be software bugs, but they could well be hardware-related. Regardless, it is surprisingly difficult to make foolproof error-detection and correction algorithms for many applications and many operating environments.

SYSTEM FAILURE AND RECOVERY

System failure of the typical embedded system is nonrecoverable for conditions other than loss of power, and loss of power is economically preventable for the most part. To preclude loss of power, generators with automatic activation features are common in hospitals, and combinations of Uninterruptible Power Supplies (UPS) and generators can prevent power loss in such environments. In critical and sophisticated medical environments there may be tandem or parallel systems that decrease probabilities of total system failure from other causes, but such fail-safe mechanisms and redundant systems have not been encountered by the author.

Speaking generally, embedded systems are designed for reliability within their intended environments and are built to withstand hardships peculiar to that environment. Within the industrialized sector, bringing down manufacturing equipment for even short periods of time can result in staggering costs to the manufacturer, and unit reliability is considered critical. Despite the economic risks, manufacturing environments do not always harbor expensive generator installations. A UPS might adequately provide for power surges, brownouts, and elegant shutdown of computer equipment, but total power loss will generally shut down the plant until power is restored.

Embedded-system recovery following power loss is usually straightforward within the context of its intended use. In some cases, data stored in NVRAM might be required in order to restart operations at a processing point that was in motion when power was lost. Regardless, the system software would typically re-initialize the unit and then branch to the appropriate functions to either totally restart operations, or to grab specific NVRAM data in order to restart operations from some previous point of operation.

To detect system failure from causes other than loss of power, many embedded systems contain "watchdog" timers that indicate (to hardware) whether or not the software appears to be functioning properly. Watchdog timers can be implemented in a variety of fashions, but one method is to use a timer ISR to toggle a specific bit of a watchdog port at a specified time interval. The time interval would have to be acceptable to the specific environment, but 10ms might be chosen. Every 10ms, the state of the specified bit could be reversed. Circuitry viewing the ultimate effects of this bit could detect the absence of state change within the specified time interval, and take appropriate action independent of the CPU. If the CPU goes awry, the software will follow. If the software goes awry, the watchdog bit will not be toggled.

If the software goes awry while operating, the watchdog timer can give pertinent notification, but safety of personnel in the vicinity of a given system is of paramount importance in the event of system failure. In environments where failed systems might lead to dangerous machinery running amuck, failure indicated by the watchdog timer could cause relays to shut down all sources of power to all related equipment. In every case where personnel safety or lives are potentially at stake, an appropriate response to system failure must be devised.

SUMMARY

Chapter 2 discussed addressing the hardware from software. In that process, CPU memory structure, ports, A/D converters, and some specific devices were addressed. Code construction techniques for table-driving hardware were assessed. A pilot's control panel is built in Appendix A.

Chapter 3 covered start-up code and looked at CPU architectural differences, as well as addressed some considerations for mixing C and assembly languages. Specific examples of start-up code for both Motorola-based systems and Intel-based systems were presented.

Chapter 4 revealed the overall simplicity of interrupt handling and presented specific interrupt service routines that are ultimately used by the example in Appendix D. Some interrupt timing issues were revealed and timer interrupts were addressed in-depth.

Chapter 5 has filled in the blanks by explaining processing control options, inter-process communications, and some overall system timing issues, as well as system errors and failure. In that process, a missile-to-aircraft interface example is presented in Appendix D. Additionally, some controversial design philosophy was presented and the creation of a software development plan was addressed in view of the United States Government's software development cycle.

With these subjects behind, the essential conceptual knowledge required in putting together an embedded system has been presented. Once these concepts have been implemented, and a given system is designed and coded, the remaining tasks are to successfully compile, link and locate, and debug the system software. Chapter 6 will look at the link-and-locate process, and Chapter 7 will address "Making It Work."

6

Linking and Locating the Code

PROMs AND BURNERS

Programmable Read Only Memory (PROM) chips are available in a variety of types. Variations include Unerasable PROMs (UPROM), Erasable PROMs (EPROM), and more recently, Electrically Erasable PROMs (EEPROM). These chips are used within embedded systems to store software programs and initialized data. Uninitialized data resides in an embedded system's RAM area. As discussed in Chapter 2, PROM and RAM are memory space components of the memory structure. Address locations of both PROM and RAM are fixed within a given embedded system, and PROM-resident programs are executed from their permanent addresses within memory space. Embedded-system PROM-resident programs are not relocatable by an operating system program loader, because no such operating system is used in an embedded system. The relocatable code normally produced as linker output when creating PC programs is replaced by non-relocatable code, which contains hard-coded addresses in anticipation of residing at the PROM's specified memory location. All of this is accomplished during the link-and-locate process and will be explained later.

For each type of PROM, a method exists for "loading" or "programming" the chips with pre-existing software programs and data. The process of placing pre-existing programs or data into an EPROM is colloquially referred to as *burning* or *blowing* the EPROM, which is terminology carried over from older techniques of chip programming. These days, EPROMs are burned by loading the chip's address pins with an appropriate address and loading the chip's data pins with the contents destined for that address, and then "pulsing" the programming pin(s) with a specified voltage for a specified period of time. Since the chip's output pins become input pins during the loading process, there are provisions for disabling chip output while burning an EPROM.

Chip-specific programming voltages, for PROMs of all types, typically range from 5V to 25V with pulse durations from under 1ms to 50ms, or even more. For some chips, the required pulse duration time is decreased by increasing chip supply voltages during pulse application period. In any case, applying improper voltages or excessive pulse durations to a given chip can damage the chip. EEPROMs can also be programmed using an EPROM burner, but EEPROMs that are made accessible to a CPU during the loading process can be "blown" by applying a specified voltage and then writing data to the chip, as if it were a part of the CPU's RAM. EEPROMs are erased in a similar fashion, but EPROMs are erased by applying ultraviolet light through a translucent opening at the top of the chip. Light-sensitive internal components generate enough voltage to deprogram the chip in an average of 15 to 45 minutes.

There are numerous commercial tools that enable programmers to burn chips with relative ease. Stand-alone EPROM burners are embedded microcomputer systems that typically have several chip socket sizes built in, along with a keypad and a small LCD display for user interface. The programmer is expected to read a user manual in order to find a series of chip-specific and burner-specific codes that will be used in conjunction with the keypad and display in identifying the chip at hand to the burner. The codes usually include a family code and pin-out code as a minimum. If the programmer selects the wrong codes, the burner may apply the wrong voltage for the wrong duration to one or more pins, and thereby damage the chip. Some burners can electronically detect such programmer errors for some chips and issue a warning; however, this capability also requires that the chip be electronically identifiable, and some are not.

Either before or after the programmer has identified the chip to the typical stand-alone burner, the desired software program can be downloaded via a serial port into the burner's RAM space. After the program is available in the burner's RAM, and after the programmer has identified the chip to the burner, pressing a start key will commence the loading of the EPROM with the desired program. The unattended process can take 15 minutes or more per 64K bytes of EPROM. (Bytes are emphasized here because PROMs of all types are typically sized by bits.) The actual loading time will vary with specific chips and burner capabilities. If the program is large and will use more than one chip, the programmer can use the keyboard and display in entering a starting address (within the burner's RAM) and length to be programmed before pressing the start key. Once the chip is programmed, it can be verified by the programmer by entering an appropriate code from the burner's keyboard. During the burning process, checksums are typically created within PROMs and are used by verification algorithms.

There are many variations of this process and many variations of burners and chips (so little time and so many EPROMs to burn), but the process as outlined is typical. Provisions for duplicating chips also exist.

As a rule, in selecting a burner, PC-based EPROM burners are much cheaper than the stand-alone units and are more convenient to use. PC-based burners typically allow full-screen viewing and editing of the programs to be loaded into EPROM, plus point-and-shoot selection of the chip to be programmed. With stand-alone units, multiple downloads to the burner may be required for large programs, but with PC-based burners the size of programs that can be accommodated is limited only by the host PC's memory. In addition, since burners only accommodate specific chips, PC-based burners are much easier to upgrade than stand-alone units. With stand-alone units, the chip-loading algorithms are contained in the burner's ROM; typically, when upgrades are needed to support newer chips, a module is removed from the burner and returned to the factory. With PC-based burners, chip-loading algorithms can be downloaded from the vendor's bulletin board, and in a much more timely manner. With new chips arriving on the market every day, this can be a desirable capability.

PROMs AND PROGRAM SPLITTING

Sometimes programs must be *split* before being placed into PROM. Within the 8-bit bus world, CPU hardware access to all bytes is sequential, and 16-bit addresses are obtained with two consecutive 8-bit reads to sequential hardware locations (in a fashion similar to the port access examples shown in Chapter 2, which accessed 16 bits from 8-bit ports). In this case, programs and data are placed into a single EPROM. Within the 16-bit and 32-bit bus worlds, CPUs manage memory differently, and programs are split between two or more EPROMs. In the 16-bit world, for example, the CPU may grab even EPROM addresses from one hardware address area, and odd addresses from another. In this case two EPROMs are needed, and the program is split with all even addresses in one program module, and all odd addresses in another. The two separate program modules are placed into two separate EPROMs.

Sometimes program splitting can be accomplished by algorithms within stand-alone burners or within In-Circuit Emulator (ICE) units, but more often is accomplished via software external to the burner (ICE units are described in Chapter 7). In any case, a tool-specific *split factor* and/or starting byte number must be provided by the programmer. The split factor tells the splitting software how many bytes to skip in the splitting process. For example, a split factor of 2 might indicate to a splitting program that every other byte is to be placed into a single program module, beginning with the starting byte number which has been supplied by the programmer. In this case, a split factor of 1 would be tantamount to no split. After programs are split into two or more modules, each resulting program module is treated as a separate program when following the loading process, as described earlier. Obviously, a good EPROM labeling scheme must be used to distinguish between the final, fully loaded PROM chips.

When program splitting is required, PC-based EPROM burners and software once again prove more convenient to use than stand-alone burners or other methods. With a PC-based burner system and splitting software, each module that is created in the splitting process can be viewed full-screen. This gives the programmer a high degree of confidence in the results of the splitting process. With other methods that split by operator commands to hardware, more time is consumed in visually verifying each created module in order to double-check the splitting process.

PROM BURNERS AND PROGRAM FORMATS

When a program is downloaded to a burner in order to be placed into a PROM chip, the format of the code to be placed in PROM must be in a form acceptable to the specific EPROM burner being used. Ultimately it must be in a format acceptable as final chip-resident code. Sometimes the formats are one and the same, but more often, the burner's programming algorithm will convert between the two. In any case, different linkers create different output formats that are largely dependent on the object module formats used for linker inputs, and the target environment for which the linker was created. For example, linkers used in programming the typical Intel-based PC program under the MS-DOS operating system will output MS-DOS-specific .EXE executable files, while linkers provided with an Intel-based embedded systems software development environment might output an Intel OMF-86 format, devoid of any MS-DOS-specific overhead constructs, and which would be acceptable to many Intel ICE units, target debuggers, and EPROM burners.

Most EPROM-burning algorithms expect various forms of object files as input, and convert these to a different and executable output contained in the EPROM. Code whose current format is acceptable to load an EPROM is called *romable*. Romable code can be produced from small .EXE programs by using the EXE2BIN utility supplied with MS-DOS. This utility can convert the hexadecimal .EXE file into a binary .BIN file which is a romable format (with hard-coded addresses and without the overhead constructs of a program header). Other utility programs exist that can convert .EXE files into other formats, such as the OMF-86 format. The typical utility that converts executable files will require both the executable and its corresponding link map file as input, in order to create the desired object output.

In addition to conversion utilities that convert executable files to romable formats, there are "locator" utility programs that accept executable files and their associated link maps as inputs and perform identical conversion functions, but also expect additional operator input. The operator input is typically accepted from the command line or via a command file, and consists of the absolute locations that the programmer wants to assign to specific code sections in order to permanently locate the final module within EPROM. In using such a locator utility, the command file created by the programmer might look like this:

```
DATA = 0x0400        ;Locate DATA segment at 400 hex
CODE = 0x1000        ;Begin CODE segment at 1000 hex
RAM  = 0x2000        ;Begin RAM segment at 2000 hex
STACKTOP = 0x2ffe    ;Initial stack pointer
LIST = x,y           ;Desired locator options
PGMSTRT = 0x1000     ;Start-up routine entry point
```

In the above case, the executable file would be placed into the desired code format with hard-coded addresses appropriately corresponding to those input by the operator.

The demarcation lines between conversion programs and locator programs can be particularly fuzzy when executable files are accepted as input, and in actual practice they are all colloquially known as locator programs. Nevertheless, in addition to conversion and locator utilities, there are translation utilities. These typically translate between various object formats that are romable. There are occasions on embedded systems projects when project tools will only provide romable formats that are not compatible with EPROM burners available to project personnel. In this case, a translation program can be used to convert from one romable format to another. For example, tools that output Intel OMF-86 format may require conversion to Tektronix Extended Tekhex format; this could be accomplished with a translation program. Previously, it was stated that locator programs accepted executable files and their associated link maps as input. This is true, but some locator programs are built to accept various romable formats as input.

There are many variations of conversion utilities, translation utilities, and locator utilities, and more will be seen in the next section. However, any given embedded software development environment targets a family of CPUs, and the range of code formats supported by that development software is limited to those that are realistically expected and useful within the world of the targeted architecture. Fortunately, the programmer typically deals with three or fewer code formats on any given project, and all of the tools and criteria necessary for any format conversions will be supplied with the embedded software development environment. All that is required of the programmer is to set up for or accept a specific format from the project linker, and then, if necessary, to convert that format into a format acceptable to the EPROM burner before splitting the file or burning the EPROM.

On the other hand EPROM burner manufacturers must support virtually all formats. To exemplify the magnitude of that problem, a far-from-exhaustive list of romable code record formats follows:

- DEC Binary Format
- ASCII Octal, Hexadecimal, or Binary Formats
- RCS COSMAC Format
- Fairchild Fairbug Format
- MOS Technology Format
- Motorola Exorciser or Exormax Formats
- Intel Intellec 8/MDS Format
- Signetics Absolute Object Format
- Tektronix Hexadecimal Format
- Intel MCS-86 Hexadecimal Object Format
- Hewlett-Packard 64000 Absolute Format
- Texas Instruments SDSMAC Format
- 5-Level BNPF Format
- Spectrum Format

Each format has very detailed and specific criteria for field locations within each record. For example, the Motorola formats mentioned above are ASCII representations of hexadecimal files and use the letter S as a new record marker to start each record. For this reason, most programmers refer to these formats as

"Motorola S format." Major record fields that follow the *S* are listed below:

- Record type (1 digit)
- Record length (2 digits)
- Load address (4, 6, or 8 hex characters depending on record type)
- Data bytes (2 hex characters each)
- Record checksum (2 hex characters)

Along similar lines, the Intel formats listed above are frequently referred to as "Intel Hex format." The records for both of the listed Intel formats are ASCII representations of hexadecimal files, and are quite similar to each other. In both cases, the new record marker that indicates the start of each record is a colon. Most of the record fields that follow the colon for the Intellec 8/MDS format are listed below:

- Record length (2 hex characters)
- Address field (4 hex characters)
- Record Type (2 hex characters)
- Data bytes (2 hex characters each)
- Checksum (2 hex characters)

All romable object formats have similar contents, and the number of data bytes in a record is usually determined from the record length field. In examining the fields of the above romable record formats, a programmer can easily see how absolute addresses are stuffed into the address fields by a locator utility, and how the entire record might be used by an EPROM-burning algorithm in order to convert and locate information into the EPROM. Typically, on any given project, programmers will only need the code format information supplied with project-specific tools; but many sources exist for detailed breakdowns of each romable format, and manufacturers of burners will likely have any unusual format that a programmer might want.

LINKING AND LOCATING THE CODE

The typical C compiler groups code, initialized data, and uninitialized data into separate memory sections, and there can be compiler-specific additional breakdowns within these groups. For example, initialized strings are often grouped together, either as a subset of the initialized data, or as a separate memory section. The number of sections is not particularly important. The fact that code, data, and uninitialized data are separated is very important; more precisely, the fact that uninitialized data (including uninitialized strings) can be totally separated from the rest is extremely important.

In Chapter 3, there was considerable mention of framework issues. Framework issues arise, in part, because different compiler (or assembler) manufacturers use different names and/or different naming conventions for the memory sections that hold code, data, and uninitialized data. They also use different naming conventions for the names of variables. For example, the Intel assembly

ISR shell routine presented in Chapter 4 uses an underscore as the first character of its name because the C compiler used places an underscore at the beginning of each function name. The ISR shell must be declared as an external function within at least one C module, and the object module ensuing from that C module would contain the name preceded by an underscore. The name used within both the assembly and C object modules must match in order to obtain a good link. If the underscore is removed from the ISR shell's name, a link is not possible. More difficult framework issues, related to more complex problems, can arise because compilers do not always allow the programmer to change either section or segment names, or naming conventions of variables; however, the more evolved embedded systems development environments permit programmer control over all of these compiler characteristics, within some confines.

The better C compilers used in embedded systems work allow specifying code sections, for specific code areas or data areas, in-line with program code. This means that the programmer can insert a compiler directive or manifest constant in-line, at any point in any C module, in order to group the desired program area into a particular section or segment of code. Along these lines, Microtec Research uses a very flexible scheme. Code sections are grouped by numbers that are freely assigned by the programmer. A very large number of code and data sections is possible, and the programmer can group code and data in a virtually endless variety of ways. At locate time, the programmer simply assigns absolute addresses to each numbered section as desired. In any case, whether the sections are named or numbered, the procedure to locate code and data sections will always be very similar to the procedure used in the preceding section in explaining locator utilities. A synopsis of the entire link-and-locate process follows:

1. After successfully compiling all software modules for the embedded system, the code is linked.
2. Using the linker map file, the programmer can determine if all code and data areas have been grouped as desired.
3. Using a locator utility and command file or command-line arguments, the programmer can assign specific system addresses to each code and data group generated in the link process.
4. The locator utility will use the operator input, the linker output, and the generated link map as its input, and will create a romable output file with permanent addresses assigned as specified by the programmer.

This is the essence of any link-and-locate process. There are minor variations to this process, and there are products that create minor variations, such as combining the link-and-locate processes into a single step. In any case, the above steps can be, and are, accomplished in some fashion. These are precisely the steps that are taken when creating romable code from small .EXE programs under MS-DOS, and without any special embedded systems development software (using EXE2BIN instead of a locator utility); generic locator utilities exist that allow the creation of romable code from larger MS-DOS executable files as well (assuming that the code is constructed to operate as embedded code).

SUMMARY

Converting, linking, locating, translating, and/or splitting code are all the possible actions that a programmer can take in creating romable modules from compiled code. Once the romable code is available in a format acceptable to both the target hardware (absolute addresses) and the EPROM burner (recognizable by burner algorithms), EPROMs can be burned with non-relocatable, executable code. Minor variations in the process are created by the capabilities of the software products available to project personnel. Some products shortcut the process and combine more than one of the detailed actions required. A synopsis of all the steps required in creating an EPROM for an embedded system might look like this:

1. Achieve a romable format by using (a) or (b) below:
   a. Convert executable code into a romable format.
   b. Link-and-locate the code into a romable format.
2. Translate the romable code, if necessary, into another romable format acceptable to the EPROM burner.
3. Split the romable code, if necessary, into more than one romable module.
4. Feed the EPROM burner with the romable module(s) and burn each respective EPROM.

Of course, during this process, RAM areas of final modules are ignored by the programmer. Only the code within the address ranges of ROM segments are placed into EPROM burners, and ultimately into EPROMs. RAM will be untouched during the EPROM burning process.

7

Making It Work

IN-CIRCUIT EMULATORS

Microcomputer technology has been exploding exponentially since the advent of IBM's PC in the early 1980s. Comparing the early PC models with the products of today, it is easy to see that the industry has made overwhelming progress in product performance, reliability, feature availability, and decreased costs.

The PC satellite industry that provides debugging tools and test equipment is making even greater strides in recent years. A large selection of debugging software and adapter board products, designed to simplify the debugging process, are currently available. No longer is the programmer locked into the level of assembly code debugging. Sophisticated software development environments allow the use of source-level debuggers with a comprehensive array of program execution choices. Switching between high-level language source code and assembly code is a breeze. Most of these products have matured only within the past several years, and the capabilities are staggering to those accustomed to less. Relatively innocuous features like breaking software execution on a write to ROM (or a specified address range), or breaking on a specified number of loop iterations, were relegated to the relatively expensive world of stand-alone In-Circuit Emulators (ICE) just a few short years ago. ICE units are still the most important tool used in making embedded systems software function properly. Assuming properly functioning hardware and an ICE unit, the programmer would not likely need additional tools to debug embedded systems software—although exceptions could exist in the form of any project-specific, specialized test equipment that might be needed.

From the programmer's focused perspective, stand-alone ICE units can easily be "black-boxed." Essentially, they are embedded microcomputer systems that contain hardware and software capable of totally emulating the function and functional characteristics of a given CPU, hence the term *emulator*. They are connected *in-circuit* by using a CPU-specific *probe*, which is a cabled connector between the ICE unit and the unit under test. At the test-unit end, the connector is physically identical to the CPU being emulated. In order to connect the ICE unit to the unit under test, the CPU is removed from its socket in the unit under test, and is replaced with the ICE unit's probe. There is no longer a CPU in the unit under test; and the CPU has been replaced, in-circuit, by the CPU emulator.

From this point forward, all CPU activities will be performed by the emulator, and the replacement will be transparent to the software and unit under test. Inside the ICE unit, critical timing is kept within close tolerances. Precise I/O pin timings and other time-critical functions are maintained across the spectrum of operating frequencies recommended by the manufacturer for a given CPU. The ICE's CPU impersonation, via realtime emulation, is essentially undetectable by the target hardware.

In the normal debug process for PC application programs, the typical debugger used will allow programmers to set breakpoints in order to stop program execution at a specified location within the code thread being debugged. When the CPU reaches the breakpoint, program execution is halted; however, other programs that may be executing and interrupts that are constantly occurring are unaffected and continue normal operation.

With an ICE unit, all CPU activity can be halted at each software breakpoint. This means that all processing can be stopped, and the programmer will have a complete "snapshot" of memory available for the given point in time. Interrupt processing ceases, and the execution of all code threads is halted. Obviously, when debugging multiple code threads, this ability to "freeze" everything currently under execution gives the programmer a highly necessary edge in determining how software components are actually interacting. In addition, CPU registers and signal lines can be analyzed for current requests and states. Few embedded projects can be successfully debugged without an ICE unit, and this is particularly true if prototype hardware is a part of the overall project. When realtime source-level debuggers are used in conjunction with an ICE unit, the combination creates an incredibly powerful debugging environment that has matured only recently.

Not too long ago, any code to be debugged had to be placed into PROM chips and inserted into the unit under test before the ICE unit could be successfully used. This meant that PROMs were constantly updated and rotated during the debug process, and this process consumed a significant amount of the programmer's time. It also limited all debugging to the assembly code level. Today, the entire memory structure of the unit under test can be mapped into the ICE unit, or selected portions of the memory structure can be mapped. This means that the code to be tested can be directly downloaded into the ICE unit with each new iteration of software. Substantial time is saved in not having to update EPROMS. The ICE unit has simply conned the unit under test into believing that its memory structure resides in the ICE unit. Also, because of the memory-mapping capability and other ICE advances, it is now possible to perform both source-level and assembly-level debugging before any target hardware is available. With I/O space mapped to the ICE unit, most of the programmer's code can be initially debugged within the ICE unit without involving any target hardware. This normally involves the relatively tedious task of stepping through and patching software, but it is a highly desirable capability when hardware and software are being developed in parallel.

Remote debugging is in vogue using today's ICE units, and cross-platform remote debugging is fairly common. For example, using an Intel-based PC for the development of a Motorola-based embedded system would require a cross-compiler. With the appropriate ICE unit and appropriately selected development software, source-level debugging at the Intel-based development machine can be accomplished via RS232 to the Motorola-based unit under test. All execution within the unit under test is in the Motorola format, but source code is being traced on the Intel-based machine by the programmer. Substantial layers of software are involved in providing these benefits, but the bottom line is that such products work, and they work well under most circumstances.

In addition to these higher-level benefits, ICE units have all the fundamental capability normally anticipated by programmers in the debug stages of a typical PC software project. Setting breakpoints by location or event, trapping under various execution conditions, the ability to assemble and disassemble code, and the ability to create execution macros are all fairly standard features of ICE units. In addition, ICE units contain timers that provide enhanced capability, whereby execution threads can be profiled by requesting "time-hacks" at specific locations within the thread. In addition, ICE profilers can provide execution speeds, number of CPU cycles per instruction, and a profile of the types of instructions executed. Normally, all of this is provided within very close timing tolerances, and with a user-selectable clock speed.

Typically, the capabilities of a given stand-alone ICE unit on today's market are mature and well-evolved. For purposes here, it is not practical to delve into more detail concerning specific ICE unit commands and capabilities as this would be tantamount to user manual duplication; however, capabilities of most ICE units are similar to one another within a given price range, and documentation accompanying specific ICE units is normally comprehensive and complete. Learning to use an ICE unit or moving from one brand to another is not especially difficult for the embedded-systems programmer.

Like all competing products in a given market, stand-alone ICE units can be purchased with different features. Many of today's more evolved ICE units can emulate a family of CPUs as a minimum, and a series of probes is supplied with the unit, or is available from the manufacturer at additional cost. Choices between specific features can be confusing, but manufacturers supply detailed information and, in some cases, personal attention, to assist users in determining the best value for their particular environment. Stand-alone ICE units represent a substantial investment, and it is wise to shop before purchasing. Costs have decreased drastically in recent years, and prices are within the reach of many small companies, but, at $7,000 to $20,000, the investment is still significant.

For greater economy, modularity, and future flexibility, ICE manufacturers are beginning to provide modular ICE units hosted by the more prevalent PCs.

With supporting software, one or more adapter boards installed in an AT-compatible PC, for example, can provide the ICE, an execution environment, a hardware profiler, and a performance simulator. Additional software support for these board-level products is available in the form of compilers, realtime source-level debuggers, and linkers and locators. These products are of very high quality, and user friendliness is comparable to that of the better PC debug environments. As market demands and programmer expectations continue to increase, even greater choices of ICE configurations with even more user-friendly features are likely to follow.

Before leaving the subject of ICE units, it should be noted that the typical ICE unit supports certain specific code formats that are associated with the target hardware environment. The appropriate code formats are usually produced by linkers and locators used during the embedded systems development cycle. Code formats, as well as linkers and locators, are addressed in Chapter 6.

PRELIMINARY TESTS USING SIMULATORS

In addition to ICE units, software simulators can sometimes be used to advantage in debugging and testing embedded systems projects. In such cases, the typical software simulator will be built to perform a subset of functionality normally performed by the hardware that it is simulating.

For example, in debugging a communications system containing the code in Appendix F, PCs were attached to the ARTIC board ports. Each PC polled the appropriate PC port looking for incoming characters. Using predefined messages from a vendor of plant-floor equipment, each PC collected incoming characters until a complete message was assembled. For each predefined incoming message, the PC did no processing pertinent to an actual application, other than to build and send the appropriate response message back to the ARTIC board, as specified by the vendor. In this way, communications between the ARTIC card and the vendor's actual equipment were realistically simulated. The PC-resident code was tantamount to a simulator of the vendor's equipment, at least as far as the communications were concerned.

Another software simulator is built in the example in appendix B. A pilot's control panel for flight demonstration purposes was built using the code in Chapter 2 and Appendix A; Appendix B builds a quick-and-dirty PC-resident software simulator for that control panel. Essentially, the simulator is built by replacing the control panel's port I/O routines with screen and keyboard routines. This allows debugging the control panel tables, switch processing, and control panel light processing on the development PC, totally apart from the VME bus hardware. An executable file for the simulator built in Appendix B is available on the accompanying diskette, and an AT-compatible machine with a color monitor is required for proper execution.

Both of the above examples are classic examples of advantageous software simulation for debug or preliminary test purposes, but not all hardware lends itself as readily to software simulation. In many cases, if simulation can be accomplished at all, it must be done with specialized hardware. In most cases, it is virtually impossible to adequately simulate analog devices without specialized hardware, and most sophisticated digital simulations involve hardware. Simulation is an engineering field unto itself, and entire careers are dedicated to simulation within specialized markets. For example, process control simulation is a full-blown industry; and specialized companies provide hardware-in-the-loop simulations for guided missile testing.

Hardware simulators typically accept a variable input in providing a variable and scaled output that allows an accurate performance analysis of the device being simulated. Applying the concept to a simpler problem encountered in embedded software testing for industrial controls, hardware engineers sometimes build small boxes with thumb-actuated wheels to simulate rotating shafts. With the box connected via an A/D device, the port can be read during testing, and values can be changed via the thumb wheel.

In some cases, test boxes are made to simulate complete machines. This is a particularly useful approach when access to actual equipment is limited or nonexistent beyond disrupting the production operations of the end-user's business. For example, in building a carpet metering and cutting machine similar to the one mentioned in Chapter 2, a simulator box might be built to simulate all pertinent timing functions of the machinery. The simulated functions might exclude bar-coded inputs and RS232 reporting, but these functions can easily be isolated and tested in other ways. Conveyers, photoeyes, the measuring wheel, and the cutting arm would be simulated. Once the software is debugged and appears to handle all controls in a proper fashion, final systems integration testing can be accomplished on the plant floor.

Some embedded systems will lend themselves to bench testing with actual equipment, or with some combination of actual equipment plus simulators. The missile-to-aircraft interface box built in Appendix D and tested in Appendix E contains a good example of bench testing with actual equipment. In one part of Appendix E, the missile manufacturer is credited with setting up a complete bench rig containing the missile computer, an actual Inertial Navigation System (INS), and all necessary interconnections. The interface box is plugged into the bench rig, and initial systems integration testing is performed indoors on the bench. Appendix E will be referenced in depth later in this chapter.

Sometimes test rigs and simulators will not be practical or economically feasible, and the programmer may have to step through the code with an ICE unit in attempting to verify as much code and function as possible. In such cases, the initial testing of hardware ISRs will sometimes be necessary without the presence of target hardware or hardware simulators. In initial testing of any ISR, a MAIN() test routine can be built to issue a software interrupt request against the interrupt type number to be tested. In this way, the programmer can simulate hardware interrupt requests by issuing software interrupt requests, and can step through hardware ISRs without having to involve the hardware. This is always a tedious process, but is certainly better than no test at all. In any case, exercising as much code as possible, with as many execution permutations as possible, is the ultimate goal of software testing at any level.

DEBUGGING AND PRELIMINARY TESTING

The typical embedded systems project deals with prototype hardware and consequently requires the expertise of two gurus, one for hardware and one for software. Software development is an extremely critical part of any project, but it is a relatively small part of the overall project. Determining how the system might fit within a particular target market, determining the benefits and features to be provided, and then specifying overall system requirements are extremely critical and time-consuming tasks seldom accomplished by a single individual. Once these things have been determined, the overall system design is accomplished by those with significant hardware expertise. Creating a bill of materials, component selection, and then physically building the hardware are not small tasks. The hardware engineer is most likely to be the project manager, and is likely to be heavily involved with schedules and project politics when software debugging peaks.

If the project has unfolded properly to the point of software debugging, the hardware will have been largely debugged in an earlier joint effort of the hardware engineer and the programmer. Despite the best efforts of both individuals, hardware glitches may still exist; sometimes it is very difficult to determine whether or not software is causing a given problem. Software personnel tend to point to hardware and vice versa, but teamwork is the key to such situations.

Because of other demands on the hardware engineer's time, the programmer should try to totally eliminate software as the source of a given problem. If this is done and the findings are reported to the hardware engineer, help will most assuredly follow. If such a determination cannot be made by the programmer, the programmer might get the hardware engineer involved a bit earlier in the determination process. Once the source of the problem is found and eliminated, the software engineer can continue alone.

Assuming no hardware glitches, problems found in debugging embedded systems software are much the same as those found in debugging other types of software. Timing issues are frequently more critical in embedded systems work, and devices must be controlled with some precision, but these considerations only require that more time be allocated to the debug process. The process itself is much the same as debugging other software except that an ICE unit is used for enhanced troubleshooting capabilities in determining the sources of problems. Isolation of functionality for test purposes is sometimes more difficult in embedded systems environments, and this is particularly true if the system is interrupt-intensive and fairly complex; but with some thought and planning, none of the challenges will prove ultimately insurmountable.

Demarcation lines between the software debugging stage and software preliminary testing are sometimes fuzzy; for many conscientious individuals they are one and the same. Until the programmer is satisfied that the code has been tested as thoroughly as possible within the lab environment (with or without actual equipment), many programmers consider the debug phase to be incomplete. Regardless of how the debugging and preliminary testing steps are formally broken down, the ultimate goal is to exercise as much code (and consequently system function) as possible under the current circumstances. If the current laboratory circumstances allow total system testing with some combination of actual equipment and simulators, then total system testing might be considered the end of preliminary tests. Of course, from a formal perspective, all of this depends on the magnitude of the project, the organizational mentality, and contractual requirements.

Embedded systems are often destined to be components of much larger systems. In this case, preliminary testing of embedded systems entails the test and integration of all component modules into the final embedded unit. Systems integration and testing entails integrating the final embedded unit into the final system and verifying its ultimate function.

PIECEMEAL PRELIMINARY TESTING

Typically, preliminary testing of embedded systems is best accomplished in a piecemeal fashion. For example, a programmer would not insert all the system adapter boards into a system bus chassis, install the software, and expect the system to function reasonably well. Ideally, the programmer would isolate those system components that can be tested as separate items, and then test each one individually. In a VME or STD bus system this might entail testing each single board and its related software. Testing each major component of an embedded system in a piecemeal fashion is the first significant testing step in embedded systems software development and can be considered a critical part of preliminary testing.

At some point following piecemeal testing of system components, all system components should be integrated together and tested, if at all possible. Assuming that this is a feasible approach, the ICE unit will be used until the complete system has been proven. After completion of tests using the ICE unit and integrated system components, EPROMS should be configured with the now-tested software, and the tests repeated while the ICE unit is still in control. After successfully testing with EPROMS and the ICE unit, the ICE unit can be replaced with the actual processor to be used, and the tests repeated.

Sometimes a project design will lend itself to integrating the system components into the final system one by one, as each is tested. When the final component is tested, all components have been integrated into the final unit. Appendix E contains a good example of such a situation. In the example in Appendix E, the missile-to-aircraft interface box that was built in Appendix D is tested. In the process, each VME bus card is individually tested starting with the CPU board. As tests are completed for each board, another board is added into the VME bus chassis, until all boards have been tested and component integration into the final unit is complete.

In the case of Appendix E, preliminary testing has been completed after piecemeal component integration into the final unit, and a good degree of confidence in the final system has been earned. Formal test plans and test procedures might be written to commence at this stage of the project. The programmer would have done everything possible within the current laboratory circumstances, and formal test procedures might verify the accomplishments to this point in the project.

THE TEST PLAN

All development projects require test plans, regardless of the nature of development or development project size. As with any journey, getting from point 'A' to point 'B' requires a road map.

Large corporate environments sometimes require lengthy, formalized documents detailing every aspect of testing, including each module test goal and the criteria for success. Usually, such plans are contractually required when the embedded system is a part of a much larger system being built, for example, to Department of Defense (DOD) specifications. Not many organizations are willing to increase project overhead with such a massive paperwork burden unless it is an integral part of deliverable documents specified in a contract. When such formal documents are necessary, the programmer typically provides input to another organizational group responsible for finalizing deliverable documents. In this case, the programmer's burden will be in conveying the detail necessary for a nonprogrammer to create the formal test plan.

For example, when contractors develop software for the United States Government, DOD contracts frequently require adherence to DOD-STD-2167A. (This standard is addressed in some detail in Chapter 5.) Overall test requirements for DOD-defined software entities include software unit testing (CSU), software component integration and testing (CSC), software configuration item (CSCI) integration and testing, and system integration and testing. Each of these test layers can require test plans, test readiness plans, test procedures, extensive documentation of results in Software Development Files (SDF), and/or Independent Verification and Validation (IV&V) by a firm with no connection to the developing firm. The process and paperwork can be massive.

Smaller engineering firms, operating on smaller budgets and without the contractual requirements of massive formality, have more latitude in creating test plans. Typically the engineering staffs of small, systems-oriented environments are competent, dedicated, and conscientious. Conscientious individuals, whether hardware or software, want their creations to work and are the best qualified people to determine meaningful test requirements, and to actually ensure proper unit function. Without contractual burdens, test plans can be as simple or as complex as the individuals involved care to make them. Appendix E tests the missile-to-aircraft interface box that was built in Appendix D; and in the process, a very simple and high-level test plan is presented in the absence of contractual test requirements. Assuming motivation on the part of the interface box creators, the simplified plan as presented could prove entirely adequate in its present state, even though all formality and a considerable amount of detail are missing.

SYSTEM INTEGRATION AND TESTING

Regardless of test plan formality, the breakdown of test phases, or the adequacy of preliminary testing, at some point systems integration and testing will occur. Systems integration and testing can be considered complete when the embedded system under construction is integrated with the actual hardware that constitutes the total system, and is successfully tested in that environment.

When in-depth preliminary testing has been accomplished using simulators and actual equipment, confidence in the unit under construction will be high when system integration begins. When preliminary testing has been accomplished under less ideal conditions, overall confidence will suffer accordingly.

In Appendix E, the missile-to-aircraft interface box is tested under almost ideal conditions. After each component is tested individually, another component is added into the system bus chassis. After component integration is complete, comprehensive tests can be conducted that approach the unit's total function in a full-blown system. Each necessary unit function, except the accuracy of the pressure altitude interface, has been reasonably well tested. A very high degree of unit confidence is gained during this preliminary testing, and system integration tests are expected to go smoothly, at least on the part of the interface box.

After preliminary testing, the interface box undergoes two additional tests, both of which can be considered system integration. The bench test at the missile manufacturer's site is conducted with actual equipment, and the pressure altitude interface is verified at that time. The interaction and proper function of all system components is verified as well. Successful completion of that test is successful completion of system integration. The test must be repeated after the equipment is installed in a test aircraft, but there is no reason to anticipate that any problems will be caused by the interface box during that *ground test*. The ground test is conducted primarily to ensure proper wiring and installation of equipment into the test aircraft. It is a second iteration of system integration and testing from the perspective of the interface box.

There are many instances when preliminary testing cannot be as thorough as the case in Appendix E. Preliminary testing is sometimes drastically limited by lack of equipment availability, and must be accomplished under less than ideal conditions. In such cases, the systems integration test is typically more tedious, more difficult, and more time consuming. The ICE unit would likely be necessary until the final stages of system integration. In some cases, system integration may be accomplished at the end-user's site while disrupting production operations, and this can be a programmer's nightmare.

In a nutshell, system integration is frequently an ultimate goal in developing embedded units. Implementation and system integration are effectively synonymous terms in many cases. The process of system integration can be tedious and time-consuming, or it can be a relatively easy part of the development process. The quantity of problems that can be anticipated during system integration is related to overall system complexity, but is inversely proportional to the quality and completeness of preliminary testing.

BETA TESTING

Beta testing, *field testing*, and *user testing* are virtually synonymous terms, and this is particularly true when discussing embedded systems. Such testing follows system integration testing; the scope of these tests largely depends on the size of the existing or anticipated user base and the overall complexity of the system being tested. Two extremes of user base are exemplified by the previously presented, one-shot missile-to-aircraft development cycle and the automobile brick-brain, described in Chapter 1. The former would undergo field testing simultaneously with each demonstration flight. The latter might be extensively tested by the manufacturer, and then implemented initially in high-end products as an add-on option. Such a scheme would introduce a relatively small number of units into the field, and would allow initial customers to unsuspectingly serve as beta test sites. This is an entirely satisfactory and practical scheme that would serve to more fully test the product before widespread distribution.

Between these two extremes there are many variations of user base size and system complexity. Consequently, there are many variations of beta test procedures and control. Typically, new products are tested in as many sites as possible, and upgraded products are tested by prior arrangement with selected and existing customers. In every case, it is unlikely that a bullet-proof product will emerge from beta tests. There are unanticipated environmental conditions and user idiocyncracies that sometimes create unexpected problems in systems that are widely distributed.

QUALITY ISSUES

Two major categories within the quality umbrella are *reliability* and *software certification*. Embedded systems software can be considered as "reliable" if its use does not result in failure of the system to perform as expected, and this definition can be interpreted within the context of time or quantitative exposures. Typically, certification of software is concerned with operational effectiveness under realistic operating conditions, and consequently, it overlaps the reliability definition. Demarcation lines can be fuzzy. In addition to these measures of functional quality, there are numerous quality issues that are highly subjective. The quality of code construction, documentation, overall design, and related maintainability are typical subjective issues that can be further decomposed into many categories. Subjective software quality issues are frequently defined by the user or customer, and in this case, there is no valid argument contrary to the customer's definition—the customer must be satisfied. The author once watched a major military contractor berate a subcontractor and the subcontractor's source code for using classic and entirely acceptable software construction techniques in building systems-level code. No amount of reasoning could change the contractor's position. The point here is that the contractor's representatives were relatively inexperienced, had little experience with software at the systems level, and simply did not understand the benefits of the software construction that they were reviewing—but the contractor was the customer. The subcontractor suffered for providing excellence and was unappreciated in a classic case of casting pearls before swine. The contractor's underlying agenda could have been political in nature, but in this case it was not. Such are the hazards of contracting.

Overall software quality is often measured using an organization's quality assurance procedures, and these vary considerably among most entities. Overall software quality is typically perceived to be good if the final product is reliable, well documented, easily maintained, and has maximized software reusability aspects. These are certainly good measurements of quality; but the detailed criteria are subjective and vary from organization to organization. Part of any given organization's quality assurance process might include software certification, as defined earlier. Because certification is never an abstract process, both correctness and robustness of software are assured to a realistic extent by the certification testing process, and the results of certification testing should be documented.

There are many issues related to software quality, but most are subjective and are defined differently by different entities, and some of the more important quality issues are frequently overlooked:

- Whether or not the work was accomplished on time
- Whether or not the development was efficient (including considerations for saving human resources at the expense of hardware and software tool purchases—not the reverse)
- Whether or not potential cross-project utilization was maximized

In any case, as with aspects of documentation and testing, formality of the quality assurance process is far less important than the qualifications, dedication, and motivation of the individuals involved. Politically, procedural changes are often credited with solving quality problems, but most often, the actual improvement comes with personnel changes and by assigning duties to individuals which are consistent with the interests and personal goals of the individuals involved.

SUMMARY

Earlier chapters covered techniques of code construction, and other specific concepts required in the building of embedded systems software. This chapter has given some insight into the process of testing and integrating an embedded system.

Using the least complex breakdown, there are five essential and major activities in the software development process: requirements gathering, design, coding, testing, and implementation. If overall project success is measured in terms of resource usage, as well as final functionality, overall project success is always the result of a domino effect. Final success and smooth implementation depend on the success of the system integration effort. The system integration effort is driven by the quality and completeness of preliminary testing. The ability to adequately conduct preliminary tests depends on system design and code construction. System design is totally dependent on the requirements specification. Therefore, each of the five essential phases of the development process are of equal importance.

The process of conducting these activities can be highly formalized or can be extremely informal. In every successful project, formality of process is far less important than the competence and dedication of the people involved. Formality is generally more important within procedure-driven environments, and project efficiency within such environments often takes a back seat to the status quo. Nevertheless, production-oriented individuals always find effective ways to accomplish project goals, in spite of artificial obstacles that may be encountered.

Results, and the adequate documentation of those results for effective future use, are the bottom-line objectives of any project. There are many procedural ways to satisfactorily achieve these objectives, and flexibility of process, in its application to a given project, can be economical in both the short and long terms.

APPENDIX A

Pilot Control Panel Example

In this appendix, a software "driver" for a pilot's push-button control panel is built. All source code necessary to operate the control panel switches, indicator lights, and associated flags is finalized here. The control panel source code is written without a comprehensive design presentation to the reader; however, control panel requirements are presented, and enough design information is provided to make the coding objectives readily apparent. In the process of building the source code, memory is mapped, data tables are designed, and code is written to interface with the data tables and to perform port I/O. These actions incorporate the essence of information contained in Chapter 2.

Appendix A shows that subsets of the code and tables can allow their use with less complex switch implementations that use consecutive bits in a single port for switch states. The requirements for the example control panel are contained in the following section. The next three sections of this appendix contain, respectively, the overall approach to be followed, the ensuing data tables, and the C functions required to manipulate the control panel lights and switches.

PILOT CONTROL PANEL REQUIREMENTS

An interface box for guided-missile-to-aircraft interface is to be built for flight demonstration purposes—not for combat. The pilot's interface to the box will be five push-button switches similar to those described in Chapter 2. The interface box will be built with an off-the-shelf VME system bus chassis. The I/O will be memory-mapped, and a Motorola 68000 CPU board will be used. The CPU board and the adapter board providing the panel's digital interface will be purchased off the shelf. Four 16-bit ports on the control panel (CP) interface board are used as follows:

1. CP status (view the requested state of switches)
2. CP control (control the current state of switches)
3. CP switch light control (control lights ON/OFF)
4. CP switch blink control (control lights BLINK/NO BLINK)

There will be a total of five switches on the control panel and each will have a three-character label, as shown in Figure A-1. Associated lights have three possible states: ON, OFF, BLINK. The switch functions are to be as follows:

1. INS (Inertial Navigation System) switch—This switch is used before takeoff. After applying power to the INS system, this switch will "start" the system internal message traffic between the INS, the INS's separate control panel, and the interface box (this control panel). It is the first switch to be used. While this switch is OFF, all switches except this switch and the panel RES switch are inhibited. If this switch is ON or IN PROCESS, no other switches are allowed until the ALN switch is pressed. When this switch is ON, it is lighted. This switch blinks if errors are detected with the INS system. This switch can be turned OFF using the RES switch.

2. ALN (Align missile's INS with aircraft's INS) switch—This switch is used after the INS switch is ON. It causes "alignment" messages to commence between the interface box and the missile's computer until the NAV or ITL switches are ON. The missile will begin "aligning" its INS with the aircraft's INS. This switch is steadily lighted when ON (indicating that the alignment is complete), and blinks while the alignment is out-of-limits (indicating that alignment is incomplete). This switch is forced OFF when the NAV or ITL switches are ON. State changes to the INS switch and this switch are inhibited while this switch is ON. (The RESET switch allows starting over with the INS switch.) The NAV switch is

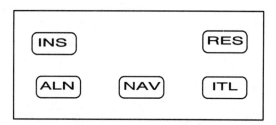

INS = Start Inertial Nav System Message Traffic
ALN = Start Alignment Message to Align Missile INS
      with Aircraft INS
NAV = Command Missile to Take Over Independent
      Navigation
ITL = Notify Missile of Pilot's Intent to Launch
RES = Control Panel Reset

Figure A-1. Pilot Control Panel Layout

inhibited while this switch is OFF. This switch can be skipped and ITL can be activated without ALN or NAV. State changes to ITL and NAV are inhibited while this switch is IN PROCESS.

3. NAV (Missile takes over its own navigation) switch—This switch is used after the ALN switch is ON. It causes a COMMAND message to be sent to the missile's computer to indicate that the missile should take over its own navigation independent of the host aircraft. When this switch is ON or IN PROCESS, the RES and ITL switches can be set ON, but no ON switches can be set OFF without RESET. When ON, this switch is steadily lighted until the missile takes over its own navigation, and then it blinks (which should be immediately). This switch can be skipped and the pilot can go directly to ITL from ALN or INS.

4. ITL (Intent to launch) switch—This switch is used at any time after the INS switch is ON. Normally, the NAV switch would be blinking (missile conducting independent navigation) when this switch is used, but NAV can be skipped. ALN can be skipped also. This switch causes a COMMAND message to be sent to the missile's computer to indicate that the pilot intends to launch the missile. When this switch is ON, no state changes of any switch is allowed (including this one)—it is a one-shot try. NAV and ALN are forced OFF by this switch. This switch blinks when ON.

5. RES (Reset Control Panel) switch—This switch is used to RESET all panel switches and start over. It is inhibited if ITL is ON. When this switch is pressed, all switches and lights (including this one) are returned to logic 0.

PILOT CONTROL PANEL APPROACH

The hardware engineer has selected the specific adapter board to be used as a panel interface, and has provided additional information about the switches and ports:

*   All four ports will be mapped identically in that the same bit mask will affect the same switch in each port. In other words, bit 9 in the status port will indicate whether or not a specific switch is currently "pressed" by the pilot. Bit 9 in the light control port will set the associated light ON or OFF for the same switch. The upper 8 bits of each port will be used.

*   The only exception to the above is that the switch control port will use the lower 8 bits to "inhibit" a switch from indicating the ON state; however, the associated mask will be the (ON-MASK >> 8).

*   The control panel is RESET by writing all inhibit bits and then writing all ON bits. This forces all bits to logic zero. An ensuing read of the status port could verify this.

*   While a switch is pressed, the appropriate mask in the control panel status port will be SET. When the switch is released, the bit will be RESET.

- The port addresses will be consecutive from hex 0x2f800 through hex 0x2f806 and in this order: CP status, CP control, switch light control, switch blink control.

For reasons that will become apparent later, the programmer has decided not to use the hardware inhibit bits at all, except for panel reset. The software will track all current and requested states from the control panel's perspective. The states will be tracked for currently ON, OFF, INHIBITED, IN PROCESS, BLINKING, PRESSED, DONE, or IN ERROR. Requested states will be tracked for REQUESTED TO LOGIC 1 and REQUESTED TO LOGIC 0 and each such request will be validated by software. After validation, software will track valid requests. This will all be accomplished in the control panel table structure. The control panel table will be a consolidation of all "current" individual switch masks in the control panel ports. The control panel table contents will be as follows:

1. Pointer to status port for CP (input) in port table
2. Pointer to status port for CP switches in port table
3. Pointer to control port for CP lights ON in port table
4. Pointer to control port for CP lights BLINK in port table
5. Mask for all switches currently SET by software
6. Mask for all switches currently pressed by pilot
7. Mask for all switches currently requested to logic 0
8. Mask for all switches currently requested to logic 1
9. Mask for all switches currently inhibited from logic 1
10. Mask for all switches currently inhibited from logic 0
11. Mask for all switches with valid logic 1 requests
12. Mask for all switches with valid logic 0 requests
13. Mask for all switches currently in DONE state
14. Mask for all switches currently in IN ERROR state
15. Mask for all switch lights currently ON
16. Mask for all switch lights currently BLINKing
17. Mask for all switches with messages SENT
18. Mask for all switches with messages DONE
19. Mask for all switches with messages IN ERROR
20. Mask for all switches with message response available
21. Mask for all switches with message response requested

Little is known at this point about the system messages; however, because message traffic will occur when certain switches are pressed, and because some of that traffic will likely entail responses, message states will also be tracked for each switch. The message states will be tracked in the control panel structure; and message states of SENT, DONE, IN ERROR, and RESPONSE AVAILABLE will be used. Provision will be made for these flags in the control panel table.

The switch state requirements appear to have flaws, and the powers-that-be are likely to change the control panel state requirements before the interface box is built. If they do, it would be easier to change the allowable states from within a single table. As some switches are inhibited while others are in various states, a table containing bit patterns for allowable switch states for given switch conditions will be built. It will also contain information about each switch's current state and other permitted switch states under the immediate conditions:

1. Bit MASK for this switch in all CP ports
2. Bit masks for switches to inhibit to logic 1 if this switch is ON
3. Bit masks for switches to inhibit to logic 0 if this switch is ON
4. Bit masks for switches to inhibit to logic 1 if this switch is OFF
5. Bit masks for switches to inhibit to logic 0 if this switch is OFF
6. Bit masks for switches to inhibit to logic 1 if this switch is IN PROCESS
7. Bit masks for switches to inhibit to logic 0 if this switch is IN PROCESS
8. Bit masks for switches to set OFF if this switch is ON or INPROCESS
9. Light ON mask while this switch is INPROCESS
10. Light BLINK mask while this switch is INPROCESS
11. Light ON mask when this switch is DONE
12. Light BLINK mask while this switch is DONE
13. Light ON mask while this switch is IN_ERR and DONE
14. Light BLINK mask while this switch is IN_ERR and DONE
15. Light ON Mask while this switch IN_ERR and INPROCESS
16. Light BLINK Mask while this switch IN_ERR and INPROCESS
17. Current state of this switch
18. Inhibit ON masks for other switches due to the current state of this switch
19. Inhibit OFF masks for other switches due to the current state of thi switch

The intent here is to provide switch processing that is "black-boxed" to a reasonable extent. The table containing individual switch information will provide bit patterns to the control panel table, which will contain current information for all switches. When other programs need to interface to the control panel, three primary methods are provided:

1. Calling a single function to obtain, filter, and validate current requests (Once a valid request occurs, the IN PROCESS or OFF flag is set as appropriate, and other switch-state flags are updated accordingly. All light-state flags are updated as well. After performing any subsequent project-specific details, the calling function can use other routines to re-update all flags and output the appropriate information to the light and blink control ports.)
2. Direct viewing of the table flags to determine current switch status
3. Calling specific routines to set switch DONE or IN ERROR conditions (OFF conditions are monitored and automated within the control panel code.)

PILOT CONTROL PANEL TABLES

```
/* -------------------- */
/* MODULE PATH: \CP\CP.H */
/* -------------------- */
```

1. Define the port table structure including port usage flags, port offsets, and port addresses.

```
/* ----------------------------------- */
/* Port table structure - System Ports */
/* ----------------------------------- */

      typedef struct port_table
  {
ULONG port_addr;   /* Port address                */
UCHAR port_imag;   /* Last image written to port  */
UCHAR port_flgs;   /* Port flag bucket            */
  } PORTBL, *PTPTR; /* New port table data types   */

        /* ---------------------- */
        /* Port Flag Bits (0 to 7) */
        /* ---------------------- */

#define INUSEP 0x8 /* Bit for port-in-use, 0 = not in use */
                   /* Bit for port-in-use, 1 = in use     */
#define READP 0x1  /* Bit for a read port, 0 = no read    */
                   /* Bit for a read port, 1 = read OK    */
#define WRITEP 0x2 /* Bit for a write port, 0 = no write  */
                   /* Bit for a write port, 1 = write OK  */
#define INITP 0x4  /* Bit for port init OK, 0 = not OK    */
                   /* Bit for port init OK, 1 = init DONE */

/* --------------------------------------------------- */
/* Offsets of specific ports in the ram/rom_ports array */
/* --------------------------------------------------- */

#define CPSTATPORT 0    /* offset CP STATUS port */
#define CPCTRLPORT 1    /* Offset CP CTRL  port  */
#define CPLITEPORT 2    /* Offset LITE CTRL port */
#define CPBLNKPORT 3    /* Offset BLNK CTRL port */

/* ------------------------------- */
/* Bit usage in control panel ports */
/* ------------------------------- */

#define ALL_LITES  0xff00    /* mask for all ON bits      */
#define INHIBITS   0x00ff    /* mask for all INHIBIT bits */
```

2. Define a structure for the control panel. The switches on the panel all

share the same control panel ports. Some buttons must be inhibited while others are pressed, and some requests will be invalid. Using flags, the requested states, current inhibits, and other switch considerations will be extensively tracked in software. Also, some buttons will initiate internal system message traffic between system components. Include provision for message requests, in process, done, and in error.

```
/* ------------------------------------------------- */
/* Control Panel Structure for ports & CP flags.  */
/*    (One of these per control panel).            */
/* ------------------------------------------------- */

typedef struct ctrl_panel {
    PTPTR   cp_stat;   /* Status port for CP (input)          */
    PTPTR   cp_ctrl;   /* Control port for CP (output)        */
    PTPTR   cp_onlt;   /* Control port for lites ON (output)  */
    PTPTR   cp_bklt;   /* Ctrl port for lites BLINK (output)  */
    USHORT cp_sets;    /* Switches with software state of SET */
    USHORT cp_press;   /* Switches currently pressed          */
    USHORT cp_req0;    /* Switches REQUESTED to logic 0       */
    USHORT cp_req1;    /* Switches REQUESTED to logic 1       */
    USHORT cp_inh1;    /* Switches INHIBITED from logic 1     */
    USHORT cp_inh0;    /* Switches INHIBITED from logic 0     */
    USHORT cp_inpr;    /* Switches w/ valid ON requests       */
    USHORT cp_unpr;    /* Switches w/ valid OFF requests      */
    USHORT cp_done;    /* Switches processed (DONE)           */
    USHORT cp_erro;    /* Switches currently IN ERROR         */
    USHORT cp_lton;    /* Lites ON (last output image)        */
    USHORT cp_ltbk;    /* Lites BLINKing (last output image)  */
    USHORT cp_msnt;    /* Message SENT flag                   */
    USHORT cp_mdon;    /* Message DONE flag                   */
    USHORT cp_merr;    /* Message IN ERROR flag               */
    USHORT cp_mres;    /* Message RESPONSE AVAILABLE flag     */
    USHORT cp_mrrq;    /* Message RESPONSE REQUESTED flag     */
} CTRLP, *CTRLPTR;
```

3. Define a structure for the individual buttons (switches) on the control panel. Some buttons must be inhibited while others are pressed, and some buttons must BLINK when ON or until a process has finished. Using flags, the predetermined valid states, ensuing inhibits, and other switch considerations will be defined to the software. This table provides switch "templates" for allowable states.

```
/* ------------------------------------------------- */
/* Structure definition for Control Panel SWITCHES */
/* (switch relationships). (1 per CP SWITCH)       */
/* ------------------------------------------------- */

typedef struct one_switch {
```

```
    USHORT  sw_mask;    /* Bit MASK for this switch in CP ports  */
    USHORT  sw_oih1;    /* Bit masks for switches to inhibit to
                           logic 1 if this switch set ON         */
    USHORT  sw_oih0;    /* Bit masks for switches to inhibit to
                           logic 0 if this switch set ON         */
    USHORT  sw_fih1;    /* Bit masks for switches to inhibit to
                           logic 1 if this switch set OFF        */
    USHORT  sw_fih0;    /* Bit masks for switches to inhibit to
                           logic 0 if this switch set OFF        */
    USHORT  sw_pih1;    /* Bit masks for switches to inhibit to
                           logic 1 if this switch set IN PROCESS */
    USHORT  sw_pih0;    /* Bit masks for switches to inhibit to
                           logic 0 if this switch set IN PROCESS */
    USHORT  sw_xoff;    /* Bit masks for switches to set OFF if
                           this switch is ON                     */
    USHORT  sw_ltei;    /* Lite ON Mask while INPROCESS          */
    USHORT  sw_lbki;    /* Lite BLINK Mask while INPROCESS       */
    USHORT  sw_lted;    /* Lite ON Mask while DONE               */
    USHORT  sw_lbkd;    /* Lite BLINK Mask while DONE            */
    USHORT  sw_ltee;    /* Lite ON Mask while IN_ERR & DONE      */
    USHORT  sw_lbke;    /* Lite BLINK Mask while IN_ERR & DONE   */
    USHORT  sw_lte2;    /* Lite ON Mask while IN_ERR & INPROCESS */
    USHORT  sw_lbk2;    /* Lite BLINK Msk while IN_ERR &INPROCES */
    USHORT  sw_cur1;    /* Sw currntly inhibited to 1 by this sw */
    USHORT  sw_cur0;    /* Sw currntly inhibited to 0 by this sw */
    USHORT  sw_curr;    /* Sw current state                      */
    } SW1, *SW1PTR;

    /* Possible values for current switch state    */

    #define  SWOFF       0    /* OFF                     */
    #define  SWDONE      1    /* DONE                    */
    #define  SWINP       3    /* IN PROCESS              */
    #define  SWERRDONE   4    /* IN ERROR & DONE         */
    #define  SWERRINP    5    /* IN ERROR & IN PROCESS   */
```

4. For each switch in the table, define its array offset for future referencing. There will be five total switches.

```
    /* ------------------------------------------------- */
    /* Switch offsets into individual switch table in ROM */
    /* ------------------------------------------------- */

    #define  INS_SW  0    /* Intertial Nav System (INS) switch */
    #define  ALN_SW  1    /* Missile ALIGN INS switch          */
    #define  NAV_SW  2    /* Missile NAV switch                */
    #define  ITL_SW  3    /* Missile INTENT TO LAUNCH switch   */
    #define  RES_SW  4    /* Control Panel RESET switch        */
```

5. For each switch in the table, define its bit mask in the control panel ports.

```
                    /* --------------- */
                    /* Switch ON masks */
                    /* --------------- */

    #define INS_MASK   0x0100      /* INS switch & lite          */
    #define ALN_MASK   0x0200      /* ALIGN switch & lite        */
    #define NAV_MASK   0x0400      /* NAV switch & lite          */
    #define ITL_MASK   0x0800      /* INTENT TO LAUNCH sw lite   */
    #define RES_MASK   0x1000      /* CP RESET switch & lite     */

                    /* --------------------- */
                    /* MODULE PATH \CP\CPDAT.C */
                    /* --------------------- */
```

6. Using the above definitions, fill in the ROM tables and define the RAM tables.

```
    /* ------------------------------------ */
    /* Port table structure - System Ports */
    /* ------------------------------------ */

    PORTBL rom_ports[] =      /* PORTS in ROM  */
    {
    0x2f8001,0,READP,         /* CP STATUS PORT */
    0x2f8021,0,WRITEP,        /* CP CTRL PORT   */
    0x2f8041,0,WRITEP,        /* LITE CTRL PORT */
    0x2f8061,0,WRITEP         /* BLNK CTRL PORT */
    };

    #define NUMPORTS ((sizeof(rom_ports))/(sizeof(PORTBL)))

    PORTBL ram_ports[NUMPORTS];/* PORTS in RAM */

    /* ----------------------------------------------- */
    /* ROM Control Panel (copied to RAM at init time) */
    /* ----------------------------------------------- */

    CTRLP rom_cp = {              /* CP in ROM              */
       &ram_ports[CPSTATPORT], /* PTPTR CP STATUS    */
       &ram_ports[CPCTRLPORT], /* PTPTR CP CTRL      */
       &ram_ports[CPLITEPORT], /* PTPTR LITE CTRL    */
       &ram_ports[CPBLNKPORT], /* PTPTR BLNK CTRL    */
       0,0,0,0,0,0,0,0,0,
       0
       };

    CTRLP ram_cp;  /* CP in RAM     */

    /* ------------------------------------------------- */
    /* ROM Individual switch table for allowable states  */
```

```
/* -------------------------------------------------- */

SW1 rom_sw[] = {

{INS_MASK,0,INS_MASK,~INS_MASK,0,~(INS_MASK  |RES_MASK),
INS_MASK,0,INS_MASK,0,INS_MASK,0,INS_MASK,INS_MASK,
INS_MASK,INS_MASK,0,0,0},

{ALN_MASK,0,INS_MASK,NAV_MASK,0,
NAV_MASK | ITL_MASK,0, NAV_MASK | ITL_MASK, ALN_MASK,
ALN_MASK,ALN_MASK,0,
ALN_MASK,ALN_MASK,ALN_MASK,ALN_MASK,0,0,0},

{NAV_MASK,ALN_MASK,INS_MASK,0,0,ALN_MASK,INS_MASK,
ALN_MASK,NAV_MASK,NAV_MASK,NAV_MASK,NAV_MASK,NAV_MASK,0,
NAV_MASK,0,0,0,0},

{ITL_MASK,ALL_LITES,ALL_LITES,0,INS_MASK,ALL_LITES,
ALL_LITES,ALN_MASK | NAV_MASK,ITL_MASK,ITL_MASK,ITL_MASK,
ITL_MASK,ITL_MASK,0,ITL_MASK,0,0,0,0},

{RES_MASK,0,0,0,0,~RES_MASK,0,ALL_LITES,
RES_MASK,0,RES_MASK,0,0,0,0,0,}
};

#define NUMCPSW     ((sizeof(rom_sw))/(sizeof(SW1)))

SW1 ram_sw[NUMCPSW];      /* Switch table in RAM */
```

At this point the tables are complete. It may seem like too many machinations for a few switches, and the structure elements do have abstract-looking names; however, the weird names are "black-boxed" for the most part, and the tables will ultimately represent an overall savings of project effort due to volatile switch requirements. The tables undoubtedly increase reusability aspects of the control panel code, and the tables represent the additional 20 percent up-front effort mentioned in Chapter 2.

Should the powers-that-be decide to change the ON light state of a switch from BLINKing to steadily ON, only the ON mask and/or the BLINK mask in the switch table need be changed. Allowable states for switches based on current switch conditions can be handled in the same fashion. Essentials of switch state and light state processing are "black-boxed" and driven by the table data.

PILOT CONTROL PANEL C FUNCTIONS

The functions required to manipulate the control panel flags and lights can be written without additional information. Routines for panel light tests, port I/O, control panel setup, and massaging the control panel bit flags for varying system conditions can be easily written with no additional project details. The consolidation of these routines will constitute the control panel driver.

The goal here is to "black-box" all switch functions, switch processing, and switch semaphores. When an application needs to interface with the control panel driver it will normally want to know if a switch is IN PROCESS, DONE, or IN ERROR; or it will want to SET one of these states. Functions will exist for setting the states, and flags exist for checking the states.

Calling trees for these functions are shown in Figures A-2, A-3, and A-4.

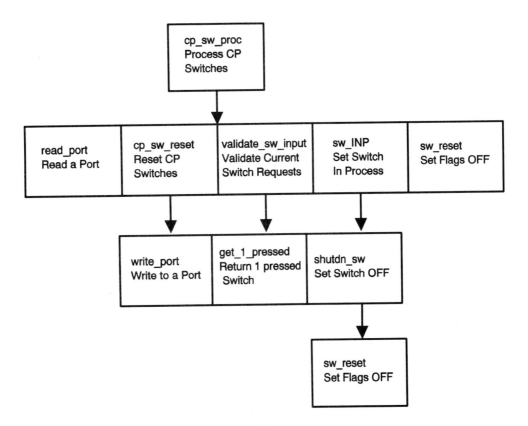

Figure A-2. Function Calling Tree for CP Switch Processing

```
/* -------------------- */
/* MODULE PATH: \CP\IO.C */
/* -------------------- */
/*
   ----------------------------------------------------------
   Routines to READ & WRITE the ports using port table.
   ----------------------------------------------------------
*/
USHORT read_port(PTPTR ptptr)        /*& READ port              */
{
```

```
    USHORT value_in;                              /* Value read from port  */

                        /*$ READ the port & RETURN value read */
        value_in = inport((USHORT far *) ptptr->port_addr);
        return(value_in);
}

VOID write_port(PTPTR ptptr, USHORT value_out)
                                                 /*& WRITE port  */
{
                        /*$ SAVE value out & WRITE value to port */
  ptptr->port_imag = value_out;
  outport((USHORT far *)ptptr->port_addr,ptptr->port_imag);
  return;/*$ RETURN */
}
```

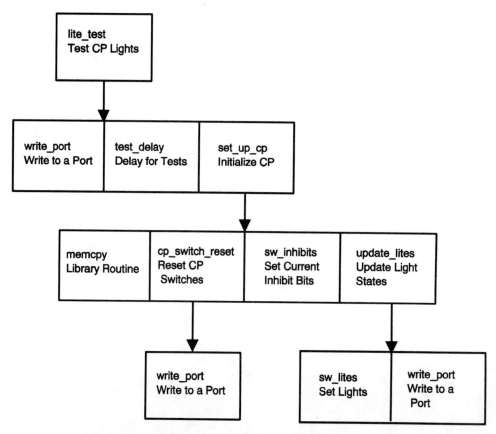

Figure A-3. Function Calling Tree for CP Light Tests

```
/* --------------------- */
/* MODULE PATH: \CP\CP.C */
/* --------------------- */
```

```
/*-----------------------------------
   Reset switch flags DONE to NOT DONE.
   -----------------------------------*/
VOID sw_reset(CTRLPTR xram_cp, SW1PTR xram_sw)
       /*& SET flags to OFF */
{
 xram_cp->cp_mrrq |= (xram_sw->sw_mask);/*$ RESET flags */
 xram_cp->cp_mrrq ^= (xram_sw->sw_mask);
 xram_cp->cp_mres |= (xram_sw->sw_mask);
 xram_cp->cp_mres ^= (xram_sw->sw_mask);
 xram_cp->cp_merr |= (xram_sw->sw_mask);
 xram_cp->cp_merr ^= (xram_sw->sw_mask);
 xram_cp->cp_msnt |= (xram_sw->sw_mask);
 xram_cp->cp_msnt ^= (xram_sw->sw_mask);
 xram_cp->cp_mdon |= (xram_sw->sw_mask);
 xram_cp->cp_mdon ^= (xram_sw->sw_mask);
 xram_cp->cp_inpr |= (xram_sw->sw_mask);
 xram_cp->cp_inpr ^= (xram_sw->sw_mask);
 xram_cp->cp_unpr |= (xram_sw->sw_mask);
 xram_cp->cp_unpr ^= (xram_sw->sw_mask);
 xram_cp->cp_sets |= (xram_sw->sw_mask);
 xram_cp->cp_sets ^= (xram_sw->sw_mask);
 xram_cp->cp_erro |= (xram_sw->sw_mask);
 xram_cp->cp_erro ^= (xram_sw->sw_mask);
 xram_cp->cp_done |= (xram_sw->sw_mask);
 xram_cp->cp_done ^= (xram_sw->sw_mask);
 xram_sw->sw_cur1 = 0;     /*$ RESET current INHIBIT to 1*/
 xram_sw->sw_cur0 = 0;     /*$ RESET current INHIBIT to 0*/
                           /*$ SET current INHIBITs */
 xram_sw->sw_cur1 = xram_sw->sw_fih1;
 xram_sw->sw_cur0 = xram_sw->sw_fih0;
 xram_sw->sw_curr = SWOFF; /*$ SET current state*/
 return;                   /*$ RETURN        */
}


/*-----------------------------------------------
   Routine to shut down a switch due to another's
   currently valid ON request.
   -----------------------------------------------
*/
VOID shutdn_sw(CTRLPTR xram_cp,
               SW1PTR xram_sw)/*& SHUTDOWN switch */
{
USHORT i;
USHORT sw;
  /*$ if any switches should be OFF, shut them OFF */
  sw = xram_sw->sw_xoff;
  for (i = 0; i < NUMCPSW; i++)
      {
       if (sw & 0x100)
             sw_reset(xram_cp,&ram_sw[i]);
```

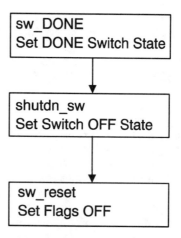

Figure A-4. Function Calling Tree for CP Switch DONE

```
        sw = (sw >> 1);
        }
  return;
}


/*----------------------------------------------------
   Routine to change any NOT DONE & NOT IN PROCESS
   switch to INPROCESS. This routine is called when
   the switch is initially set ON. (CP Flags Only).
   ----------------------------------------------------
*/
VOID sw_INP(CTRLPTR xram_cp, SW1PTR xram_sw)
                          /*& SET switch INPROCESS flags */
{
 xram_cp->cp_inpr |= (xram_sw->sw_mask);/*$ SET INPROC    */
 xram_cp->cp_sets |= (xram_sw->sw_mask);/*$ SET ON flag    */
 xram_cp->cp_done |= (xram_sw->sw_mask);/*$ RESET flags    */
 xram_cp->cp_done ^= (xram_sw->sw_mask);
 xram_cp->cp_erro |= (xram_sw->sw_mask);
 xram_cp->cp_erro ^= (xram_sw->sw_mask);
 xram_cp->cp_unpr |= (xram_sw->sw_mask);
 xram_cp->cp_unpr ^= (xram_sw->sw_mask);
 xram_cp->cp_mrrq |= (xram_sw->sw_mask);
 xram_cp->cp_mrrq ^= (xram_sw->sw_mask);
 xram_cp->cp_mres |= (xram_sw->sw_mask);
 xram_cp->cp_mres ^= (xram_sw->sw_mask);
 xram_cp->cp_merr |= (xram_sw->sw_mask);
 xram_cp->cp_merr ^= (xram_sw->sw_mask);
 xram_cp->cp_msnt |= (xram_sw->sw_mask);
 xram_cp->cp_msnt ^= (xram_sw->sw_mask);
```

```
    xram_cp->cp_mdon |= (xram_sw->sw_mask);
    xram_cp->cp_mdon ^= (xram_sw->sw_mask);
    xram_sw->sw_cur1 = 0;              /*$ RESET current INHIBIT*/
    xram_sw->sw_cur0 = 0;              /*$ RESET current INHIBIT*/
    if (xram_sw->sw_xoff)             /*$ IF any must be OFF    */
        shutdn_sw(xram_cp, xram_sw); /*$ SET them to OFF       */
                                      /*$ SET current INHIBITs  */
    xram_sw->sw_cur1 |= (xram_sw->sw_oih1 | xram_sw->sw_pih1);
    xram_sw->sw_cur0 |= (xram_sw->sw_oih0 | xram_sw->sw_pih1);
    xram_sw->sw_curr = SWINP;         /*$ SET IN PROCESS state */
    return; /*$ RETURN*/
}
/*---------------------------------
  Set switch flags INPROCESS to DONE.
  ---------------------------------
*/
VOID sw_DONE(CTRLPTR xram_cp,SW1PTR xram_sw)
              /*& SET DONE switch flags */
{
  xram_cp->cp_done |= (xram_sw->sw_mask);/*$ SET DONE        */
  xram_cp->cp_sets |= (xram_sw->sw_mask);/*$ SET switch ON   */
  xram_cp->cp_inpr |= (xram_sw->sw_mask);/*$ RESET flags     */
  xram_cp->cp_inpr ^= (xram_sw->sw_mask);
  xram_cp->cp_unpr |= (xram_sw->sw_mask);
  xram_cp->cp_unpr ^= (xram_sw->sw_mask);
  xram_cp->cp_mrrq |= (xram_sw->sw_mask);
  xram_cp->cp_mrrq ^= (xram_sw->sw_mask);
  xram_cp->cp_mres |= (xram_sw->sw_mask);
  xram_cp->cp_mres ^= (xram_sw->sw_mask);
  xram_cp->cp_merr |= (xram_sw->sw_mask);
  xram_cp->cp_merr ^= (xram_sw->sw_mask);
  xram_cp->cp_msnt |= (xram_sw->sw_mask);
  xram_cp->cp_msnt ^= (xram_sw->sw_mask);
  xram_cp->cp_mdon |= (xram_sw->sw_mask);
  xram_cp->cp_mdon ^= (xram_sw->sw_mask);
  xram_sw->sw_cur1 = 0;     /*$ RESET current INHIBIT     */
  xram_sw->sw_cur0 = 0;     /*$ RESET current INHIBIT     */
  if (xram_sw->sw_xoff)    /*$ IF any must be OFF        */
  shutdn_sw(xram_cp,xram_sw); /*$ SET them to OFF        */
                            /*$ SET current INHIBITs      */
  xram_sw->sw_cur1 |= (xram_sw->sw_oih1 | xram_sw->sw_pih1);
  xram_sw->sw_cur0 |= (xram_sw->sw_oih0 | xram_sw->sw_pih1);
  xram_sw->sw_curr = SWDONE;/*$ SET DONE state           */
  return;                  /*$ RETURN                   */
}


/* ----------------------------------
   Set switch flags to ERROR condition.
   ---------------------------------
*/
```

```
VOID sw_ERRO(CTRLPTR xram_cp, SW1PTR xram_sw)
        /*& SET switch ERR flag        */
        /*$ SET switch ERR bit & RETURN */
{ xram_cp->cp_erro |= (xram_sw->sw_mask);
  xram_sw->sw_curr += 3;
  return;
}


/*-----------------------------------------------------
  Routine to set INHIBIT bits based on switch state
  -----------------------------------------------------
*/
VOID sw_inhibits(CTRLPTR xram_cp)/*& SET current INHIBITs */
{
USHORT i;
USHORT inhibit0;
USHORT inhibit1;
SW1PTR xram_sw;

  inhibit1 = 0;                        /*$ INIT INHIBIT buckets */
  inhibit0 = 0;

 for (i = 0; i < NUMCPSW; i++)     /*$ RUN the switch table */
   { xram_sw = &ram_sw[i];         /*$ GET current INHIBITs */
    switch(xram_sw->sw_curr)
        {
          case(SWDONE):
   xram_sw->sw_cur1 = xram_sw->sw_oih1;
   xram_sw->sw_cur0 = xram_sw->sw_oih0;
          break;
          case(SWINP):
   xram_sw->sw_cur1 = xram_sw->sw_pih1;
   xram_sw->sw_cur0 = xram_sw->sw_pih0;
          break;
          case(SWOFF):
   xram_sw->sw_cur1 = xram_sw->sw_fih1;
   xram_sw->sw_cur0 = xram_sw->sw_fih0;
          break;
          default:
   xram_sw->sw_cur1 = 0;
   xram_sw->sw_cur0 = 0;
          break;

        }
          inhibit1 |= xram_sw->sw_cur1;
          inhibit0 |= xram_sw->sw_cur0;
   }

  inhibit1 |= INHIBITS;
  inhibit1 ^= INHIBITS;
  inhibit0 |= INHIBITS;
```

```
    inhibit0 ^= INHIBITS;

    xram_cp->cp_inh1 = inhibit1;/*$ SET current INHIBIT in CP */
    xram_cp->cp_inh0 = inhibit0;
    return;
}

/*----------------------------------------
   Set LIGHT bits for current switch state
   ----------------------------------------
*/
VOID sw_lites(CTRLPTR xram_cp)
                /*& Set lights current switch state */
{
USHORT lite0;
USHORT lite1;
USHORT i;
USHORT align_done;
SW1PTR xram_sw;

    lite1 = 0;   /*$ INIT lite buckets   */
    lite0 = 0;
    for (i = 0; i < NUMCPSW; i++)/*$ RUN the switch table */
  {
   xram_sw = &ram_sw[i];
   switch(xram_sw->sw_curr)
     {
     case(SWDONE):
           lite1 |= xram_sw->sw_lbkd;/*$ SET lite BLINK */
           lite0 |= xram_sw->sw_lted;/*$ SET lite ON mask*/
     break;
     case(SWINP):
           lite1 |= xram_sw->sw_lbki;/*$ SET lite BLINK */
           lite0 |= xram_sw->sw_ltei;/*$ SET lite ON mask*/
     break;
     case(SWERRINP):
           lite1 |= xram_sw->sw_lbk2;/*$ SET lite BLINK */
           lite0 |= xram_sw->sw_lte2;/*$ SET lite ON mask*/
     break;
     case(SWERRDONE):
           lite1 |= xram_sw->sw_lbke;/*$ SET lite BLINK */
           lite0 |= xram_sw->sw_ltee;/*$ SET lite ON mask*/
     break;
           }
    }
    lite1 |= INHIBITS;
    lite1 ^= INHIBITS;
    lite0 |= INHIBITS;
    lite0 ^= INHIBITS;
    xram_cp->cp_lton = lite0;/*$ PUT output val in CP tbl */
    xram_cp->cp_ltbk = lite1;
```

```
        return;     /*$ RETURN      */
    }

    /*----------------------------------------------------
       Routine to SET light states to current desired states
       ----------------------------------------------------
    */
    VOID update_lites(CTRLPTR xram_cp)
                         /*& UPDATE lights */
    {
    PTPTR ptptr;
       ptptr = xram_cp->cp_onlt;            /*$ ASSIGN pointer    */
       sw_lites(xram_cp);                   /*$ SET-UP bits       */
       write_port(ptptr,xram_cp->cp_lton);  /*$ WRITE lite ON/OFF */
       ptptr = xram_cp->cp_bklt;            /*$ ASSIGN port ptr   */
       write_port(ptptr,xram_cp->cp_ltbk);  /*$ WRITE lite BLINK  */
       return;                              /*$ RETURN */
    }
    /*-----------------------------------------
       Routine to reset Control Panel switches
       -----------------------------------------
    */

    VOID cp_switch_resets(CTRLPTR xram_cp)
                         /*& RESET CP Switches  */
    {
    PTPTR ptptr;
    SW1PTR xram_sw;
    USHORT i;
       ptptr = xram_cp->cp_ctrl;       /*$ ASSIGN port pointer */
       write_port(ptptr,INHIBITS);     /*$ WRITE INHIBIT mask  */
       write_port(ptptr,~INHIBITS);    /*$ WRITE NOT INHIBIT   */
       return;                         /*$ RETURN              */
    }

    /*-------------------------------------------------
       This routine will initialize the Control Panel.
       The control panel is copied from RAM to ROM.
       All switches and lights are RESET
       -------------------------------------------------
    */

    VOID set_up_cp(CTRLPTR xram_cp,SW1PTR xram_sw)/*&INIT CP*/
    {
                                       /*$ COPY tables To RAM */
       memcpy((UCHAR *) xram_cp,(UCHAR *) &rom_cp, sizeof(CTRLP));
       memcpy((UCHAR *) xram_sw,(UCHAR *) &rom_sw, sizeof(rom_sw));

       cp_switch_resets(xram_cp);      /*$ RESET CP switches   */
       sw_inhibits(xram_cp);           /*$ SET INHIBITS        */
```

```
    update_lites(xram_cp);              /*$ UPDATE lights        */

    return;                             /*$ RETURN               */
}

/*
    ------------------------------------
    Coarse DELAY routine for light tests.
    ------------------------------------
*/
VOID test_delay(VOID)/*& DELAY loop for tests */
{
USHORT i;
USHORT n;
USHORT m;
        for (i = 0; i < 100; i++)
                {
                for (n = 0; n < 100; n++)
                        {
                        for (m = 0; m < 100; m++);
                }
        }
        return;       /*$ DELAY & RETURN */
}

/*
    ------------------------------------------------
    This routine tests the control panel lights by
    setting all lights to BLINK for a brief period,
    then steady ON, then OFF.
    ------------------------------------------------
*/
VOID lite_test(CTRLPTR xram_cp,SW1PTR xram_sw)
                                /*& TEST CP lights */

{
PTPTR ptptr;

    xram_cp->cp_lton = ALL_LITES;           /*$ SET lite ON msks   */
    xram_cp->cp_ltbk = ALL_LITES;           /*$ SET blink masks    */
    ptptr = xram_cp->cp_onlt;               /*$ ASSIGN port ptr    */
    write_port(ptptr,xram_cp->cp_lton);     /*$ WRITE ON           */
    test_delay();                           /*$ PAUSE for tests    */
    ptptr = xram_cp->cp_bklt;               /*$ ASSIGN port ptr    */
    write_port(ptptr,xram_cp->cp_ltbk);     /*$ WRITE blink        */
    test_delay();                           /*$ PAUSE for tests    */
    xram_cp->cp_lton = 0;                   /*$ SET lite OFF msk   */
    xram_cp->cp_ltbk = 0;                   /*$ SET blink OFF      */
    set_up_cp(xram_cp,xram_sw);             /*$ REINIT CP          */
    return;
```

```
}

/*-------------------------------------------------
   This routine looks at all switches currently
   PRESSED and accepts the first one encountered,
   ignoring all others. (~0 = BAD or NONE.)
   Returns PRESSED switch offset in switch table.
   -----------------------------------------------
*/
USHORT get_1_pressd(USHORT *value)/*& GET 1 PRESSED switch */
{
USHORT i;
USHORT sw_offset;
SW1PTR xram_sw;

  sw_offset = ~0;

  /*$ RUN the switch table looking for a mask match      */
  /*$ USE the first mask found & remove others           */

  for (i = 0; i < NUMCPSW; i++)
  { xram_sw = &ram_sw[i];               /*$ SET curr ptr   */
  if ((*value) & xram_sw->sw_mask)      /*$ If MATCH found */
   { *value |= ~(xram_sw->sw_mask);     /*$ REMOVE others  */
    *value ^= ~(xram_sw->sw_mask);
    sw_offset = i;    /*$ GRAB offset    */
    i = NUMCPSW;      /*$ EXIT loop      */
   }
  }
  return(sw_offset);    /*$RETURN grabbed switch offset */
}

/*-------------------------------------------------------------
   Routine to validate currently pressed switch. If more
   than one is pressed, only one will be used or validated.
   Returns switch offset in table or ~0 for none valid.
   -----------------------------------------------------------
*/
UCHAR validate_sw_input(CTRLPTR xram_cp, USHORT sw_req_in)
                    /*& VALIDATE current sw request */
{
USHORT diff;        /* Differences from last read  */
USHORT work;        /* Work area                   */
USHORT to_ON;       /* Valid ON requests           */
USHORT to_OFF;      /* Valid OFF requests          */

  to_OFF = 0; to_ON = 0; work = 0;
  diff = sw_req_in;
  if (diff)         /*$ IF any requests input      */
  {
```

```
                        /*$ GET requests to logic 0,OFF*/
        to_OFF = (diff & xram_cp->cp_sets);
                        /*$ GET requests to logic 1, ON */
        to_ON = (diff ^ to_OFF);
                        /*$ REMOVE invalid requests    */
        work = (to_ON & xram_cp->cp_inh1);
        work |= (to_ON & xram_cp->cp_done);
        work |= (to_ON & xram_cp->cp_inpr);
        to_ON ^= work;
                        /*$ REMOVE invalid requests    */
        work = (to_OFF & xram_cp->cp_inh0);
        work |= (to_OFF & ~(xram_cp->cp_done));
        work |= (to_OFF & ~(xram_cp->cp_inpr));
        to_OFF ^= work;
                        /*$ REDUCE requests to 1       */
        if (to_ON)
         { to_OFF = 0;
         work = get_1_pressd(&to_ON);
        }
        else
        {
        if (to_OFF)
   { to_ON = 0;
  work = get_1_pressd(&to_OFF);
  }

        else         /*$ NO changes to switch states    */
                     /*$ SET no-valid-changes code      */
             work = ~0;
      }
   }                 /*$ UPDATE masks in CP table       */
   xram_cp->cp_req0 = to_OFF;
   xram_cp->cp_req1 = to_ON;

   return(work);     /*$ RETURN ~0 i,f BAD or sw OFFSET    */
}

/*-------------------------------------------
  Routine to process Control Panel switches
  -------------------------------------------
*/
VOID cp_sw_proc(CTRLPTR xram_cp)/*& PROCESS CP switches */
{
UCHAR sw_offset;
SW1PTR xram_sw;
USHORT temprd;
PTPTR ptptr;
   ptptr = xram_cp->cp_stat;       /*$ ASSIGN status port ptr  */
   temprd = xram_cp->cp_press;     /*$ SAVE last PRESSED value */
   xram_cp->cp_press = read_port(ptptr); /*$ READ switches     */
```

```
        xram_cp->cp_press |= INHIBITS; /*$ REMOVE curr INHIBITs    */
        xram_cp->cp_press ^= INHIBITS;
        cp_switch_resets(xram_cp);      /*$ RESET switches          */

                                /*$ REMOVE unchanged logic 1   */
                                /* (operator holding sw)       */
        temprd &= xram_cp->cp_press;
        temprd ^= xram_cp->cp_press;
            /*$ GET current requests                          */
      sw_offset = validate_sw_input(xram_cp,temprd);

      if ((sw_offset != ((UCHAR)~0))/*$ If VALID request        */
      && ((xram_cp->cp_req1) || (xram_cp->cp_req0)))
        {                       /*$ ASSIGN ptr for request       */
        xram_sw = &ram_sw[sw_offset];
                                /*$IF request is ON,process      */
        if (xram_cp->cp_req1) sw_INP(xram_cp,xram_sw);
        else                    /*$IF reqst is OFF,process       */
            if (xram_cp->cp_req0) sw_reset(xram_cp,xram_sw);
        }
      return; /*$ RETURN */
}
```

COMPILING THE PILOT CONTROL PANEL ROUTINES

A module for consolidating the control panel work accomplished could look like this:

```
/* --------------------------   */
/*   MODULE PATH: \CP\CPMAIN.C    */
/* --------------------------   */

#include <stdio.h>
#include <string.h>
#define XINTEL 1

#include <\cp\newdat.h>   /* Data types   */
#include <\cp\cp.h>       /* CP equates   */

VOID write_port(PTPTR port_adr, USHORT value);
USHORT read_port(PTPTR port_adr);
VOID outport(USHORT far *port_adr, USHORT value);
USHORT inport(USHORT far *port_adr);

#include <\cp\cpdat.c>   /* Control Panel data tables   */
#include <\cp\cp.c>      /* C fcns for Control Panel     */
#include <\cp\io.c>      /* C routines for port I/O      */
```

USING THE SWITCH TABLE MESSAGE FLAGS

Since project message requirements are currently unknown, the message flags that are included in the control panel table have been largely ignored until now. The routines that initially set a switch to the DONE, IN PROCESS, or OFF conditions will reset all message flags, as they should; however, the initial setting of message flags has not been addressed.

Normally, a code thread will call CP_SW_PROC() to determine if the pilot has currently pressed any panel buttons that are valid for the current switch states. If there is a valid ON request, the switch is set IN PROCESS by CP_SW_PROC(). Another code thread could be responsible for actually sending messages. If so, it might check for new IN PROCESS states that require message traffic. For example:

```
/* If switch IN PROCESS and message not sent */

if ((cptblptr->cp_inpr & ALN_MASK)
 && !(cptblptr->cp_msnt & ALN_MASK))
    {
            send_message(ALN_MSK_mssg_ptr); /* SEND message */
            ctblptr->cp_msnt |= ALN_MASK;   /* SET sent bit */

/*
If a response is necessary, set the RESPONSE REQUESTED bit
*/

        ctblptr->cp_mrrq |= ALN_MASK;          /* SET resp req */
    }
```

After successful transmission of a message that requires no response, the code thread that checks for transmission complete could call SW_DONE() to set the switch to the DONE state. If the outbound message required a response, the code thread that accepts responses could set the RESPONSE AVAILABLE bit when the response is received:

```
        ctblptr->cp_mres |= ALN_MASK /* SET resp avail */
```

The main code thread might check the RESPONSE AVAILABLE bit, process any available responses, and set the switch to DONE:

```
if (ctblptr->cp_mres & ALN_MASK)
    {
    get_&_process_response(msg_location);
    sw_DONE(ALN_SW);
    }
```

If a timeout value is reached before the response becomes available, the code might call SW_ERRO() to set the switch condition to ERROR.

There are many ways to implement message traffic semaphores, and the flags contained in the control panel table will handle a number of approaches. Expansion of the table is always a possibility, and can be done easily if required.

APPENDIX B

Pilot Control Panel Test and Simulation

In this appendix, a PC-based "simulator" is built for the control panel. The simulator allows testing most of the control panel logic that processes switch states and data-table-based switch flags.

Simulation is accomplished by replacing the I/O module of Appendix A with an I/O module that reads the keyboard and writes the console. An executable version of the final simulator is on the accompanying diskette as \CPTEST\TESTCP.EXE. The executable module was compiled using Borland's C compiler version 3.1, and requires an AT-compatible machine with a color monitor for proper execution.

SIMULATOR BACKGROUND

By tracking all switch states and allowable switch states in software, and by not using the hardware "inhibit" bits provided in the control port, control panel simulation becomes a snap.

A PC screen layout, as shown in Figure B-1, is needed to approximate the actual control panel design. Once the screen has been built, the control panel's port I/O routines can be replaced with routines that simply input from the keyboard and output to the console. The resulting control panel simulator can be distributed to the powers-that-be in order to enhance the decision-making process and ensure that the panel's buttons are accomplishing the desired end.

The entire simulator should not require much time to write and test, but the final screen should be reasonably appealing to the eye. Project time is precious, so a really quick-and-dirty version is written—in color, but with no graphics or bells and whistles.

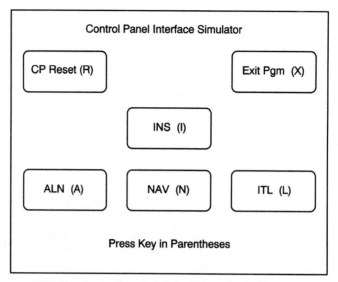

Figure B-1. Control Panel Simulator Screen

SIMULATOR SCREEN CODE AND MAIN ROUTINE

```c
/* ---------------------------- */
/* MODULE PATH: \CPTEST\CPTMAIN */
/* ---------------------------- */

CHAR fmt1x[] = "%*.*s";

VOID say_cursr(SHORT,SHORT);
typedef struct names {
  USHORT msk;
  CHAR name[19];
  USHORT xxx;
  USHORT yyy;
        }Xnames;

/* DEFINE BUTTONS */
Xnames sws[9] = {
0,        " (X)   EXIT PGM  ",50,10,
RES_MASK, " (R)   CP RESET  ",6,10,
INS_MASK, " (I)   INS       ",28,14,
ALN_MASK, " (A)   ALN       ",6,20,
NAV_MASK, " (N)   NAV       ",28,20,
ITL_MASK, " (L)   ITL       ",50,20
};

#define NUMCPBUTTS ((sizeof(sws))/(sizeof(Xnames)))

VOID say_cursr(SHORT, SHORT);
```

```
CHAR title[] = "          Control Panel Interface Simulator --
Version 0.00        ";
CHAR titl1[] = "
";
VOID video_init(USHORT mode);

SHORT main()
{
SHORT i;
   /* DRAW main CONTROL PANEL */
   video_init(3);
   textattr(0x20);
   say_cursr(6,1);
   cprintf(&fmt1x[0],strlen(titl1),strlen(titl1),
                                     &titl1[0]);
   say_cursr(6,2);
   cprintf(&fmt1x[0],strlen(title),strlen(title),
                                     &title[0]);
   say_cursr(6,3);
   cprintf(&fmt1x[0],strlen(titl1),strlen(titl1),
                                     &titl1[0]);
   normvideo();
   textattr(0x17);
   say_cursr(19,5);
   cprintf(&fmt1x[0],3,3,&titl1[0]);
   normvideo();
   textattr(0x07);
   say_cursr(22,5);
   cprintf(&fmt1x[0],13,13," = Light OFF");
   normvideo();
   textattr(0x47);
   say_cursr(42,5);
   cprintf(&fmt1x[0],3,3,&titl1[0]);
   normvideo();
   textattr(0x07);
   say_cursr(45,5);
   cprintf(&fmt1x[0],13,13," = Light ON   ");
   normvideo();
   for (i = 0; i < NUMCPBUTTS; i++)
         {
         textattr(0x17);
         say_cursr(sws[i].xxx,sws[i].yyy-1);
         cprintf(&fmt1x[0],strlen(&sws[i].name[0]),
              strlen(&sws[i].name[0]),&titl1[0]);
         say_cursr(sws[i].xxx,sws[i].yyy);
         cprintf(&fmt1x[0],strlen(&sws[i].name[0]),
              strlen(&sws[i].name[0]),&sws[i].name[0]);
         say_cursr(sws[i].xxx,sws[i].yyy+1);
         cprintf(&fmt1x[0],strlen(&sws[i].name[0]),
              strlen(&sws[i].name[0]),&titl1[0]);
```

```
                        normvideo();
                        }
                textattr(0x07);
                say_cursr(25,24);
                cprintf(&fmt1x[0],25,25," Light tests in process. ");
                normvideo();
                set_up_cp(&ram_cp,&ram_sw[0]);
                lite_test(&ram_cp,&ram_sw[0]);
                set_up_cp(&ram_cp,&ram_sw[0]);
                /* PROCESS buttons */
                while (1)
                        {
                        cp_sw_proc(&ram_cp);
                        textattr(0x07);
                        say_cursr(25,23);
                        cprintf(&fmt1x[0],25,25,&titl1[0]);
                        normvideo();
                        if ((ram_cp.cp_inpr & INS_MASK)
                        ||  (ram_cp.cp_sets & INS_MASK))
                                sw_DONE(&ram_cp,&ram_sw[INS_SW]);

                        if ((ram_cp.cp_inpr & NAV_MASK)
                        ||  (ram_cp.cp_sets & NAV_MASK))
                                sw_DONE(&ram_cp,&ram_sw[NAV_SW]);

                        if ((ram_cp.cp_inpr & ITL_MASK)
                        ||  (ram_cp.cp_sets & ITL_MASK))
                                sw_DONE(&ram_cp,&ram_sw[ITL_SW]);

                        if ((ram_cp.cp_inpr == 0)
                        &&  (ram_cp.cp_sets == 0)
                        &&  (ram_cp.cp_done == 0))
                                set_up_cp(&ram_cp,&ram_sw[0]);
                        sw_inhibits(&ram_cp);
                        sw_lites(&ram_cp);
                        update_lites(&ram_cp);
                        }
        }
```

SIMULATOR I/O CODE

```
/* ---------------------------- */
/* MODULE PATH: \CPTEST\CPTIO.C */
/* ---------------------------- */

union REGS r_in;
union REGS r_out;
struct SREGS seg_regs;
```

```
CHAR donemssg[] = "    DONE    ":
CHAR inprmssg[] = " IN PROCESS ";
CHAR erromssg[] = "  IN ERROR  ";

VOID say_cursr(SHORT,SHORT);

CHAR dummy[] = "                  ";
/* ------------------- */
/* Routine to init video */
/* ------------------- */
VOID video_init(mode)
USHORT mode;
{
  r_in.h.ah = 0;
  r_in.h.al = mode;
  int86(0x10,&r_in,&r_out);
}
/* ------------------------------------------------- */
/* Routine to replace port READ with KEYBOARD input */
/* ------------------------------------------------- */

USHORT read_port(PTPTR port_adr)
{
USHORT xx;
  xx = 0;
  if (ram_cp.cp_inpr & ALN_MASK)
  {
  textattr(0x07);
  say_cursr(25,23);
  cprintf(&fmt1x[0],29,29,"(A) again to 'finish' ALIGN: ");
  normvideo();
}
else
{
textattr(0x07);
say_cursr(25,23);
cprintf(&fmt1x[0],29,29,&titl1[0]);
normvideo();
}
textattr(0x07);
say_cursr(25,24);
cprintf(&fmt1x[0],25,25,"Enter letter in brackets: ");
normvideo();
xx = getch();
xx = toupper(xx);
switch(xx)
  {
  case('I'):
        xx = INS_MASK;
```

```
                  ram_cp.cp_press &= INS_MASK;
                  ram_cp.cp_press ^= INS_MASK;
          break;
          case('A'):
                  xx = ALN_MASK;
                  ram_cp.cp_press &= ALN_MASK;
                  ram_cp.cp_press ^= ALN_MASK;
                  if (ram_cp.cp_inpr & ALN_MASK)
                  sw_DONE(&ram_cp,&ram_sw[ALN_SW]);

          break;
          case('N'):
                  xx = NAV_MASK;
                  ram_cp.cp_press &= NAV_MASK;
                  ram_cp.cp_press ^= NAV_MASK;
          break;
          case('L'):
                   xx = ITL_MASK;
                  ram_cp.cp_press &= ITL_MASK;
                  ram_cp.cp_press ^= ITL_MASK;
          break;
          case('R'):
                  xx = RES_MASK;
                  ram_cp.cp_press &= RES_MASK;
                  ram_cp.cp_press ^= RES_MASK;
          break;
          case('X'):
                  exit(0);
          break;
          default:
                  xx = 0;
          break;
          }
  textattr(0x07);
  say_cursr(25,24);
  cprintf(&fmt1x[0],25,25,&titl1[0]);
  normvideo();
  return(xx);
  }


  /* ------------------------- */
  /* Routine to position cursor */
  /* ------------------------- */
  VOID say_cursr(xx,yy)
  SHORT xx;
  SHORT yy;
  {
          r_in.x.ax = 0x200;
          r_in.h.bh = 0;
          r_in.h.dl = xx;
```

```
          r_in.h.dh = yy;
          int86(0x10,&r_in,&r_out);
          return;

}

/* ------------------------------------------------- */
/* Routine to replace port WRITE with CONSOLE output */
/* ------------------------------------------------- */

VOID write_port(PTPTR port_adr, USHORT value)
{
USHORT i;
USHORT tmp;

   for (i = 0; i < 6; i++)
          {
          textattr(0x07);
          tmp = sws[i].yyy+2;
          say_cursr(sws[i].xxx,tmp);
          cprintf(&fmt1x[0],strlen(dummy),strlen(dummy),
                                    &dummy[0]);
          say_cursr(sws[i].xxx,tmp);
          if (ram_cp.cp_inpr & sws[i].msk)
                cprintf(&fmt1x[0],strlen(inprmssg),
                      strlen(inprmssg),&inprmssg[0]);

          say_cursr(sws[i].xxx,tmp);
          if (ram_cp.cp_done & sws[i].msk)
                cprintf(&fmt1x[0],strlen(donemssg),
                      strlen(donemssg),&donemssg[0]);

          say_cursr(sws[i].xxx,tmp);
          if (ram_cp.cp_erro & sws[i].msk)
                cprintf(&fmt1x[0],strlen(erromssg),
                      strlen(erromssg),&erromssg[0]);
          normvideo();
          if (ram_cp.cp_lton & sws[i].msk)
          {
          textattr(0x47);
          say_cursr(sws[i].xxx,sws[i].yyy-1);
          cprintf(&fmt1x[0],strlen(&sws[i].name[0]),
                strlen(&sws[i].name[0]),&titl1[0]);
          say_cursr(sws[i].xxx,sws[i].yyy);
          cprintf(&fmt1x[0],strlen(&sws[i].name[0]),
                strlen(&sws[i].name[0]),&sws[i].name[0]);
          say_cursr(sws[i].xxx,sws[i].yyy+1);
          cprintf(&fmt1x[0],strlen(&sws[i].name[0]),
                strlen(&sws[i].name[0]),&titl1[0]);
          normvideo();
          }
```

```
            else
                    {
                    textattr(0x17);
                    say_cursr(sws[i].xxx,sws[i].yyy-1);
                    cprintf(&fmt1x[0],strlen(&sws[i].name[0]),
                            strlen(&sws[i].name[0]),&titl1[0]);
                    say_cursr(sws[i].xxx,sws[i].yyy);
                    cprintf(&fmt1x[0],strlen(&sws[i].name[0]),
                            strlen(&sws[i].name[0]),&sws[i].name[0]);
                    say_cursr(sws[i].xxx,sws[i].yyy+1);
                    cprintf(&fmt1x[0],strlen(&sws[i].name[0]),
                            strlen(&sws[i].name[0]),&titl1[0]);
                    normvideo();
                    }

            if (ram_cp.cp_ltbk & sws[i].msk)
                    {
                    textattr(0x47 | 0x80);
                    say_cursr(sws[i].xxx,sws[i].yyy-1);
                    cprintf(&fmt1x[0],strlen(&sws[i].name[0]),
                            strlen(&sws[i].name[0]),&titl1[0]);
                    say_cursr(sws[i].xxx,sws[i].yyy);
                    cprintf(&fmt1x[0],strlen(&sws[i].name[0]),
                            strlen(&sws[i].name[0]),&sws[i].name[0]);
                    say_cursr(sws[i].xxx,sws[i].yyy+1);
                    cprintf(&fmt1x[0],strlen(&sws[i].name[0]),
                            strlen(&sws[i].name[0]),&titl1[0]);
                    normvideo();
                    }
            }
    say_cursr(1,24);
    return;
}
```

COMPILING THE SIMULATOR CODE

This module is virtually identical to the corresponding sample module for the "real" control panel code, except that a MAIN() thread now exists and the I/O routines have been changed.

```
/* ----------------------------- */
/*   MODULE PATH: \CPTEST\CPSIM.C   */
/* ----------------------------- */
#include <stdio.h>
#include <string.h>
#define XINTEL 1

#include <\CP\newdat.h>
```

```
#include <\CP\cp.h>

/* Function declarations */
VOID write_port(PTPTR port_adr, USHORT value);
USHORT read_port(PTPTR port_adr);

#include <\CP\cpdat.c>
#include <\CP\cp.c>

/* ============== */
/* FOR TESTING CP */
/* ============== */

#include <conio.h>
#include <dos.h>
#include <stdlib.h>
#include <ctype.h>

#include <\cptest\cptmain.c>/* C routines for CP test    */
#include <\cptest\cptio.c>  /* CP test, replace port I/O */
```

APPENDIX C

1553 Aircraft Bus and 1553 Adapter

The purpose of this appendix is to introduce concepts related to the 1553 Aircraft Bus and the typical application-level machinations required to transfer message traffic among 1553 bus terminals. A hypothetical 1553 bus adapter interface card is used, but it is very similar in function to a 65522 board which is manufactured by ILC Data Device Corporation of Bohemia, NY, and which makes low-level details of the 1553 interface transparent. The information contained in this appendix becomes an integral part of the missile-to-aircraft project example contained in Appendix D.

1553 BUS BACKGROUND

There is a "military standard" data bus used in inter-connecting avionics equipment within military aircraft. It is normally referred to as the *1553 aircraft bus*. For those interested, every detail of bus architecture, terminal connections, and essential message requirements are delineated in a military standard publication called MIL-STD-1553X, where *X* indicates a revision level. For purposes here, less formal definitions will be used, with emphasis on conveying essential information. The revision level that is considered most current (or is most often used) is MIL-STD-1553B. In this book *1553* and *1553B* are synonymous terms.

The 1553 aircraft bus is a twisted-pair of shielded cables with a specified data transfer rate of one megabit per second. It is a *time-division command/ response multiplexed data bus*. The *time division* and *multiplexed* aspects deal with the physical methodologies of data signal transmission and really do not concern programmers at the subsystem application level. The *com-*

mand/response characteristic means that remote terminals (RTs) only transfer data when commanded to do so by the bus controller (BC).

Only one terminal in the system is designated as a bus controller (BC). All others are remote terminals (RTs), with one exception. Distinction is made for a "bus monitor" terminal that can receive all bus traffic. One BC and as many as twenty-nine RTs can exist on a system. Five bits are used for terminal addresses, but address 0 and address 31 are reserved for special purposes. Typically, all units are transformer-coupled to the 1553 bus; however, direct coupling is sometimes used.

Message traffic can be transferred BC-to-RT, RT-to-BC, or RT-to-RT; but in all cases, transfers are commanded by the BC. The essential 1553 bus message consists of a *command word* and a *status word* plus any specified *data words*. The command word contains a terminal address, message "subaddress," message length, and the type of transfer. When RT-to-RT transfers are used, there must be two command words and two status words in a single message. All words for 1553 bus are 16-bit.

Essentially, all 1553 bus terminals look at every 1553 message placed on the bus, and accept those with the appropriate terminal address in the command word. If a message indicates that the receiving unit should transfer information to another terminal, that transfer occurs immediately. This would happen if the BC issued an RT-to-RT command to an Inertial Navigation System (INS), for example to send something to the INS's console display unit.

Standard military subsystems have predefined 1553 bus messages delineated in military publications devoted to these specific units or types of units. These messages are typically identified by alphanumeric designation such as "I01" or "I07P." Such pre-definitions have very specific formats for word locations and content. The adapter board discussion that follows will look at details of messages, subaddresses, and message formats, as well as 1553 bus message transfers among bus terminals.

ADAPTER BOARD OVERVIEW

The selected hypothetical 1553 bus interface card is presumed to be well-known and popular in military engineering circles. Extensive documentation is presumed to accompany the board. The adapter has two channels for 1553 bus traffic, and both channels can operate in either BC or RT mode; however, this example will use only channel A. The adapter hides low-level details of the 1553 interface from programmers, including some aspects of the 1553 messaging requirements. The adapter board hosts a number of 1553-specific registers as well as VME bus registers in order to allow configuration under software control.

These registers must be initially set up for project-specific requirements. A number of acceptable configurations are possible, depending on project design goals. Board self-tests are available, and their usage is specified in great detail in the adapter's documentation. When executed, these tests ensure proper board function in a given system.

The board has 16K of on-board RAM for programmer use. Board RAM is accessed by 2-byte word offsets from board RAM location zero, with a typical layout as shown in Figure C-1. Board RAM offset location zero is the beginning of a 256-word *descriptor stack*. Each descriptor stack entry contains four words which are a "Block Status Word (BSW)," a time tag, a word for programmer use, and a message block pointer in that order. Board RAM word location hex 100 is the current stack pointer into the descriptor stack, and word location hex 101 is the message count associated with the current stack pointer.

Board RAM word hex 140 is the beginning of *look-up tables* used in RT mode only. The look-up tables are sixty-four total words. The first thirty-two are for inbound messages, and the second thirty-two are for outbound mes-

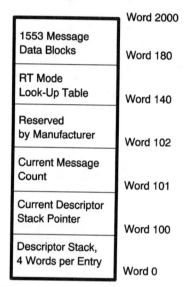

Figure C-1   1553 Aircraft Bus, Interface Adapter RAM model

sages. Speaking relatively within the look-up tables, word 1 would point to the receive block for subaddress 1 messages, and word 33 would point to the transmit block for subaddress 1 messages. In BC mode, these tables are not used.

Word location hex 180 starts the message block area. The message block area is divided into separate sections which correspond to specific 1553-bus message subaddresses. Each 1553 message is expected to be sent from, or received into, a specific section of board RAM. The programmer determines the size and location of each section, but normally they are of equal size and are contiguous in board memory. As mentioned, the physical size of data blocks is at programmer discretion, but the first data block must start at word location hex 180, as specified above.

During the project design phase, specific 1553 messages are assigned to specific 1553 subaddresses. During software design, the programmer assigns appropriately sized data blocks within adapter RAM for each subaddress. Messages assigned to a given subaddress will reside in the corresponding datablock. The size of each data block is normally determined by the number of messages anticipated. Assuming fixed lengths of messages or fixed lengths reserved for each message, the starting point of a data block might be calculated as follows:

Data Block Start for a given subaddress = (DB1 address +
(MESSAGE_SIZE * number of preceding messages)

In order to transfer an outbound message, the programmer simply defines the message in accordance with 1553 adapter criteria, sets the correct subaddress into the message, places the message at the appropriate location in adapter RAM, and starts the transfer by writing a specified mask into the adapter's Start/Reset register.

Transfer-complete can be indicated via an End Of Message (EOM) interrupt generated by the 1553 adapter. The ISR for this interrupt will normally set a flag indicating that the 1553 transfer has completed. Interrupts for EOM and for ERRORS are selected during board configuration by using the appropriate mask in the adapter's 1553 interrupt mask register. The ERROR interrupt is only valid in RT mode. When additional interrupts are selected in this fashion, consecutive interrupts (up to four) are used, beginning with the vector type-number placed by the programmer into the 1553 interrupt vector register.

The adapter requires that a *control word* precede the 1553 bus command word in each 1553 message. There is a mask in this control word that indicates the type of transfer that is to occur—whether RT-to-RT, BC-to-RT, or RT-to-BC. While in BC mode and in order to obtain a specific message from an RT, the same "outbound" message procedure can be followed that was delineated above. The correct mask in the message control word indicates to the adapter that this is a request for message transfer from an RT back to the BC; and the 1553 command word gives the same information to the RT. The ensuing response is immediate.

The adapter board also has a "block transfer" mode whereby messages from different subaddresses can be transferred as a block while in BC mode. This mode can generate a single EOM interrupt for the entire block. The setup for block transfer entails configuring the descriptor stack with consecutive entries for each message to be sent. The stack pointer is set to point to the beginning of the block, and a specific mask is written to the adapter's Start/ Reset register. When the entire block has been transferred, the EOM is generated.

The programmer is required to initially set up the entire on-board RAM in a fashion that coincides with the selected board mode, whether BC or RT.

ADAPTER BOARD CONSTANTS

Adapter board equates are available from the manufacturer and from engineering bulletin boards. A header module has been obtained, and the programmer has edited the header to reduce its size and become familiar with the contents:

```
/* MODULE PATH: \X1553\ADAPTER.H */

/* RT = Remote Terminal */
/* BC = Bus Controller   */

#define BDRAMSIZ 0x3fff

/* --------------------------------
    Adapter Board Register Addresses
   --------------------------------
   */
/* Offsets from base register to access 1553 registers  */
/*                                             INITIAL VALUES */
#define REG_ID 0     /* Identification            0xff00 */
#define REG_DT 2     /* Device type               0xff00 */
#define REG_SC 4     /* Status/control            0x6000 */
#define REG_RA 6     /* Ram base address          0xffff */
#define REG_VE 8     /* Vector - enable - level   0xffff */
#define REG_DE 10    /* Device-type extension     0xff00 */
#define REG_RT 12    /* 1553 RT address           0xffff */
#define REG_TT 14    /* 1553 Time tag - counter   0x0000 */
#define REG_IM 16    /* 1553 Interrupt mask       0xff00 */
#define REG_CG 18    /* 1553 Configuration        0x00ff */
#define REG_NU 20    /* NOT USED                  0xff00 */
#define REG_SR 22    /* 1553 Start/reset          0xff00 */

/*Offsets of registers into adapter board register table*/
#define AREGX_ID 0     /* Identification              */
#define AREGX_DT 1     /* Device type                 */
#define AREGX_RA 3     /* Ram base address            */
#define AREGX_VE 4     /* Vector - enable - level     */
#define AREGX_DE 5     /* Device = type extension     */
#define AREGX_RT 6     /* 1553 RT address             */
#define AREGX_TT 7     /* 1553 Time tag - counter     */
#define AREGX_IM 8     /* 1553 Interrupt mask         */
#define AREGX_CG 9     /* NOT USED                    */
#define AREGX_SR 11    /* 1553 Start/reset            */

/* --------------------------------
   Register Bit Maps for Adapter
   --------------------------------
   */
```

```
/* Status/Control register */
#define GR_LITE 0x8000  /* Green LED 'ON' if bit set.       */
#define INT1553 0x0800  /* 1553 Interrupt.                  */
#define SC_RSET 0x0001  /* Reset                            */

/* Start/Reset Register */
#define SR_NOTU 0xfffc  /* Unused bits                      */
#define SR_STRT 0x0002  /* Initiates tx of 1553 mssgs (BC)  */
#define SR_RSET 0x0001  /* Issued by CPU to reset 1553      */
                        /* Configuration , Start/reset, &   */
                        /* Interrupt msk regs are reset=0   */


/* Vector/Enable/Level Register */
#define I_LEVEL6 0x4000 /* Select interrupt level 6         */
#define I_1553   0x0800 /* Select 1553 interrupt            */
#define I_BITS   0x0200 /* Select built-in test interrupt   */
#define I_VECT   0x00ff /* Interrupt vector TYPE number     */

/* Interrupt Mask Register */
#define IM_BEOM 0x0008  /* Bus Controller EOM, adapter SETs */
#define IM_FERR 0x004   /* Format Err/Stat, adapter SETs    */
#define IM_EOMS 0x001   /* End of Message (EOM), adapter    */
                        /* SETs when any 1553 mssg txmttd   */

/* Configuration Register */
#define CR_NOTU 0x00ff  /* Unused Bits, either SET or RESET */
#define RT_MODE 0x8000  /* 1553 MODE, RT = 1, BC = 0        */
#define MT_MODE 0x4000  /* Monitor mode select              */
#define CU_AREA 0x2000  /* Select current area, B=1, A=0    */
#define ST_ERRO 0x1000  /* Stop on error = 1, no stop = 0   */

#define MODE_FOR_RT (RT_MODE | 0x700)
                        /* WRITE this value to select RT    */
#define MODE_FOR_BC  0x700
                        /* WRITE this value to select BC    */

/* Adapter's Descriptor Stack */
/* The descriptor stack is 4 consecutive word entries       */
#define DS_SIZE 4       /* Descriptor Stack Size in WORDs   */
/* Locations (WORD offsets) in on-board RAM                 */
#define DS_CHNA 0       /* Channel A DS location in on-bd RAM */
#define DS_STKA 0x100   /* Stack Pointer, Channel A         */
#define DS_MCTA (DS_STKA + 1)     /* Channel A message count */
#define DS_DBLK (DS_STKA + 0x80)  /* Channel A data bocks    */
#define DS_RTLU (DS_STKA + 0x40)  /* Channel A look up tbl   */
#define DS_MSIZ 32      /* Max message size for 1553 messages */
/* Descriptor Stack CONTENTS - WORD offsets (not BYTES):    */
#define DS_BSW 0        /* Block Status Word                */
#define DS_TAG 1        /* Time Tag (WHEN started is over-  */
```

```
                            /* written by WHEN completed)         */
#define DS_NOT 2            /* Not used                           */
#define DS_MSG 3            * Message address - only field that is */
                            /* SET by user. (BC)                  */
#define DS_CMD 3            /* For RT MODE - 1st received command  */

/* Adapter's Block Status Word */
#define BSW_EOM 0x8000      /* End of Message                     */
#define BSW_CHN 0x2000      /* Message Channel, A=0, B=1          */
#define BSW_ERR 0x1000      /* Error Flag                         */
#define BSW_LTF 0x0100      /* Loop test failed                   */
#define BSW_NOT 0x00ff      /* Unused bits of BSW                 */

/* Adapter RAM Access for Self-Test */
/* Off-line Self-test Word Addresses (board RAM offsets)         */
#define WA_DSP 100          /* Descriptor Stack Pointer           */
#define WA_CNT 101          /* Message Count                      */


/* -------------------------------------------------- */
/* Bit Map - 1553 Messages - Control/Information Words */
/* -------------------------------------------------- */

/* Message Control Word */
#define CW_BUSC 0x0080      /* Channel select, 1=A, 0=B           */
                            /* If bits used for count             */
#define CW_BCST 0x0002      /* Sets 1553 BC mode                  */
#define CW_RTRT 0x0001      /* Sets RT to RT comm mode            */

/* Message Command Word */
#define CD_TXRX 0x0400 /* Transmit/receive, 1=tx, 0=rx */
```

ADAPTER BOARD TABLES

An application-level "driver" will be needed for the 1553 bus interface adapter board. Using information contained in the documentation, the necessary data tables are designed as follows:

```
/* MODULE PATH: \X1553\ADPTABLS.H */

/* Adapter Board Register structure (One per Register)  */
typedef struct adptregs {
  USHORT far *ar_addr;      /* Adapter Register Address           */
  USHORT  ar_mval;          /* Mask for unused bits               */
  USHORT  ar_mpdb;          /* Mask for predefined bits           */
  } CTRLREGS, *AREGSPTR;

/* Adapter Board structure */
typedef struct adapter {
  AREGSPTR ab_regs;         /* Register table addr this reg       */
```

```
    USHORT  ab_intx;          /* Interrupt #,level,type for board */
    USHORT  far *ab_RAMs;  /* RAM starting addr for board        */
    USHORT  far *ab_rbas;  /* Register base addr for board       */
    }ABOARD, *ABPTR;

/* Adapter register initialization sequence table */
typedef struct init_seq {
    USHORT is_off;      /* Offset in regs table               */
    USHORT is_val;      /* Init value to write                */
    } BDINIT, *BIPTR;

/* Struct for initial self-test of adapter */
typedef struct data_block {
    USHORT db_start;    /* Start of data block (word offset)  */
    USHORT db_point;    /* Location of DB start word offset   */
    } ADB, *ADBPTR;

/* 1553 Message Block */
typedef struct msg_block {
    USHORT mctrl_wrd; /* Control word for test mssg 1st word  */
    USHORT mcmmd_wrd; /* Command word for test mssg 2nd word  */
    USHORT mloop_wrd; /* Loop word for test mssg 3rd word     */
    USHORT mlclr_wrd; /* CLR loop location(test msg 4th word) */
    USHORT mrbsw_wrd; /* Location to check BSW for IN mssg    */
    USHORT mvbsw_wrd; /* Expected value of BSW returned       */
    }AMSGBLK, *MBLKPTR;



/* MODULE PATH: \X1553\ADPTROM.C */

/* ---------------------------
   Tables for board self-tests
   --------------------------- 
*/
/* Adapter INIT register sequence */
BDINIT regseq[] = {
  AREGX_SC, SC_RSET,/* Status/Control RESET                   */
  AREGX_SC, GR_LITE,/* Enable ON-BOARD RAM                    */
                    /* SET 4 status bits CONFIG reg           */
  AREGX_CG, (RT_MODE | MT_MODE | CU_AREA | ST_ERRO),
  AREGX_SR, SR_RSET,/* RESET 1553 Start/Reset reg             */
  AREGX_RA, 0,        /* SET RAM base addr, RAM reg (hi)      */
  AREGX_VE, 0,        /* SET 1553 INT in Vector reg           */
  AREGX_IM, 0         /* MASK 1553 interrupts, INT MASK reg   */
};

#define MAXINIT ((sizeof(regseq))/(sizeof(BDINIT)))

/* Self-test data blocks for adapter */
```

```
ADB tdblks[] = {
        0x0140,0x03, /* DB1 for self-test  */
        0x0180,0x07, /* DB2 for self-test  */
        0x01c0,0x0b, /* DB3 for self-test  */
        0x0200,0x0f  /* DB4 for self-test  */
        };

#define MAXDBLKS  ((sizeof(tdblks))/(sizeof(ADB)))

/* Self-test message blocks for adapter */
AMSGBLK tstmsgs[] = {
        0xffc0, 0x0821, 0xaaaa, 0,  0,  (0x92ff ^ BSW_NOT),
        0xff40, 0x0821, 0xaaaa, 0,  4,  (0x92ff ^ BSW_NOT),
        0xffe2, 0x0821, 0x5555, 0,  8,  (0x80ff ^ BSW_NOT),
        0xff62, 0x0821, 0x5555, 0, 12,  (0x80ff ^ BSW_NOT)
        };

#define MAXTSTMSG  ((sizeof(tstmsgs))/(sizeof(AMSGBLK)))



/* MODULE PATH: \X1553\ MSGTBLS.H */

/* 1553 Message Structure */
typedef struct mssgs {
  USHORT msg[DS_MSIZ];
  } M1553, *M1553PTR;

  /* 1553 Descriptor Stack Structure */
typedef struct des_stack {
        USHORT d_stk[DS_SIZE];
             }DSTK, *DSTKPTR;
```

ADAPTER SELF-TEST ROUTINES

With the table definitions in place, the routines for adapter self-test can be written as recommended in the board documentation. The tests can be executed prior to configuring the board for a specific application. These tests are highly device-specific and device-convention-specific; however, the example code below is representative of programmer effort in building board self-tests. After the test routines are executed, an external lighted indicator on the board will be steady ON if the tests were successful. Various BLINK rates indicate specific problems in accordance with the board documentation.

```
/* MODULE PATH: \X1553\TEST.C */

/* ---------------------------
   Initialize adapter registers
```

```
    ---------------------------
*/

VOID initregs(ABPTR board, BIPTR iseq)/*& Init adapter registers
*/
{
AREGSPTR crptr;
USHORT temp;
UCHAR  i;
BIPTR insqc;

        /* initialize adapter registers */
        for (i = 0; i < MAXINIT; i++)
            {
            insqc = iseq + i;  /*$ FOR each init entry    */
                               /*$ POINT to CTRL reg      */
                               /*$ INIT register as appr  */
            crptr = ((board->ab_regs) + (insqc->is_off));
            switch(insqc->is_off)
                {
                case(AREGX_RA):
                    temp = ((((ULONG) board->ab_RAMs) >> 16));
                break;
                case(AREGX_VE):
                    temp =    board->ab_intx;
                break;
                default:
                    temp = insqc->is_val;
                break;
                }
            temp |= crptr->ar_mpdb;
            outport(crptr->ar_addr,temp);
            }
            /*$ READ STATUS/CNTL to enable interrupts */
        crptr =  board->ab_regs + AREGX_SC;
        inport(crptr->ar_addr);
        return;
    }
  /* ----------------------------------------
     Adapter initial self-test messages SENDs
     ----------------------------------------
  */
VOID selftest(ABPTR board, MBLKPTR startmsgs,
              ADBPTR tdbs)/*$ PERFORM board self-tests      */
{
USHORT *db_curr;
USHORT *msg_ptr;
ADBPTR db_ptr;
MBLKPTR dm_ptr;
AREGSPTR crptr;
```

```
USHORT i;
                    /*$ SET ptr to current desc stack & INIT DS    */
          db_curr = ((board->ab_RAMs) + WA_DSP);
          *db_curr = 0;

          /*$ Set up all test messages and pointers into RAM */
          for ( i = 0; i < MAXDBLKS; i++)
                  {
                  dm_ptr = startmsgs + i;
                  db_ptr = tdbs + i;

                  /*$ SET offset of DBstart into data block */
                  db_curr = ((board->ab_RAMs) + db_ptr->db_point);
                  *db_curr = db_ptr->db_start;

                  /*$ SET message VALUES into data block */
                  msg_ptr = (( board->ab_RAMs) + db_ptr->db_start);
                  *msg_ptr = dm_ptr->mctrl_wrd;
                  ++msg_ptr;
                  *msg_ptr = dm_ptr->mcmmd_wrd;
                  ++msg_ptr;
                  *msg_ptr = dm_ptr->mloop_wrd;
                  ++msg_ptr;
                  *msg_ptr = 0;
                  }
          /*$ GET mssg count area addr & init--1's complement*/
          db_curr = ((board->ab_RAMs) + WA_CNT);
          *db_curr = ~(MAXTSTMSG);

          crptr = (board->ab_regs) + AREGX_SR;/* Status/Reset  */
          i = (SR_STRT | crptr->ar_mpdb);/*$ SET start-value    */
          outport(crptr->ar_addr,i);   /*$ WRITE to start mssgs */

          return;
}
/* ---------------------------------------------------------
   Verify values of BSW and LOOP word after adapt INIT.
   Returns zero = GOOD, any other = BAD
   ---------------------------------------------------------
*/
USHORT chk_bsw_loop(ABPTR board, MBLKPTR startmsgs,
                    ADBPTR tdbs)/*$ VERIFY BSW/Loop Words*/
{
USHORT *loopwrd;
USHORT *bsw;
ADBPTR db_ptr;
MBLKPTR dm_ptr;
USHORT retcod1;
USHORT retcod2;
USHORT i;
```

```
            retcod1 = 0;
            retcod2 = 0;
            /*$ FOR each data block */
            for ( i = 0; i < MAXDBLKS; i++)
                    {
                    dm_ptr = startmsgs + i;
                    db_ptr = tdbs + i;

                    /*$ GET pointer to Loop Word & BSW */
                    loopwrd =  board->ab_RAMs + db_ptr->db_start + 3;
                    bsw =  board->ab_RAMs + dm_ptr->mrbsw_wrd;

                    /*$ VERIFY values */
                    retcod1 |= (((*bsw & dm_ptr->mvbsw_wrd) ^
dm_ptr->mvbsw_wrd));
                    retcod2 |= ((*loopwrd) - (*(loopwrd-1)));
                    }
            retcod1 |= retcod2;
            return(retcod1);
}
/* ---------------------
   Initial Adapter Reset
   ---------------------
*/
VOID adptreset(ABPTR board, MBLKPTR startmsgs,
                    ADBPTR tdbs, BIPTR iseqstrt)
                    /*& RESET adapter */
{
        initregs(board,iseqstrt);/*$ INIT Adapt regs        */
        /*$ DO self-test mssgs   */
        selftest(board,startmsgs,tdbs);
        return;
}


/* -------------------------
   Check Initial Adapter Reset
   -------------------------
*/
USHORT chkreset(ABPTR board, MBLKPTR startmsgs,
                    ADBPTR tdbs)/*& CHECK test mssgs OK      */
{
USHORT retcode;
        retcode = 0;
                            /*$ CHECK test mssgs OK           */
        retcode |= chk_bsw_loop(board,startmsgs,tdbs);
        return(retcode);
}

/* -------------------
```

```
      RESET Adapter Board
      -------------------
*/
VOID reset_board(ABPTR board)/*& RESET adapter */
{
AREGSPTR crptr; /* Pointer to regs struct for this board   */
    crptr = (board->ab_regs + AREGX_SC); /* Status/Control */
    outport(crptr->ar_addr,SC_RSET);        /*$ ISSUE RESET   */
    crptr = (board->ab_regs + AREGX_SR); /* Start/Reset    */
    outport(crptr->ar_addr,SR_RSET);        /*$ ISSUE RESET   */
    return;
}
```

ADAPTER INITIALIZATION

Following the self-tests, the board can be initialized for either BC or RT modes. Typical routines for on-board RAM initialization and for initial register configuration are shown below, but other board configurations are possible in either mode.

```
/* MODULE PATH: \X1553\ADPTINIT.C */

/* -------------------------------------------
   Routine to init ON-BOARD RAM for BC mode
   -------------------------------------------
*/
VOID bc_meminit(ABPTR board)/*& INIT memory for BC mode */
{
AREGSPTR cregs;

    reset_board(board);        /*$ RESET adapter              */

                               /*$ INIT board RAM to 0's      */
    memset((UCHAR *) board->ab_RAMs,0,BDRAMSIZ);

            /*$ COPY msg blocks to board RAM      */
    memcpy((UCHAR *) (board->ab_RAMs + DS_DBLK),
            (UCHAR *) msgs1553, sizeof(msgs1553));

            /*$ COPY descriptor stack to bd RAM   */
    memcpy((UCHAR *) board->ab_RAMs, (UCHAR *) dstk_a,
               sizeof(dstk_a));

    *(board->ab_RAMs+DS_MCTA) = 0;    /*$ SET message cnt = 0  */
    *(board->ab_RAMs + DS_STKA) = DS_CHNA;/*$ INIT stack PTR   */
    cregs = (board->ab_regs + AREGX_IM);/* INT MASK register   */
    outport(cregs->ar_addr, IM_BEOM);/*$ SET BC EOM interrupt  */
    return;
```

```
}

/* ---------------------------------------
   Routine to init ON-BOARD RAM for RT mode
   ---------------------------------------
*/
#define RT_PARITY 0x20
#define DBLKSIZE  (DS_MSIZ << 1)

VOID rt_meminit(ABPTR board)/*& INIT memory for RT mode        */
{
USHORT *tmptr;
AREGSPTR cregs;
USHORT i;
        reset_board(board);    /*$ RESET adapter                 */

                               /*$ INIT board RAM to 0's         */
        memset((UCHAR *) board->ab_RAMs,0,BDRAMSIZ);

                               /*$ SET RT addr into reg          */
        cregs = (board->ab_regs + AREGX_RT);
        outport(cregs->ar_addr,(BOX_ADR | RT_PARITY));

        for (i = 0; i < 64; i++) /*$ INIT RT look-up tables       */
                {
                tmptr = (board->ab_RAMs + DS_RTLU) + i;
                *tmptr = (DS_DBLK + (i * DBLKSIZE));
                }

                                /*$ INIT descriptor stack ptr    */
        *(board->ab_RAMs + DS_STKA) = DS_CHNA;

                                /*$ SELECT ERR & EOM interrupts  */
        cregs = (board->ab_regs + AREGX_IM);
        outport(cregs->ar_addr, IM_FERR | IM_EOMS);
        return;
}

/* ----------------------
   Select 1553 board mode
   ----------------------
*/
VOID select_mode(ABPTR board, USHORT mode)
                                /*& SELECT board mode      */
{
AREGSPTR cregs;

        switch(mode)
                {
```

```
                case(MODE_FOR_RT):
                        rt_meminit(board);/*$ INIT for RT */
                break;
                default:
                case(MODE_FOR_BC):
                        mode = MODE_FOR_BC;
                        bc_meminit(board);/*$ INIT for BC */
                break;
                }
        /*$ SELECT mode in config register */
        cregs = (board->ab_regs + AREGX_CG);
        outport(cregs->ar_addr,mode);
        return;
}
```

MESSAGE BLOCK SEND ROUTINE

In order to transfer a block of 1553 messages using the selected adapter board, the bus controller might use the following routine:

```
/* Send a block of 1553 messages */

VOID snd_blk(ABPTR board, USHORT msgcount)
                /*& SEND 1553 block of messages      */
{

USHORT *ramptr;
USHORT *tmptr;
USHORT *portbase;
                        /*$ SET base RAM & base reg ar      */
    ramptr = board->ab_RAMs;
    portbase = board->ab_rbas;
                        /*$ SET descriptor stck pointer     */
    tmptr = ramptr + DS_STKA;
    *tmptr = DS_CHNA;     /*$ INIT the stack pointer          */
                        /*$ SET message count address       */
    tmptr = ramptr + DS_MCTA;
    *tmptr = ~msgcount;  /*$ SET msg cnt, 1's complement     */
                        /*$ PERFORM block transmit          */
    *(portbase + AREGX_SR) = SR_STRT;
}
```

COMPILING THE ADAPTER INITIALIZATION AND SELF-TESTS

After the adapter has been defined with an ABOARD structure, the following module can be used to test the board configuration and to compile all adapter routines shown in this section.

```
/* ------------------------------- */
/*   MODULE PATH: \X1553\TESTMAIN.C   */
/* ------------------------------- */
#include <stdio.h>
#include <string.h>
#include <\cp\newdat.h>
#include <\x1553\adapter.h>
#include <\x1553\adptabls.h>
#include <\x1553\msgtbls.h>

VOID outport(USHORT far *port_adr, USHORT value);
USHORT inport(USHORT far *port_adr);

/* Just for compile */
extern ABOARD bd1553;
extern M1553 msgs1553[1];
extern DSTK dstk_a[1];
extern DSTK ram_dstka[1];
#define BOX_ADR 15

#include <\x1553\adptrom.c>    /* Adapter ROM tables */
#include <\x1553\test.c>       /* Adapter self-tests */
#include <\x1553\adptinit.c>   /* Adapter INIT       */
#include <\x1553\sndblock.c>   /* Block Mssg SEND    */


/* ---------------------
   MAIN Self Test Routine
   ---------------------
*/
USHORT main()
{

USHORT retcode;
      reset_board(&bd1553); /*$ RESET apapter                 */
                            /*$ PERFORM self-tests            */
      adptreset(&bd1553,&tstmsgs[0],&tdblks[0],&regseq[0]);

                            /*$ CHECK results of self-tests */
      retcode = chkreset(&bd1553,&tstmsgs[0],&tdblks[0]);
      if (!retcode)
            select_mode(&bd1553,  MODE_FOR_BC);
      return(retcode);      /*$ RETURN retcode                */
}
```

1553 BUS MONITOR

In addition to the selected adapter board, the manufacturer makes an AT bus
board that allows AT-compatible PCs to be terminals on a 1553 bus. This

board can operate in either BC or RT modes, but also has a "Bus Monitor" mode capability. When the board is operating as a bus monitor, the host PC can display or capture all 1553 bus message traffic. This board is a highly desirable piece of test equipment in any 1553 bus project.

APPENDIX D

Missile-to-Aircraft Interface

The example presented here is somewhat simplified, but is conceptually sound from a programmer's perspective in dealing with the 1553 bus interface and the overall project issues as specified. System functionality, component interaction, and fail-safe mechanisms would be more complex in an actual flight demonstration, and the resulting code would be larger and more complex. Nevertheless, this example provides programmer insight into an embedded software development project for military applications, as well as insight into the implementation of a 1553 bus interface.

For those not familiar with the 1553 Aircraft Bus, and for those wanting the specifics of the 1553 Bus Interface Card, refer to Appendix C. Appendix C is an introduction to the 1553 Aircraft Bus and is an in-depth look at the 1553 adapter board used in this example. Appendix A contains the example that builds the pilot control panel.

REQUIREMENTS

An interface box (IBOX) for guided-missile-to-aircraft interface is to be built for flight demonstration purposes–not for combat. The pilot's interface to the box will be five push-button switches, as described in Appendix A. The interface box will be built with an off-the-shelf VME system bus chassis. The I/O will be memory-mapped, and a Motorola 68000 CPU board will be used. The CPU will operate at a clock speed of 8MHz. System boards will be as follows:

1. CPU board with a Motorola 68000 processor and the hypothetical timer discussed in Chapter 4. (The board has provisions for up to 256K of on-board memory structure. There will be 64K of EPROM and 64K of RAM utilized.)

2. Digital I/O interface board for pilot's control panel as described in Appendix A.
3. Custom board for synchro-to-digital pressure altitude interface for servicing the aircraft's INS system.
4. 1553 aircraft bus interface board as described in Appendix C. (This board contains 16K of on-board RAM.)

The 1553 aircraft bus interface board will operate in Bus Controller (BC) mode throughout processing. Remote terminals on the 1553 bus will be an INS unit, the INS control panel, and a guidance computer which is on board a missile. The IBOX-BC will reside at 1553 bus address 15. Remote terminal addresses will be as follows:

1. INS unit, address 24
2. INS display unit, address 23
3. Missile's computer, address 22

An overview of the entire system is shown in Figure D-1, and a system memory map is shown in Figure D-2. The INS unit will be a standard medium-accuracy unit using predefined 1553 bus messages. Military standard messages pertaining to medium accuracy INS systems are found (oddly enough) in a U.S. Air Force publication called *USAF Standard for Form, Fit and Function for Medium Accuracy Intertial Navigation Systems*. The following standard messages are used, and will be transferred (commanded) by the interface box, as 1553 Bus Controller (BC), at 32Hz (every 31.25ms):

1. DO1 at message subaddress 26
2. I01 at message subaddress 16
3. I06 at message subaddress 25
4. 07 at message subaddress 27

In addition, the missile manufacturer has specified four user-defined 1553 bus messages. When activated, these messages are also transferred at 32Hz:

1. Alignment message at subaddress 8 (sent from the BC to the missile RT after the ALN switch is activated).
2. Navigation message at subaddress 4 (sent from the BC to the missile RT after the NAV switch is activated).
3. Intent to launch message at subaddress 2 (sent from the BC to the missile RT after the ITL switch is activated).
4. Status message at subaddress 10 (sent from the missile RT to the BC when either the ALN, NAV, or ITL switch is activated).

Requirements for the overall function of the control panel are given in Appendix A, as are the detailed requirements of control panel switch and light states. Specifics of the 1553-bus message traffic, corresponding to unique switch selections, follow:

1. When INS is pressed, all four INS messages between the INS and the INS display will be transferred 32 times per second, as long as the INS switch is ON or ACTIVE. The "I07" message requires that a current pressure altitude reading be provided into word five.

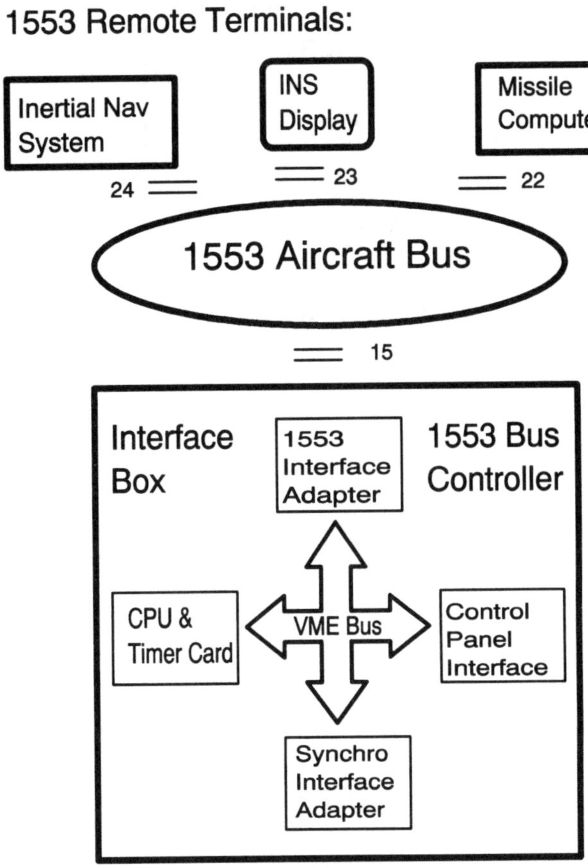

1553 Remote Terminals:

Figure D-1.   System Overview of Missile-to-Aircraft Interface Box

2. When ALN is pressed, the current pressure altitude reading is placed into the alignment message at word five, and this message is subsequently transferred to the missile's computer. A missile status message is transferred from the missile's computer to the interface box. A specific response mask in the received status message will indicate when the alignment is complete. When ALN is OFF (including when ITL or NAV are ACTIVE), this activity ceases.

3. When either the NAV or ITL switch is pressed, the alignment message is replaced with the appropriate command message (either Navigation or Intent to Launch) from the IBOX to the missile's computer, and the status message from the missile to the IBOX continues. Specific status response masks indicate when NAV or ITL are complete.

4. At any time that ALN, NAV, or ITL are ON or IN PROCESS, a status message is transferred from the missile's computer to the IBOX at 32Hz. Pertinent conditions are contained in a single word of this message, and always indicate current switch states of DONE or switch IN ERROR.

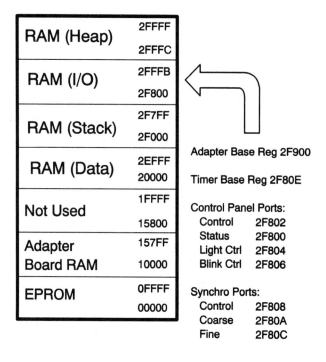

Figure D-2.   System Memory Map for Missile-to-Aircraft Interface Box

OVERALL SOFTWARE DESIGN

In separating functionality and attempting to create a modular design, it appears that the following software items will be needed:

- Control Panel driver for CP configuration, initialization, and CP switches and light functions.
- 1553 Adapter driver for configuration, initialization, and self-tests, plus 1553 message transfer routines for sending and receiving.
- Synchro-to-digital routine to obtain pressure altitude data.
- Timer initialization routines and timer restart capability. (A timer interrupt will be required at 32Hz.)

Most of these items have been addressed earlier. Chapter 2 and Appendix A address the control panel requirements and code, Appendix C addresses the adapter and all necessary code except the message receive routine(s), and Chapter 4 contains an ISR routine to read a synchro-to-digital device, as well as all necessary timer routines to request an interrupt at 32Hz. The start-up code of Chapter 3 can be used virtually "as is," and the vector table of Chapter 2 will require only minor modification. The complete software system overview is depicted in Figure D-3.

1553 ADDRESSES

Using the supplied memory map, the 1553 addresses and message subaddresses can be mapped. The base register address (port) for the 1553 adapter is also specified:

```
/* MODULE PATH: \MTA\ADR1553.H */

#define I_REGADR 0x2f900 /* base register for adapter */

/* --------------------
     1553 Address Equates
   --------------------
*/
/* 1553 Bus Addresses of All 1553 terminals */
#define MSL_ADR 7      /* Missile Computer Address - RT      */
#define DIS_ADR 22     /* INS Display Address - RT           */
#define INS_ADR 25     /* INS (LN-93) Address  - RT          */
#define BOX_ADR 15     /* Interface Box Address - BC         */

/* 1553 Bus Message Subaddresses */
#define D01_SUBA    26
#define I01_SUBA    16
#define I06_SUBA    25
#define I07_SUBA    27
#define NAV_SUBA    4
#define ITL_SUBA    2
#define ALN_SUBA    8
#define STA_SUBA    10
```

ADAPTER DEFINITIONS

With the memory map supplied, the starting point of the board RAM is known, as is the base register address (port) for the adapter board. Using the table definitions of Appendix C, the adapter and its registers can be defined. The BC EOM interrupt will be selected by the board initialization routines, and the vector type 66 will be specified into the adapter's interrupt mask register at interrupt level 6.

```
/* MODULE PATH: \MTA\ADPTDEFS.C */

/* -------------------------------------------
     Adapter board tables (board definition)
```

```
            --------------------------------------
   */

   /* Control Registers for board */
   CTRLREGS cntlregs[] ={
   ((USHORT *)(I_REGADR + REG_ID)),0,0,/* ID              */
   ((USHORT *)(I_REGADR + REG_DT)),0,0,/* Device type      */
   ((USHORT *)(I_REGADR + REG_SC)),0,0x6000,/* Status/Ctrl  */
   ((USHORT *)(I_REGADR + REG_RA)),0,0,/* Ram base address  */
   ((USHORT *)(I_REGADR + REG_VE)),0,0,/* Vector/enable/lev */
   ((USHORT *)(I_REGADR + REG_DE)),0,0,/* Device type       */
   ((USHORT *)(I_REGADR + REG_RT)),0,0,/* 1553 RT address   */
   ((USHORT *)(I_REGADR + REG_TT)),0,0,/* 1553 time tag     */
   ((USHORT *)(I_REGADR + REG_IM)),0xfff2,0,/* INT mask      */
   ((USHORT *)(I_REGADR + REG_CG)),0x00ff,0,/* Config        */
   NULL,0,0,                           /* Not used          */
   ((USHORT *)(I_REGADR + REG_SR)),0xfffc,0/* Start/reset    */
   };
   /* --------------------
      Adapter board in ROM
      --------------------
   */
   ABOARD bd1553 = { &cntlregs[0],(I_LEVEL6 | I_1553 | 66),
             (USHORT *) 0x100001,(USHORT *) I_REGADR
             };
```

1553 MESSAGES

Missile data words and error condition flags have been supplied by the missile manufacturer, and so have the specific 1553 message formats for missile messages. The appropriate military document can be researched to get the I01, I06, I07, and D01 message formats. Using this information and the structures defined in Appendix C, an initialized message table can be built to contain all system messages in ROM.

In Appendix C it was learned how to map adapter RAM to hold the 1553 system messages. The programmer has decided to place a dummy message between each system message in the message table and to map adapter RAM to hold two messages per subaddress. This will allow the programmer to directly copy the initialized message table from ROM into the adapter RAM, beginning at the first available adapter RAM data block address.

Since all messages are to be sent at 32Hz, the adapter's block transfer mode can be used for all message transfers. An initialized descriptor stack table can be built in ROM to point to all system messages in adapter RAM. This ROM descriptor stack table can be refreshed to RAM before each block transfer. The fifth message in the message table can be either ALN, NAV, or ITL, depending on which button the pilot has selected. Before sending the 1553 message block, the refreshed RAM copy of the descriptor stack can be adjusted based on current control panel switch settings.

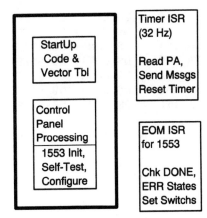

Figure D-3.   Software System Overview of Missile-to-Aircraft Interface Box

Using the block transfer mode for all 1553 messages will preclude the use of the individual message flags in the switch table. The missile response is constantly available after each block transfer. There will be no need to send a message and subsequently wait for its transfer or for its status response. These buckets could be eliminated from the switch structure.

Mapping known information with the programmer's message layout scheme and subsequently defining the 1553 messages would look like this:

```
/* MODULE PATH: \MTA\MSG1553.H */

/* RT = Remote Terminal
   BC = Bus Controller
   IBOX = Interface Box
*/
/* --------------------
   1553 Message Equates
   --------------------
*/

/* WD offsets, 1553 msg Data Block Address in board RAM */
#define DBA_D01    (DS_DBLK+(DS_MSIZ *   0))
#define DBA_I06    (DS_DBLK+(DS_MSIZ *   2))
#define DBA_I07    (DS_DBLK+(DS_MSIZ *   4))
#define DBA_I01    (DS_DBLK+(DS_MSIZ *   6))
#define DBA_ALN    (DS_DBLK+(DS_MSIZ *   8))
#define DBA_STA    (DS_DBLK+(DS_MSIZ * 10))
#define DBA_NAV    (DS_DBLK+(DS_MSIZ * 12))
#define DBA_ITL    (DS_DBLK+(DS_MSIZ * 14))


/* WD offsets, descriptor stack, in board RAM */
#define DSA_D01    (DS_CHNA+(DS_SIZE *   0))
```

```c
#define DSA_IO6     (DS_CHNA+(DS_SIZE *  1))
#define DSA_IO7     (DS_CHNA+(DS_SIZE *  2))
#define DSA_IO1     (DS_CHNA+(DS_SIZE *  3))
#define DSA_ALN     (DS_CHNA+(DS_SIZE *  4))
#define DSA_STA     (DS_CHNA+(DS_SIZE *  5))
#define DSA_NAV     (DS_CHNA+(DS_SIZE *  6))
#define DSA_ITL     (DS_CHNA+(DS_SIZE *  7))

/* From Missile Response mssg data word masks, to IBOX      */
#define MSL_ITL 0x1000 /* Missile has received ITL CMMD     */
#define MSL_ALN 0x0800 /* Missile has finished ALN           */
#define MSL_NAV 0x2000 /* Missile NAV is complete            */
#define MSL_ERR 0x4000 /* Missile Error Detect               */

/* TO Missile COMMAND messages (data), FM IBOX */
#define CMD_ALN     0x0001
#define CMD_NAV     0x0004
#define CMD_ITL     0x0008




/* MODULE PATH: \MTA\M1553DAT.C  */

/* --------------------------------
   1553 Message definitions for BC
   (One dummy mssg follows each)
   --------------------------------
*/
M1553 msgs1553[] =
   {
     {/* DO1 MSSG - RT-RT - Display to INS */
         (CW_BUSC | CW_RTRT), /* 1553 Control word          */
                              /* 1553 Receive command word  */
         ((INS_ADR << 11) |   (DO1_SUBA << 5)  | DS_MSIZ ),
                              /* 1553 Transmit command word */
         ((DIS_ADR << 11) |   (DO1_SUBA << 5)  |
                              DS_MSIZ | CD_TXRX),
         0,                   /* 1553 loop word             */
         0,                   /* 1553 status word           */
         0,                   /* 1553 data word             */
         0                    /* Remaining data             */
     },{0},

   {/* IO6 MSSG - RT-RT - INS to Display */
     (CW_BUSC | CW_RTRT),
     ((DIS_ADR << 11)  | (IO6_SUBA << 5)  | DS_MSIZ ),
     ((INS_ADR << 11)  | (IO6_SUBA << 5)  | DS_MSIZ |
     CD_TXRX), 0,0,0},{0},

   {/* IO7 MSSG - RT-RT - INS to Display */
     (CW_BUSC | CW_RTRT),
```

```
       ((DIS_ADR << 11)  | (I07_SUBA << 5)  | DS_MSIZ ),
       ((INS_ADR << 11)  | (I07_SUBA << 5)  | DS_MSIZ |
                                                 CD_TXRX),
       0,0,0,},{0},

    {/* I01 MSSG - RT-BC - INS to IBOX */
       CW_BUSC,
       ((INS_ADR << 11)  | (I01_SUBA << 5)  | DS_MSIZ | CD_TXRX),
       0,0,0,},{0},

    {/* ALIGN MSSG - BC-RT - IBOX to Missile */
       CW_BUSC,
       ((MSL_ADR << 11)  | (ALN_SUBA << 5)  | DS_MSIZ ),
       0,0,0,},{0},

    {/* STATUS - RT-BC - Missile to IBOX */
       CW_BUSC,
       ((MSL_ADR << 11)  | (STA_SUBA << 5)  | DS_MSIZ | CD_TXRX),
       0,0,0,},{0},

    {/* COMMAND NAV - BC-RT - IBOX to Missile */
       CW_BUSC,
       ((MSL_ADR << 11)  | (NAV_SUBA << 5)  | DS_MSIZ ),
       CMD_NAV,0,0,},{0},

    {/* COMMAND ITL - BC-RT - IBOX to Missile */
       CW_BUSC,
       ((MSL_ADR << 11)  | (ITL_SUBA << 5)  | DS_MSIZ ),
       CMD_ITL,0,0,},{0},
};

#define  NUMBLKMSG  (((sizeof(msgs1553))/(sizeof(M1553)))>>1)

/* Needed Message offsets in mssg tbl & dstk tbl */
#define MSG_I07 2
#define MSG_ALN 4
#define MSG_STA 5
#define MSG_NAV 6
#define MSG_ITL 7


/* ---------------------------
   1553 Message descriptor stack
   ---------------------------
*/
DSTK dstk_a[NUMBLKMSG] =
    {
    0,0,0,DBA_D01,
    0,0,0,DBA_I06,
    0,0,0,DBA_I07,
    0,0,0,DBA_I01,
    0,0,0,DBA_ALN,
```

```
           0,0,0,DBA_STA,
           0,0,0,DBA_NAV,
           0,0,0,DBA_ITL
           };

     #define NUMDSTK ((sizeof(dstk_a))/(sizeof(DSTK)))
```

32HZ INTERRUPT

In Chapter 4, the timer was initialized to use interrupt vector hex 60 and to request interrupts at 31.25ms intervals. According to project requirements, the ISR whose entry point will be placed into the vector table at absolute memory location hex 180 must accomplish the following details:

1. Re-initialize the timer's counter for the next interrupt to occur 31.25ms later.
2. Lock the synchros in order to read the current synchro value.
3. Refresh the descriptor stack for the block message transfer.
4. Read the synchros and massage the value read into an altitude data value (in feet above sea level).
5. Unlock the synchros.
6. Determine which messages are to be transferred in accordance with current control panel switch settings, and adjust the descriptor stack if necessary.
7. Set the correct message count to be transferred.
8. Set the massaged pressure altitude value into one or more messages.
9. Transfer the message block.

```
/* MODULE PATH: \MTA\INTERRPT.C */

/* --------------------------------
   32 Hz Interrupt Service Routine
   --------------------------------
*/

/* 16-bit ports used by this ISR */
#define SYNCCTRL ((USHORT *) 0x02f8081)
#define SYNCOARS ((USHORT *) 0x02f80a1)
#define SYNCFINE ((USHORT *) 0x02f80c1)

/* Mask indicating synchros locked (in control port)   */
#define SYNLKD 0xe000

/* Assembly routine to reset timer for next interrupt   */
extern VOID RECNT32(VOID);

/* 'C' fcn to convert synchro input to altitude (feet)   */
extern USHORT massage_data
                    (SFLOAT coarse_read, SFLOAT fine_read);
```

```
#ifdef XMOTO /* if compiling under Microtek */
#define $INTERRUPT
#endif

VOID far int_hz32(VOID)
{
USHORT PActrlIN;
SFLOAT coarse;
SFLOAT fine;
USHORT count;

  RECNT32();                    /*$ RESET timer (assembly)    */
  PActrlIN = *SYNCCTRL;         /*$ LOCK synchro reading      */
                                /*  (LATCH value)             */

                    /*$ REINIT descriptor stack table        */
    memcpy((UCHAR *) (bd1553.ab_RAMs), (UCHAR *) dstk_a,
                                              NUMDSTK);


                                    /*$ CHECK synchros LOCKED */
    if ((PActrlIN & SYNLKD) == SYNLKD)
      {

                                    /*$ READ coarse then fine */
      coarse = *SYNCOARS;
      fine   = *SYNCFINE;

                                    /*$ MASSAGE values input  */

                                    /*$ SAVE desired altitude */

                    *(bd1553.ab_RAMs + DBA_IO7 + 5) =

                        massage_data(coarse, fine);

      }
    *SYNCCTRL = 0;                      /*$ RELEASE synchros      */

                /*$ SETUP correct mssgs and counts for Block */
    count = MSG_STA+1;
                            /* ITL in process or DONE, use ITL */
      if  ((ram_cp.cp_sets & ITL_MASK)
      ||   (ram_cp.cp_inpr & ITL_MASK))
          memcpy((UCHAR *) (bd1553.ab_RAMs+(MSG_ALN*DS_SIZE)),
                          (UCHAR *) dstk_a+MSG_ITL,DS_SIZE);
      else
                            /* NAV in process or DONE, use NAV */
          if ((ram_cp.cp_sets & NAV_MASK)
          ||  (ram_cp.cp_inpr & NAV_MASK))
```

```
                    memcpy((UCHAR *) (bd1553.ab_RAMs+

                                   (MSG_ALN*DS_SIZE)),
                              (UCHAR *) dstk_a+MSG_NAV,DS_SIZE);
          else
                              /* ALN in process or DONE, use ALN */
                              if ((ram_cp.cp_sets & ALN_MASK)
                              || (ram_cp.cp_inpr & ALN_MASK))
                              {
                              memcpy((UCHAR *) (bd1553.ab_RAMs+

                                          (MSG_ALN*DS_SIZE)),
                                 (UCHAR *) dstk_a+MSG_ALN,DS_SIZE);
                              *(bd1553.ab_RAMs + DBA_ALN + 5) =
                                   *(bd1553.ab_RAMs + DBA_IO7 + 5);
                              }
                              else
                                             count = MSG_STA;
          snd_blk(&bd1553, count);
}

#ifdef XMOTO /* if compiling under Microtek */
#undef $INTERRUPT
#endif
```

EOM INTERRUPT

The adapter initialization routines of Appendix C configured the board to BC
mode and to generate an EOM interrupt at the end of each 1553 message
block transmission. The ISR type is selected as 66. The ISR whose address
will be placed into the vector table at absolute location hex 108 must accomplish the following:

  1. Check the missile status message word for ERROR, ALN DONE, NAV
     DONE, or ITL DONE. If INS is operating and ALN, NAV, and ITL are all
     OFF, this word will have been refreshed to zero. If ALN, NAV, or ITL are
     ON, this word will have been updated by the transparent acceptance of
     the response message into adapter RAM.
  2. If ALN, NAV, or ITL are DONE, set the DONE switch condition.
  3. If an error exists, set the ERROR switch condition.

```
/* MODULE PATH: \MTA\ISREOM.C */

#ifdef XMOTO /* if compiling under Microtek */
#define $INTERRUPT
#endif
/* ---------------------------------------------
    ISR for EOM (transmission DONE, End Of Msg)
```

```
      Process CP flags indicating 1553 mssg DONE
      ------------------------------------------------
*/
VOID eom1553(VOID)
{
USHORT retcode;
SW1PTR this_sw;
         retcode = 0;
                                /*$ DETERMINE current status    */

   switch(*((USHORT *) (bd1553.ab_RAMs + DBA_STA + 5)))
               {
               case(MSL_ALN):
                       this_sw = &ram_sw[ALN_SW];
                       last_sw = ALN_SW;
               break;
               case(MSL_NAV):
                       this_sw = &ram_sw[NAV_SW];
                       last_sw = NAV_SW;
               break;
               case(MSL_ITL):
                       this_sw = &ram_sw[ITL_SW];
                       last_sw = ITL_SW;
               break;
               case(MSL_ERR):
                       retcode = 1;
                       sw_ERRO(&ram_cp, &ram_sw[last_sw]);
               break;
               default:
                       retcode = 1;
               break;
               }
         if (!retcode)
                       /*$ SET bit for any DONE switch */
               sw_DONE(&ram_cp,this_sw);
   }

#ifdef XMOTO /* if compiling under Microtek */
#undef $INTERRUPT
#endif
```

VECTOR TABLE

The Motorola example vector table of Chapter 4 will be used. The system will have only two active interrupts, and there is no danger of interrupt contention. The timer will interrupt at 32Hz in order to transfer 1553 messages, and the EOM interrupt will occur after the message block has been transferred.

The timer interrupt's entry point will be set into the table at absolute location hex 180. The 1553 EOM interrupt will use hex address 108. All other vector table entries will point to the "dummy" ISR example of Chapter 4.

START-UP CODE

The Motorola start-up code example of Chapter 3 can be used, but the starting and ending points of RAM must be changed to hex 20000 and 2FFFF respectively. Adapter board RAM will be initialized by C functions after the self-tests are executed.

Interrupts will not be enabled inside the start-up code, but MAIN() will call ENABLI() for that purpose.

MAIN CODE THREAD

The MAIN code thread will use routines defined in Appendices A and C in order to test the adapter board, initialize the board to BC mode, test the control panel lights, and reset the control panel, before falling into a repetitive processing loop. Once inside the loop, the CP_SW_PROC() routine defined in Appendix A will transparently take care of all project-specific switch processing except the DONE states and ERROR states.

As soon as the INS switch is pressed by the pilot, the CP_SW_PROC() function will set the switch to the software IN PROCESS state. Subsequently, the main code thread will start the 32Hz timer and set the INS switch state to DONE. INS message traffic will continue throughout processing. The MAIN thread will not have to be concerned with DONE states for ALN, NAV, and ITL. They are set by the EOM interrupt when the status message indicates that they are DONE.

If the CP's RES switch is pressed under conditions that allow its use, all flags will be reset to zero by CP_SW_PROC(). Subsequently, the MAIN code thread will stop the 32Hz timer until the INS switch is once again pressed. At the bottom of the infinite processing loop, the switch patterns and lights are updated in order to reflect changes accomplished after leaving CP_SW_PROC().

```
/*   MODULE PATH: \MTA\CMDMAIN.C   */

#include <stdio.h>
#include <string.h>
#include <\cp\newdat.h>
#include <\cp\cp.h>
#include <\x1553\adapter.h>
#include <\x1553\adptabls.h>
#include <\x1553\msgtbls.h> /* 1553 messages */
#include <\mta\adr1553.h>
#include <\mta\msg1553.h>
```

```
/* Function declarations */
VOID outport(USHORT far *port_adr, USHORT value);
USHORT inport(USHORT far *port_adr);
VOID enablei(VOID);

USHORT last_sw;        /* Last switch processed via EOM */

#include <\cp\io.c>           /* Port table I/O          */
#include <\cp\cpdat.c>        /* CP tables               */
#include <\mta\m1553dat.c>    /* 1553 messages           */
#include <\mta\adptdefs.c>    /* Adapter ROM tables      */
#include <\x1553\adptrom.c>   /* Adapter ROM tables      */
#include <\cp\cp.c>           /* CP code                 */
#include <\x1553\test.c>      /* Adapter self-tests      */
#include <\x1553\adptinit.c>  /* Adapter INIT            */
#include <\x1553\sndblock.c>  /* Block Mssg SEND         */
#include <\mta\interrpt.c>    /* 32Hz processing         */
#include <\mta\isreom.c>      /* EOM processing          */

/* Assembly routines located in timer & start-up modules */
extern VOID ENABLEI(VOID);
extern VOID INITMR(VOID);
extern VOID HLTMR(VOID);

USHORT main()/*& Main IBOX Processing */
{
USHORT retcode;

    reset_board(&bd1553);     /*$ RESET adapter          */
    last_sw = INS_SW;         /*$ INIT global data       */
    ENABLEI();
                              /*$ ENABLE interrupts      */

                              /*$ PERFORM self-tests     */
    adptreset(&bd1553,&tstmsgs[0],&tdblks[0],&regseq[0]);

                              /*$ CHECK results of self-tests  */
    retcode = chkreset(&bd1553,&tstmsgs[0],&tdblks[0]);
    if (!retcode)
       {                      /*$ INIT board memory and SET mode  */
       select_mode(&bd1553,  MODE_FOR_BC);

                              /*$ SET UP & TEST CP       */
       set_up_cp(&ram_cp,&ram_sw[0]);
       lite_test(&ram_cp,&ram_sw[0]);
       set_up_cp(&ram_cp,&ram_sw[0]);
       }
    while (1)
```

```
        {
cp_sw_proc(&ram_cp);/*$ PROCESS panel switches         */
if (ram_cp.cp_inpr & INS_MASK)
                {               /*$ If INS INPROC        */
                INITMR();       /*$ START timer (assembly) */

                                /*$ SET INS DONE         */
                sw_DONE(&ram_cp,&ram_sw[INS_SW]);
                }
                                /*$ IF no ACTIVE switch   */
                                /*$ RESET CP, stop timer  */
if ((ram_cp.cp_inpr == 0)
&& (ram_cp.cp_sets == 0)
&& (ram_cp.cp_done == 0))
                {
                HLTMR();        /*$ STOP timer (assembly)  */
                set_up_cp(&ram_cp,&ram_sw[0]);
                }
                                /*$ UPDATE bits & lights  */
sw_inhibits(&ram_cp);
sw_lites(&ram_cp);
update_lites(&ram_cp);
}
        }
```

APPENDIX E

Testing the Missile-to-Aircraft Interface

This appendix is an overview of one approach that could be used in testing the software routines used in the missile-to-aircraft interface example in Appendix D.

TEST PLAN

In testing the example project of Appendix D, the goal is to verify each VME system bus card and its associated software in a piecemeal fashion. Starting with the CPU/timer board and subsequently adding one board at a time into the VME bus chassis could accomplish the desired result.

It seems feasible to test the CPU/Timer card first, and then to add the control panel board, the 1553 bus interface adapter, and the pressure-altitude interface card, in that order. If all goes well, major component integration will have been accomplished at the end of preliminary testing of all system adapters.

For test equipment, an In-Circuit Emulator (ICE) unit will be required, as will an AT-compatible PC configured with the 1553 aircraft bus "bus monitor" adapter board of Appendix C. A logic analyzer may or may not be necessary, depending on the debugged state of the hardware.

Some type of synchro or synchro-simulator hardware is desirable. The hardware engineer has provided a small simulator box with knobs that will allow the programmer to change either coarse or fine synchro readings manually. The box also simulates the "locking" mechanism to latch the current reading.

CPU/TIMER PRELIMINARY TESTING

The CPU chip can be removed from its socket on the CPU board, and can be replaced with the ICE unit probe. The start-up code, vector table, timer routines, and dummy ISR can be used "as is." The MAIN() C function of Appendix D can be replaced with a test routine that simply enables external interrupts and starts the timer:

```
USHORT main()/*& Main IBOX Processing */
{
  last_sw = INS_SW;          /*$ INIT global data      */
  ENABLEI();                 /*$ ENABLE interrupts     */
  INITMR();                  /*$ START timer (assembly)*/
  while (1);
}
```

The ISR for the timer (the 32Hz ISR) must be replaced with a test ISR. The test ISR should do nothing more than reset the timer for the next interrupt. The EOM ISR can be modified to contain the dummy ISR code. This allows a good link without changing any "externs" related to the ISRs.

```
VOID far int_hz32(VOID)
{
  RECNT32();                 /*$ RESET timer (assembly) */
}
VOID eom1553(VOID)
{
  ++(dmmy_cnt);              /*$ INCREMENT bucket      */
}
```

Using this configuration, initialization of RAM to zeros by the start-up code can be verified, as can the enabling of external interrupts. Using the ICE unit, timer intervals can be checked by triggering a time hack with each ISR iteration, or by using a logic analyzer connected to the appropriate interrupt request lines of the CPU. Any needed adjustments to the calculated timer "counts" can be made in order to get the desired interval. A breakpoint can be set in the dummy ISR routine to check for spurious or unexpected interrupt occurrences.

After successful completion of this test, the start-up code will have been verified, along with at least one vector table entry and the timer interrupt request interval of 31.25ms.

CONTROL PANEL PRELIMINARY TESTING

Most of the control panel (CP) code has been tested in building the control panel simulator in Appendix B. Little more can be done without having the actual control panel installed. The CPU/Timer test has been successful and the control panel interface board can be added into the system bus chassis and the actual control panel can be connected to the installed card.

The MAIN() test function used in the CPU/Timer tests can be expanded to setup and test the control panel using logic extracted from the final MAIN() module in Appendix D. Logic can be inserted to set any IN PROCESS switch to the DONE state. When the switches are pressed, they should remain in their normal ON state. All panel functions can be tested in this fashion.

```
USHORT main()/*& Main IBOX Processing */
{
  last_sw = INS_SW;          /*$ INIT global data      */
  ENABLEI();                 /*$ ENABLE interrupts     */
                             /*$ PERFORM self tests    */

                 /*$ SETUP & TEST CP             */
        set_up_cp(&ram_cp,&ram_sw[0]);
        lite_test(&ram_cp,&ram_sw[0]);
        set_up_cp(&ram_cp,&ram_sw[0]);

  while (1)
        {
        cp_sw_proc(&ram_cp);/*$ PROCESS panel switches   */
        if (ram_cp.cp_inpr & INS_MASK)
              {              /*$ If INS IN PROC          */
              INITMR();      /*$ START timer (assembly)  */
                             /*$ SET INS DONE            */
              sw_DONE(&ram_cp,&ram_sw[INS_SW]);
              }
        if (ram_cp.cp_inpr & ALN_MASK)
                             /*$ If ALN IN PROC          */
                             /*$ SET ALN DONE            */
              sw_DONE(&ram_cp,&ram_sw[ALN_SW]);
        if (ram_cp.cp_inpr & NAV_MASK)
                             /*$ If NAV IN PROC          */
                             /*$ SET NAV DONE            */
              sw_DONE(&ram_cp,&ram_sw[NAV_SW]);
        if (ram_cp.cp_inpr & ITL_MASK)
                             /*$ If ITL IN PROC          */
                             /*$ SET ITL DONE            */
              sw_DONE(&ram_cp,&ram_sw[ITL_SW]);

                             /*$ IF no ACTIVE switch     */
                             /*$ RESET CP, stop timer    */
        if ((ram_cp.cp_inpr == 0)
        && (ram_cp.cp_sets == 0)
        && (ram_cp.cp_done == 0))
              {
              HLTMR();  /*$ STOP timer (assembly) */
              set_up_cp(&ram_cp,&ram_sw[0]);
              }
```

```
                                /*$ UPDATE bits & lights      */
                 sw_inhibits(&ram_cp);
                 sw_lites(&ram_cp);
                 update_lites(&ram_cp);
                 }
      }
```

When the above tests are complete, the logic that sets ALN, NAV, and ITL to DONE can be moved to the 32Hz ISR:

```
USHORT main()/*& Main IBOX Processing */
{
   last_sw = INS_SW;        /*$ INIT global data      */
   ENABLEI();               /*$ ENABLE interrupts     */
                            /*$ PERFORM self tests*/

                  /*$ SETUP & TEST CP                */
         set_up_cp(&ram_cp,&ram_sw[0]);
         lite_test(&ram_cp,&ram_sw[0]);
         set_up_cp(&ram_cp,&ram_sw[0]);

   while (1)
         {
         cp_sw_proc(&ram_cp);/*$ PROCESS panel switches*/
         if (ram_cp.cp_inpr & INS_MASK)
                  {            /*$ If INS IN PROC        */
                  INITMR();   /*$ START timer (assembly)*/
                              /*$ SET INS DONE          */
                  sw_DONE(&ram_cp,&ram_sw[INS_SW]);
                  }

                              /*$ IF no ACTIVE switch   */
                              /*$ RESET CP, stop timer  */
         if ((ram_cp.cp_inpr == 0)
         &&   (ram_cp.cp_sets == 0)
         &&   (ram_cp.cp_done == 0))
                  {
                  HLTMR();    /*$ STOP timer (assembly) */
                  set_up_cp(&ram_cp,&ram_sw[0]);
                  }
                              /*$ UPDATE bits & lights  */
         sw_inhibits(&ram_cp);
         sw_lites(&ram_cp);
         update_lites(&ram_cp);
         }
}

VOID far int_hz32(VOID)
{
   RECNT32();                           /*$ RESET timer (assembly) */
```

```
      if (ram_cp.cp_inpr & ALN_MASK)
                              /*$ If ALN IN PROC            */
                              /*$ SET ALN DONE              */
                       sw_DONE(&ram_cp,&ram_sw[ALN_SW]);
      if (ram_cp.cp_inpr & NAV_MASK)
                              /*$ If NAV IN PROC            */
                              /*$ SET NAV DONE              */
                       sw_DONE(&ram_cp,&ram_sw[NAV_SW]);
      if (ram_cp.cp_inpr & ITL_MASK)
                              /*$ If ITL IN PROC            */
                              /*$ SET ITL DONE              */
                       sw_DONE(&ram_cp,&ram_sw[ITL_SW]);
}
```

After successful completion of the above tests, all control panel functions will have been tested, along with the additional 32Hz ISR function.

1553 BUS INTERFACE ADAPTER TESTING

With the timer, timer interrupt interval, and control panel tested, the 1553 bus interface adapter card can be installed into the system chassis. The PC 1553 bus monitor should be coupled to the 1553 bus and placed into "monitor" mode, and should be set to capture or monitor all 1553 bus traffic.

The final MAIN() module of Appendix D can be used, and the final ISRs can also be used. A breakpoint can be set in the MAIN() thread at a point following the initial adapter tests and before selecting the board mode. This way, the return code from the board test can be checked, and the board's external light indicator can be checked, and both checks verify proper board configuration for the system.

After verifying correct board configuration, the programmer can trace through the routine that selects the board's operating mode. This will ensure that the correct masks are being written to the correct registers.

With the board configuration and mode verified, the 1553 messages can be tested. It would be a good idea to place breakpoints at the beginning of both the 32Hz and EOM ISRs. Pressing INS will start the 32Hz interrupt processing, and the four INS messages should be sent as a block with each interrupt. The EOM interrupt should occur after each block send.

The breakpoint within the 32Hz ISR will be encountered first. This verifies that the interrupt occurred as expected. The programmer might opt to step through the remaining ISR code to the point of the block message send. This would verify that the pressure-altitude logic appears to work OK, even though the board is not currently installed. Test values can be patched into the synchro readings.

When the block message send is activated, the EOM breakpoint should halt processing. The 1553 bus monitor can be checked for correct message formats, addresses, and codes. The appropriate INS "done" code can be patched into the adapter board RAM location corresponding to status message word 5.

When the current breakpoint is released, the INS will be in the DONE state, and the 32Hz breakpoint should once again halt processing.

The programmer could now place a breakpoint in the MAIN() thread at the point of reading the switch panel. The code returned from the switch panel could be patched to the ALN value, and the breakpoint could be removed. The next time that the 32Hz ISR is stopped, the ALN state of IN PROCESS should be active.

The programmer might opt to step through 32Hz processing a second time in order to ensure that the block count is adjusted to include the ALN message. After the block send, the EOM will once again halt processing. After checking the bus monitor to ensure that the ALN message is correct, the programmer could opt to step through the EOM routine to patch in the ALN done mask, and then release the breakpoint.

The programmer could now, once again, place a breakpoint in the MAIN() thread at the point of reading the switch panel. The code returned from the switch panel could be patched to the NAV value, and the breakpoint could be removed. The next time that the 32Hz ISR is stopped, the NAV state of IN PROCESS should be active.

The programmer might opt to step through 32Hz processing a third time in order to ensure that the ALN message is properly replaced with the NAV message prior to the block send. After the block send, the EOM will once again halt processing. After checking the bus monitor to ensure that the NAV message is correct, the programmer could opt to step through the EOM routine to patch in the NAV done mask, and then release the breakpoint.

The NAV test could be repeated using the ITL message. Once all messages, message block sends, and codes have been verified in this fashion, the bus monitor terminal can be configured to respond as an RT with the missile computer address. This way, the terminal can be used to manually insert DONE codes into the status message, which is checked by the EOM interrupt.

With all breakpoints removed, it should be possible to set each switch IN PROCESS using the switch panel and to set each switch DONE using the PC bus monitor terminal.

After successful completion of this test, preliminary testing of everything except the pressure-altitude interface has been accomplished. The massaging of pressure-altitude values has been tested to some degree.

INTERRUPT EXECUTION TIMES

Using the ICE unit with a triggered time-hack at the beginning and ending points of the ISRs, the programmer can determine the execution time required for both ISRs. It is discovered that the 32Hz ISR requires 4 to 5ms for execution. This is presumed to be because of the floating-point emulation and memory block copies used within that routine. This will not be a problem in that there is a full 31.25ms between executions; and certainly, the pilot will hold a depressed button for several hundred milliseconds as a minimum. The EOM ISR only requires a few microseconds for completion.

PRESSURE-ALTITUDE INTERFACE TESTING

This is not a highly productive test, but it will ensure that port numbers are correct and that the synchro simulator actually provides viable readings and will give some variety to raw pressure altitude readings.

Adding the synchro-to-digital interface board into the 1553 bus chassis and connecting the synchro simulator will allow the operator to vary the pressure-altitude readings to the upper and lower anticipated limits. This will allow checking bucket sizes and data manipulation functions related to massaging the synchro readings into a pressure altitude measurement. If negative readings are anticipated (due to equipment calibration) these should also be checked.

THE NEXT STEP

After the above preliminary tests have been successful, EPROMS can be configured with the successfully tested software, as detailed in Chapter 6. After installing the EPROMS into the unit under test, tests of the fully configured interface box (IBOX) can be repeated with the ICE unit still in control. After tests are successful using the installed EPROMS and the ICE unit, the ICE unit probe can be removed from the unit under test and replaced with the Motorola 68000 processor. Stand-alone tests of the fully configured IBOX can now be conducted using the EPROMS and the final processor.

BENCH TESTING

After the above preliminary tests have been successful using the actual processor and EPROMS on a stand-alone IBOX, component integration into the final embedded unit has been tested and verified, and little more can be done without connecting to actual equipment. The missile manufacturer has rigged a complete bench-test system at the manufacturing location. The entire IBOX and all test equipment (possibly including the ICE unit and all EPROM tools) must be packaged and shipped to the manufacturer's site.

At the manufacturer's site, the bench-test configuration is absolutely complete. There is an inertial navigation system identical to the unit to be used in flight tests, the actual missile computer, and all associated interfaces.

The bus monitor is added as an extra 1553 terminal and tests are conducted with actual equipment. Following successful completion, total system integration has been verified, and nothing more can be done until the interface box and missile are installed on a test aircraft.

GROUND TESTING

It will take a minimum of one month to properly wire, configure, and test the wiring of the selected aircraft, if this chore has not been accomplished in parallel with interface box (IBOX) development. Once all equipment is installed on the test aircraft, final system integration is complete, and functional tests can be conducted while the aircraft is on the ground. Such tests can ensure all interface box function except Intent to Launch (ITL). ITL can only be conducted while the aircraft is airborne over the test range's drop zone. A high degree of confidence has been gained from the bench tests and from this ground test. The first test flight will verify proper ITL function.

APPENDIX F

Multiport Zilog 8530 SCC Driver in C

RS232 environments are frequently encountered by embedded-systems programmers. The primary purpose of this appendix is to provide an example of an interrupt-intensive environment found in multiport, asynchronous, interrupt-driven, character I/O. The example uses Zilog 8530 Serial Communications Controllers (SCCs), which are popular in such implementations. The code shows in great detail what is required in using a software ISR to build an API to background communications conducted by hardware ISRs. It also reveals what is typically found in an application program's communication control block, which is used in conjunction with the software ISR interface. Initialization of the 8530 chip is also included in the example. The code construction is consistent with Figures 4-1 through 4-5.

This code is written to execute on IBM's Multiport or Multiport/2 Asynchronous Realtime Interface Coprocessor (ARTIC) board under IBM's proprietary Realtime Control Microcode (RCM) multitasking capability which is available for that board. The two Multiport ARTIC boards are Intel 80186 coprocessor boards that use Zilog 8530 SCCs to oversee as many as eight serial communications ports. The example code is a subset of a larger system, and IBM products are required to compile or use the code "as is"; however, relatively minor modification can allow its use in a number of 8530 environments. A MAKE file for Microsoft's C compiler version 5.1 is included.

The example code does not use the RTS and DTR lines for handshaking. Connectors are presumed to be wired as shown in Figure F-1. By using short cable "stubs" attached to the ARTIC connector and wired as shown in Figure F-1, longer "straight" cables can be connected between the stubs and an AT-compatible PC, which might host equipment-specific emulators for testing.

To compile and modify this code for other boards and other environments, the user might want to delete the "#include <icadeclt.h>" statement from

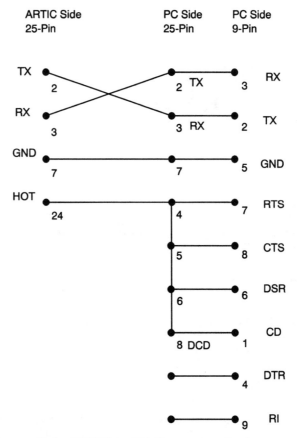

Figure F-1. ARTIC-to-PC Connector Stubs

source files. The file, ICADECLT.H, is a header supplied with IBM's C language support for the ARTIC board. Subsequent compiles will produce errors primarily related to the CPU vector table, and setting the specific vectors into the table. Data structures and routines using IBM-defined tables can be modified for user-defined tables. Conventions are followed that are suitable for use with CLEAR Software's (Brookline, MA) CLEAR+ for C product. This means that reverse engineering for calling trees and flow charts is possible using that software package.

HEADERS

```
/* MODULE PATH: \RS232\JFBIXX.H -- header module */

/* For MSC 5.1 compatibility without using STDIO.H */
#define NULL OL
    /* Same as MS'C' ver 5.1 definition in stdio.h */

/* ------------------*/
```

```
/* STANDARD TYPEDEFS */

typedef int INT;
typedef unsigned int UINT;
typedef unsigned char UCHAR;
typedef char CHAR;
typedef unsigned long ULONG;
typedef long LONG;
typedef float FLOAT;
typedef double DOUBLE;

#define OK 0    /* GOOD return code */

/* MISCELLANEOUS SYSTEM HOOKS */

#define BOARDTYPE 0 /* Type of ARTIC board   */
#define XDOSSYS 0    /* Type of host software */
#define SYSTEMTYPE 0 /* Type of host system   */

/* MISCELLANEOUS IMPLEMENTATION-SPECIFIC EQUATES    */

/* Task priority equates for RCM on ARTIC board    */
#define PRI_COMM 2  /* COMM_TSK (highest below RCM) */

/* Task number equates for DOS interface       */

#define RIC_EXEC 0 /* IBM-supplied multitasking    */
#define COMM_TSK 1 /* SCC communications (Port IO) */

#define NUMCOMMPARM 10/* Number of comm parm in COMMINFO  */
                      /* NUMCOMMPARM must be even number  */

/* ARTIC board hardware limitations    */
#define MAXPORTS 8  /* Hardware limitation of Multiport  */

/* SYSTEM BUFFER SIZES */

/* User-defined low-level communications buffer sizes
   (defined for each port).
   ("transmit" & "receive" defined from application task
   perspective).
*/

#define TXBUFFSIZ 256    /* Size of transmit buffer */
#define RXBUFFSIZ 256    /* Size of receive  buffer */

/* Application Communication buffer sizes
   (defined for each application).
   ("Transmit" & "receive" defined from application
   task perspective).
*/
```

```
#define ACTXBUFFSIZ TXBUFFSIZ /* Size of transmit buffer */
#define ACRXBUFFSIZ RXBUFFSIZ /* Size of receive  buffer */

/* INTERRUPT VECTOR ALLOCATION */

/* On the PC-side, any vector may be used that does not
   conflict with others.
   Software vector number for PC-side ISR interface to
   ARTIC Communications.
*/
#define VECTORNMBR 0x61

/* On the ARTIC side: */
/* IBMs RCM allows use of ODD vector numbers
   from 0x21 - 0xff.
   The below vector spacing is arbitrary within
   these confines.
*/

#define VSPACE 6 /* spacing of vectors for allocation */

/* Software starting vector number for comm services
   (nine total vectors reserved from COMMVECTOR to
   (COMMVECTOR + VSPACE + (MAXPORTS * VSPACE))
   (the vectors are spaced by a count of VSPACE).
*/
#define COMMVECTOR 0x21
/* MODULE PATH: \RS232\RXFLAGS.H */

/* Codes used by COMM_TSK requests -- bit flags */
#define FLGFORRESET       0x01 /* port reset request */
#define FLGFORINTDIS      0x08 /* init with interrupts disabled
*/

/* MODULE PATH: \RS232\COMMPRM.H
   Communications parameter equates for system
*/

/* Communications parameter codes for system messages &
   processing. These values represent table offsets.
*/

/* Supported baud rates */
#define BAUD110 0    /* 110 baud   */
#define BAUD300 2    /* 300 baud   */
#define BAUD600 4    /* 600 baud   */
#define BAUD1200 6   /* 1200 baud  */
#define BAUD2400 8   /* 2400 baud  */
#define BAUD4800 10  /* 4800 baud  */
#define BAUD9600 12  /* 9600 baud  */
```

```
#define BAUD19200 14 /* 19200 baud */


/* Supported parities */
#define PARITY0 0     /* no parity bits */
#define PARITY1 1     /* 1 parity bits  */
#define PARITY2 2     /* 2 parity bits  */


/* Supported numbers of stop bits */
#define STOPBITS1     0 /* one stop bit   */
#define STOPBITS2     1 /* two stop bits  */
#define STOPBITS1HALF 2 /* one and a half */


/* Supported numbers of data bits */
#define DATABITS5 0  /* 5 data bits */
#define DATABITS6 1  /* 6 data bits */
#define DATABITS7 2  /* 7 data bits */
#define DATABITS8 3  /* 8 data bits */


/* Supported communications protocols */
#define RS232XX 0
#define RS422XX 1 /* not currently supported */


/* Supported port-to-equipment protocols   */
#define HSHAKE0 0 /* no special handshake   */
/* no other handshakes currently supported */

/* MODULE PATH \RS232\SCC.h
   Equates specific to 8530 SCC
*/
#define IUSRESET 0x38/* mask to reset highest IUS       */
#define TXPRESET 0x28/* mask to reset tx int pending     */
#define TXURESET 0xc0/* mask to reset transmit underrun  */
#define SPERESET 0x30/* mask to reset sp rx condition int */
#define EXSRESET 0x10/* mask to reset extrnl/status int   */


/* SCC read register codes returned */
#define RR1 1         /* read reg 1 mask */

#define BUFFOVRN 0x20/* rx buffer overrun (read reg 1) */
#define PARTYERR 0x10/* rx parity error (read reg 1)   */
#define FRAMEERR 0x40/* rx frame error (read reg 1)    */
#define TIMEOERR 0x80/* rx unknown/timeout error       */
#define TXBUFMTY 0x04/* mask for tx empty (read reg 0) */

/* SCC write register masks */

#define WR0               0x00
#define WR1               0x01
#define WR3               0x03
#define WR4               0x04
```

```c
#define WR5              0x05
#define WR6              0x06
#define WR7              0x07
#define WR8              0x08
#define WR10             0x0A
#define WR11             0x0B
#define WR12             0x0C
#define WR13             0x0D
#define WR14             0x0E
#define WR15             0x0F


/* MODULE PATH: \RS232\SFTSCC.H */

/* Request codes for software ISR interface to comm */
#define RETNINFO 0/* return avail information */
#define RESETPRT 1/* reset port */
#define SENDCHAR 2/* put 1 or more chars to tx buff & xmit*/
#define RECVCHAR 3/* get/put 1 or more chars from rx buff */
#define RESETBUF 4/* clear desired comm buffer (tx/rx)     */
#define SET_RTSX 5/* for supported handshakes (send)       */
#define SET_DTRX 6/* for supported handshakes (receive)    */

/* Codes used by RESETBUF request */
#define DOTXBUFF 0x01     /* operation is for TX buffer */
#define DORXBUFF 0x02     /* operation is for RX buffer */
#define DO2BUFF (DOTXBUFF | DORXBUFF) /* both buffers   */

/* Codes returned by software ISR interface to comm */
#define BADPORTNUM 100       /* invalid port number */
#define BADREQUEST 101       /* invalid request number */
#define NOBUFSPACE 102       /* no buffer space for request */
#define BADRXTXVAL 103       /* invalide rxtxcode */
#define PORTNOINIT 104       /* port is not initialized */
#define BADCOMMPRM 105       /* invalid comm parameter */
#define NOCOMMINIT 106       /* COMMINFO structure not INIT */
#define BADXXCOUNT 107       /* bad count for rx or tx */
#define RESETIMOUT 108       /* RESET request timed out */
#define BADHSHAKEC 109       /* Bad special handshake code */
#define BAD232422C 110       /* Bad RS232/422 indicator code */

/* Port Control Block—one for each port in system */
/* Structure for port control (PCB), located in COMM_TSK */
/* Passed FAR between COMM_TSK and COMMINFO structure
   in application */

typedef struct xxpcb {
/* tx & rx management */
UINT datareg;  /* data register addr    */
UINT ctrlreg;  /* control register addr */
UCHAR cxparm[NUMCOMMPARM];/* curr comm values for port    */
```

```
void (far *tx_inth)();/* transmit hdwr interrupt handler   */
void (far *rx_inth)();/* receive  hdwr interrupt handler   */
void (far *er_inth)();/* error    hdwr interrupt handler   */
void (far *st_inth)();/* status   hdwr interrupt handler   */
void (far *sft_inth)();/* software interrupt handler       */
UCHAR rxflg;/* rx interrupt occurred at least once flag    */
UCHAR txflg;/* tx interrupt occurred at least once flag    */
UCHAR spflg;/* err interrupt occurred at least once flag   */
UCHAR exflg;/* ex/stat interrupt occurred at least once
                flag (should not) */
UCHAR sftflg;/* software interrupt occurred flag */
UCHAR badport;/* badport flag (set to 0xff before SCC init,
                if 0, port is good */
/* transmit buffer management */
UINT tx_remcnt;/* tx internal buff byte cnt to transmit    */
UINT tx_curcnt;/* tx byte cnt (cnt actually transmitted)   */
UCHAR *tx_usrptr;/* addr of next user put in tx buffer      */
UCHAR *tx_comptr;/* addr of next char to tx in tx buffer    */
UCHAR tx_errstat;/* tx error status       */
UCHAR tx_numerr; /* number tx errors      */
UCHAR *txbstart; /* tx buffer starting addr     */
        /* receive buffer management        */
UINT rx_remcnt;/* rx internal buff byte cnt not in use     */
UINT rx_curcnt;/* rx byte cnt (curr buffer cnt received)   */
UCHAR *rx_usrptr;/* addr of next user access in rx buffer */
UCHAR *rx_comptr;/* addr of next char put into rx buffer  */
UCHAR rx_errstat;/* rx error status       */
UCHAR rx_numerr;/* number of chars in error in rx buffer    */
UCHAR rx_flags; /* rx flags        */
UCHAR *rxbstart;/* rx buffer starting addr     */
/* init tables */
UCHAR *scc_tbl;
/* IBM-defined structure (defined in RIC C support) */
struct rs232rbstruct *IBMPRBPTR;/*       pointer to rs232
                                         Port Request Block */
struct rs422rbstruct *IBM422PTR;/*       pointer to rs422 Port
                                         Request Block (not
                                         currently supported)*/
} XPCB, *XPCBPTR, far *XPCBPTRF;

/* COMMINFO passed FAR between application & COMM_TSK
   located in application task only
*/
typedef struct xsftint {
UINT taskno;          /* invoking task number */
UCHAR far *dataptr; /* far pointer to user data area */
UCHAR commparm[NUMCOMMPARM];  /* communications parm */
INT  descnt;          /* desired count this operation  */
UINT retcnt;          /* actual count this operation   */
UINT rettxcnt; /* returned tx total count in buffer   */
```

```
    UINT retrxcnt; /* returned rx total count in buffer  */
    UINT errtxcnt; /* returned tx err count in buffer    */
    UINT errrxcnt; /* returned rx err count in buffer    */
    UINT retreqst; /* request status for COMMTSK requests*/
    UCHAR txcode;  /* returned tx status code in buffer  */
    UCHAR rxcode;  /* returned rx status code in buffer  */
    UCHAR retcode; /* returned int status this operation */
    UCHAR operation;/* desired op code this operation */
    UCHAR rxtxcode; /* operate on rx or tx or both       */
    UCHAR portnum;  /* port number for operation         */
    struct vrbstruct *vrbsftptr;/* pointer to software services
                                    VRB Vector Request Block */
    UCHAR cinitf;  /* COMMINFO initialization DONE flag */
    UCHAR cinitx;  /* COMMINFO initialization TYPE flag
                      (1=keep interrupts disabled) */
    XPCBPTRF chldstrc;/* hold addr for beginning XPCB array */
    } COMMINFO, *COMMPTR, far *COMMPTRF;
```

MAIN(), SCC INITIALIZATION UNDER RCM

```
/* MODULE PATH: \RS232\SCCINIT.C
   Hardware initialization & communications functions.
   This task provides "background" RS232 communications
   for a IBM Multiport/2 board.
*/
/*
This task installs all interrupt handlers and
OWNS ALL PORTS. This task is provided to initialize the
hardware and to determine which ports are available.
This task OWNS the COMMVECTOR for software service.
The ONLY valid COMMVECTOR calls from this task change port
personality. The COMMVECTOR is also used to pass the
software ISR address to other tasks as they are loaded.
This is the only task servicing the ARTIC hardware.
Hardware vectors are stored in the RCM. Interrupts are
first vectored to the RCM by the IBM Microcode, then back
to the handler address.

All resource blocks must be in the same segment as the TCB
of the owning task.

User services are via software interrupt and are documented
elsewhere. All tasks utilize the same code for interfacing
to the communciations buffers.  Unique vectors (pointing to
identical code) are defined for each task in order to
prevent excessive dispatch exercise under the existing
IBM RCM.
*/
```

```
/* Notes:
        This task should be compiled with the LARGE model.
        This task is known to the RCM as COMM_TSK by number.
        The executable module is known as COMMTSK by name.
        This task should be loaded AFTER the RCM task
            and BEFORE any task that uses any port.
        This task should be a higher priority than any other
            task except the RCM control code task
            (multitasking control).
        The task is made up of the following modules:
            SCCINIT.C --This module, the MAIN COMM_TSK mod.
            ISRRX.C   ---Receiver hardware interrupts
            ISRTX.C   ---Transmitter hardware interrupts
            ISRSP.C   ---Special RX err hdwr interrupts
            ISREX.C   ---External/Status hardware interrupts
            ISRSFT.C ---Software ISR for comm services
            SFTISR.C ---Routines used by ISRSFT
            HDWISR.C ---Routines used by hdwr interrupts
            INTERSFT.C -Application interface to software ISR
            ONESHOT.C --One-Shot Software Timer module
*/


/*
Basic operation:

This task OWNs all ports and RS232 request blocks and
hardware ISRs. When loaded, it sets hardware vectors,
initializes all ports with interrupts disabled, and then
suspends itself until requested to reinitialize a port to
specified communications parameters and enable interrupts
for the specified port.

After performing its request, the task suspends itself
again. Communications are always active in the "background"
for ports with interrupts enabled.  Each port has four unique
hardware interrupt vectors, a buffer in which to receive
characters from the port, and a buffer from which to
transmit characters. All application interface to
communications is via the Software ISR, which is also a part
of this module.  Applications desiring to send or receive
characters issue a software interrupt, which is ultimately
vectored to this routine. As viewed by the application,
communications are a matter of getting or putting
characters to/from the transmit and receive buffers which
are filled/emptied by the hardware ISRs.

An API library of "C" routines is provided to make even the
software interrupt transparent to users.  All application
functions necessary for robust communications are contained
in the API (which consists of INTERSFT.OBJ and ONESHOT.OBJ)
```

```
*/

#include <icadeclt.h>
                /* IBM RIC (Realtime Interface Coprocessor)
                   C language support header */
#include <jfbixx.h>
#include <sftscc.h>
#include <sfcndecs.h>
#include <scc.h>
#include <interfcn.h>
#include <rxflags.h>

extern XPCB port_tbl[MAXPORTS];
extern VECTOR cvecthold;
extern XPCBPTRF cvecth2ld;
/*-------------------------------------------*/
/*         Global data for this module       */
/*-------------------------------------------*/

/* IBM-defined structure (pointers to IBM-defined
control blocks for this task) */
struct cbptr cb;

/*-------------------------------------------*/
/*         MAIN ROUTINE for PORT IO          */
/*         Init SCCs and standby             */
/*-------------------------------------------*/
INT main(void)
{
COMMPTR cptr;          /* pointer to COMMINFO */
struct cbptr *ptrcb; /* pointer to struct with tsk ptrs */
UINT i;                /* loop counter */
XPCBPTR pcbxptr;       /* entry in port table for port */
                       /*$ set addr of ISR & addr of struct
                              into VECTHOLD buckets */
   cvecthold = (VECTOR) sft_isr;
   cvecth2ld = (XPCBPTRF) &port_tbl[0];
   ptrcb = &cb;/*$ get addr global struct for pointers */
   get_ptrs(ptrcb);/*$ return task cb ptrs into cb struct */
   cptr = get_cptrinit(ptrcb);/*$ init COMMINFO, allocate
          software vector (for this task only, init all ports) */
   initpri(PRI_COMM);/*$ set task priority */
   svcinitc(0);     /*$ tell RCM that init done */
   get_ptrs(ptrcb);/*$ return task cb ptrs into cb struct*/
   while(1)
          {
                                 /*$ post in order to resume */
       svcpost((UCHAR) cptr->taskno,0x20);
                          /*$ remove task from dispatch que */
       svcsspnd((UCHAR) cptr->taskno);
```

```
        for ( i = 0; i < MAXPORTS; i++)
              {
              cptr->portnum = (UCHAR) i;
              pcbxptr = &port_tbl[i];
   /*$ if any requests exist for COMM_TSK, service them */
              if (pcbxptr->rx_flags & FLGFORRESET)
               {
              switch(pcbxptr->badport)
                  {
                  case(0):/* $ is a good port, issue reset */
                        resetport(0xff,0xff,0xff,0xff,0,0);
                  break;
                  default:/*$ is a bad port */
                  break;
                  }
              }
             }
        cptr->portnum = 0;
        }
 return(0);
}
```

HARDWARE ISRs

```
        /* MODULE PATH: \RS232\HDWISR.C
           Routines used by hardware ISRs
        */
        #include <icadeclt.h>
                 /* IBM RIC (Realtime Interface Coprocessor)
                    C language support header */
        #include <jfbixx.h>
        #include <sftscc.h>
        #include <sfcndecs.h>
        #include <scc.h>
        #include <conio.h>

        extern XPCB far port_tbl[MAXPORTS];
        /* ----------------------------------------- */
        /* This routine is shared by all ext/status ISRs  */
        /* ----------------------------------------- */
        /* Routine to get external/status & manage buffer */
        /* ----------------------------------------- */
        void ex_char(XPCBPTR pcbx)/*& GET error & manage tx buffer */
        {
                pcbx->tx_errstat |= 1;          /*$ OR err into buff    */
                ++(pcbx->tx_numerr);            /*$ INCREMENT err cnt   */
                pcbx->exflg |= 1;               /*$ SET interrupt flag  */
                outp(pcbx->ctrlreg,EXSRESET);   /*$ RESET ext/stat int  */
```

```c
                outp(pcbx->ctrlreg,IUSRESET);  /*$ RESET highest IUS  */
    }
    /* ------------------------------------------ */
    /* This routine is shared by all receiver ISRs */
    /* ------------------------------------------ */
    /* Routine to get a character from the receiver*/
    /* and place it in the internal buffer         */
    /* and perform buffer management functions      */
    /* ------------------------------------------ */

void rx_char(XPCBPTR pcbx)
                /*& RECEIVE character & manage rx buffer        */
{
    if (pcbx->rx_remcnt > 0)/*$ ENSURE room in buffer          */
    {
                        /*$ PUT char into next buff position    */
        *(pcbx->rx_comptr) = (UCHAR) inp(pcbx->datareg);
        ++(pcbx->rx_comptr);   /*$ INCREMENT buff position       */
        ++(pcbx->rx_curcnt);   /*$ INCREMENT received count      */
        --(pcbx->rx_remcnt);   /*$ DECREMENT count available     */
                /*$ CHECK for buffer wrap (circular buffer)     */
        if ((ULONG) pcbx->rx_comptr ==
            ((ULONG) pcbx->rxbstart + RXBUFFSIZ))
                pcbx->rx_comptr = pcbx->rxbstart;
    }
    else                          /* No more room in buffer       */
    {
        pcbx->rx_errstat |= BUFFOVRN; /*$ SET buffer overrun       */
        ++(pcbx->rx_numerr);          /*$ INCREMENT err cnt        */
    }
    pcbx->rxflg |= 1;
    outp(pcbx->ctrlreg,IUSRESET);/*$ RESET SCC highest IUS  */
}
/* --------------------------------------------- */
/* This routine is shared by all special rx ISRs */
/* --------------------------------------------- */
/* Routine to get special condition code into    */
/* buffer & manage buffer                        */
/* --------------------------------------------- */

void sp_char(XPCBPTR pcbx) /*& GET err & manage tx buffer   */
{
    pcbx->rx_errstat |= 1;     /*$ OR err into buff             */
    ++(pcbx->rx_numerr);       /*$ INCREMENT err cnt            */
    pcbx->spflg |= 1;          /*$ SET interrupt occurred       */
    outp(pcbx->ctrlreg,SPERESET); /*$ UNLATCH flag              */
    outp(pcbx->ctrlreg,IUSRESET); /*$ RESET highest IUS         */
}
/* --------------------------------------------- */
/* This routine is shared by hdwr & sfwr tx ISRs */
```

```
/* ------------------------------------------- */
/* Routine to send a character from the internal */
/* buffer into the transmitter & manage buffer   */
/* ------------------------------------------- */

void tx_1_char(XPCBPTRF pcbx)
                /*& TRANSMIT char & manage tx buffer */
{
UINT sendata;
      sendata = *(pcbx->tx_comptr);/*$ SAVE send character */
      if (pcbx->tx_remcnt > 0)      /*$ # CHARS to transmit */
         {
          ++(pcbx->tx_comptr); /*$ INCREMENT to next addr */
          --(pcbx->tx_remcnt); /*$ DECREMENT cnt to send  */
          ++(pcbx->tx_curcnt); /*$ INCREMENT sent count   */
             /*$ CHECK for buffer wrap (circular buffer) */
          if ((ULONG) pcbx->tx_comptr ==
             ((ULONG) pcbx->txbstart + TXBUFFSIZ))
                pcbx->tx_comptr = pcbx->txbstart;

          outp(pcbx->datareg,sendata);/*$ OUTPUT 1 char   */
          }
}

/* -------------------------------------------- */
/* This routine is shared by all transmitter ISRs */
/* -------------------------------------------- */
/* Routine to put a character from the internal   */
/* buffer into the transmitter & manage buffer    */
/* -------------------------------------------- */

void tx_char(XPCBPTR pcbx)
                /*& TRANSMIT char & manage tx buffer */
{
                     /*$ OUTPUT char & handle buffer */
      tx_1_char((XPCBPTRF) pcbx);
      if (pcbx->tx_remcnt == 0)
         {
          outp(pcbx->ctrlreg,TXPRESET);
                       /*$ SEND DONE, RESET count sent */
          pcbx->tx_curcnt = 0;
          }
                    /*$ IF no more, reset tx pending */
      pcbx->txflg |= 1;      /*$ SET interrupt occurred */
      outp(pcbx->ctrlreg,IUSRESET); /*$ RESET highest IUS */
}
/* MODULE PATH: \RS232\ISREX.C
   Hardware external/status interrupt service routines.
*/
```

```c
#include <icadeclt.h>
            /* IBM RIC (Realtime Interface Coprocessor)
                C language support header */
#include <jfbixx.h>
#include <sftscc.h>
#include <sfcndecs.h>
#include <scc.h>

extern XPCB port_tbl[MAXPORTS];

/* These interrupts should not occur - for system testing*/

/* ------------------------------------------------- */
/* One of these routines for each RS232 port          */
/* Special receive condition                          */
/* ------------------------------------------------- */
void far ex_port0() /*& Hardware external/status cond ISR*/
{
      int_ntry();       /*$ Save entry state */
      sti();            /*$ Re-enable interrupts */
      nseoi();          /*$ Issue non-specific EOI to 80186*/
      ex_char(&port_tbl[0]);/*$ Get err & buff management*/
      int_exit();       /*$ Restore entry state */
}
void far ex_port1() /*& Hardware external/status cond ISR*/
{
      int_ntry();       /*$ Save entry state */
      sti();            /*$ Re-enable interrupts */
      nseoi();          /*$ Issue non-specific EOI to 80186*/
      ex_char(&port_tbl[1]);/*$ Get err & buff management */
      int_exit();       /*$ Restore entry state */
}
void far ex_port2() /*& Hardware external/status cond ISR*/
{
      int_ntry();       /*$ Save entry state */
      sti();            /*$ Re-enable interrupts */
      nseoi();          /*$ Issue non-specific EOI to 80186*/
      ex_char(&port_tbl[2]);/*$ Get err & buff management*/
      int_exit();       /*$ Restore entry state */
}
void far ex_port3()  /*& Hardware external/status cond ISR*/
{
      int_ntry();       /*$ Save entry state */
      sti();            /*$ Re-enable interrupts */
      nseoi();          /*$ Issue non-specific EOI to 80186*/
      ex_char(&port_tbl[3]);/*$ Get err & buff management */
      int_exit();       /*$ Restore entry state */
}
```

```
void far ex_port4()  /*& Hardware external/status cond ISR*/
{
     int_ntry();      /*$ Save entry state */
     sti();           /*$ Re-enable interrupts */
     nseoi();         /*$ Issue non-specific EOI to 80186*/
     ex_char(&port_tbl[4]);/*$ Get err & buff management */
     int_exit();      /*$ Restore entry state */
}
void far ex_port5()  /*& Hardware external/status cond ISR*/
{
     int_ntry();      /*$ Save entry state */
     sti();           /*$ Re-enable interrupts */
     nseoi();         /*$ Issue non-specific EOI to 80186*/
     ex_char(&port_tbl[5]);/*$ Get err & buff management */
     int_exit();      /*$ Restore entry state */
}
void far ex_port6()  /*& Hardware external/status cond ISR*/
{
     int_ntry();      /*$ Save entry state */
     sti();           /*$ Re-enable interrupts */
     nseoi();         /*$ Issue non-specific EOI to 80186*/
     ex_char(&port_tbl[6]);/*$ Get err & buff management */
     int_exit();      /*$ Restore entry state */
}
void far ex_port7()  /*& Hardware external/status cond ISR*/
{

     int_ntry();      /*$ Save entry state */
     sti();           /*$ Re-enable interrupts */
     nseoi();         /*$ Issue non-specific EOI to 80186*/
     ex_char(&port_tbl[7]);/*$ Get err & buff management */
     int_exit();      /*$ Restore entry state */
}

/* MODULE PATH: ISRSP.C
   Hardware special receive interrupt service routines
*/
#include <icadeclt.h>  /* IBM RIC (Realtime Interface
Coprocessor)
                 C language support header */
#include <jfbixx.h>
#include <sftscc.h>
#include <sfcndecs.h>
#include <scc.h>

extern XPCB port_tbl[MAXPORTS];

/* -------------------------------------------------- */
/* One of these routines for each RS232 port          */
/* Special receive condition                          */
```

```c
/* --------------------------------------------------- */
void far sp_port0() /*& Hardware special rx cond ISR */
{
  int_ntry(); /*$ Save entry state */
  sti();      /*$ Re-enable interrupts */
  nseoi();    /*$ Issue non-specific EOI to 80186 */
  sp_char(&port_tbl[0]);/*$ Get err & do buffer management */
  int_exit(); /*$ Restore entry state */
}
void far sp_port1() /*& Hardware special rx cond ISR */
{
  int_ntry(); /*$ Save entry state */
  sti();      /*$ Re-enable interrupts */
  nseoi();    /*$ Issue non-specific EOI to 80186 */
  sp_char(&port_tbl[1]);/*$ Get err & do buffer management */
  int_exit(); /*$ Restore entry state */
}
void far sp_port2() /*& Hardware special rx cond ISR */
{
  int_ntry(); /*$ Save entry state */
  sti();      /*$ Re-enable interrupts */
  nseoi();    /*$ Issue non-specific EOI to 80186 */
  sp_char(&port_tbl[2]);/*$ Get err & do buffer management */
  int_exit(); /*$ Restore entry state */
}
void far sp_port3() /*& Hardware special rx cond ISR */
{
  int_ntry(); /*$ Save entry state */
  sti();      /*$ Re-enable interrupts */
  nseoi();    /*$ Issue non-specific EOI to 80186 */
  sp_char(&port_tbl[3]);/*$ Get err & do buffer management */
  int_exit();/*$ Restore entry state */
}
void far sp_port4() /*& Hardware special rx cond ISR */
{
  int_ntry(); /*$ Save entry state */
  sti();      /*$ Re-enable interrupts */
  nseoi();    /*$ Issue non-specific EOI to 80186 */
  sp_char(&port_tbl[4]);/*$ Get err & do buffer management */
  int_exit(); /*$ Restore entry state */
}
void far sp_port5() /*& Hardware special rx cond ISR */
{
  int_ntry(); /*$ Save entry state */
  sti();      /*$ Re-enable interrupts */
  nseoi();    /*$ Issue non-specific EOI to 80186 */
  sp_char(&port_tbl[5]);/*$ Get err & do buffer management */
  int_exit(); /*$ Restore entry state */
}
void far sp_port6() /*& Hardware special rx cond ISR */
{
```

```
   int_ntry();  /*$ Save entry state */
   sti();       /*$ Re-enable interrupts */
   nseoi();     /*$ Issue non-specific EOI to 80186 */
   sp_char(&port_tbl[6]);/*$ Get err & do buffer management */
   int_exit();  /*$ Restore entry state */
}
void far sp_port7() /*& Hardware special rx cond ISR */
{
   int_ntry();  /*$ Save entry state */
   sti();       /*$ Re-enable interrupts */
   nseoi();     /*$ Issue non-specific EOI to 80186 */
   sp_char(&port_tbl[7]);/*$ Get err & do buffer management */
   int_exit();  /*$ Restore entry state */
}

/* MODULE PATH: \RS232\ISRRX.C
   Hardware receive interrupt service routines
*/

#include <icadeclt.h>
            /* IBM RIC (Realtime Interface Coprocessor)
               C language support header */
#include <jfbixx.h>
#include <sftscc.h>
#include <sfcndecs.h>
#include <scc.h>
extern XPCB port_tbl[MAXPORTS];
/* ------------------------------------------------ */
/* One of these routines for each RS232 port        */
/* ------------------------------------------------ */
/* ISR to receive character into internal buffer    */
/* ------------------------------------------------ */
void far rx_port0()          /*& Hardware receive ISR */
{
        int_ntry();          /*$ Save entry state */
        sti();               /*$ Re-enable interrupts */
        nseoi();             /*$ Issue non-specific EOI to 80186*/
        rx_char(&port_tbl[0]);/*$ Get char & buff management*/
        int_exit();          /*$ Restore entry state */
}
void far rx_port1()          /*& Hardware receive ISR */
{
        int_ntry();          /*$ Save entry state */
        sti();               /*$ Re-enable interrupts */
        nseoi();             /*$ Issue non-specific EOI to 80186*/
        rx_char(&port_tbl[1]);/*$ Get char & buff management*/
        int_exit();          /*$ Restore entry state */
}
void far rx_port2()          /*& Hardware receive ISR */
{
        int_ntry();          /*$ Save entry state */
```

```
        sti();                  /*$ Re-enable interrupts */
        nseoi();                /*$ Issue non-specific EOI to 80186*/
        rx_char(&port_tbl[2]);/*$ Get char & buff management*/
        int_exit();             /*$ Restore entry state */
}
void far rx_port3()             /*& Hardware receive ISR */
{
        int_ntry();             /*$ Save entry state */
        sti();                  /*$ Re-enable interrupts */
        nseoi();                /*$ Issue non-specific EOI to 80186*/
        rx_char(&port_tbl[3]);/*$ Get char & buff management*/
        int_exit();             /*$ Restore entry state */
}
void far rx_port4()             /*& Hardware receive ISR */
{

        int_ntry();             /*$ Save entry state */
        sti();                  /*$ Re-enable interrupts */
        nseoi();                /*$ Issue non-specific EOI to 80186*/
        rx_char(&port_tbl[4]);/*$ Get char & buff management*/
        int_exit();             /*$ Restore entry state */
}
void far rx_port5()             /*& Hardware receive ISR */
{

        int_ntry();             /*$ Save entry state */
        sti();                  /*$ Re-enable interrupts */
        nseoi();                /*$ Issue non-specific EOI to 80186*/
        rx_char(&port_tbl[5]);/*$ Get char & buff management*/
        int_exit();             /*$ Restore entry state */
}
void far rx_port6()             /*& Hardware receive ISR */
{

        int_ntry();             /*$ Save entry state */
        sti();                  /*$ Re-enable interrupts */
        nseoi();                /*$ Issue non-specific EOI to 80186*/
        rx_char(&port_tbl[6]);/*$ Get char & buff management*/
        int_exit();             /*$ Restore entry state */
}
void far rx_port7()             /*& Hardware receive ISR */
{

        int_ntry();             /*$ Save entry state */
        sti();                  /*$ Re-enable interrupts */
        nseoi();                /*$ Issue non-specific EOI to 80186*/
        rx_char(&port_tbl[7]);/*$ Get char & buff management*/
        int_exit();             /*$ Restore entry state */
}
```

```
/* MODULE PATH: \RS232\ISRTX.C
   Hardware transmit interrupt service routines
*/
#include <icadeclt.h>
             /* IBM RIC (Realtime Interface Coprocessor)
                 C language support header */
#include <jfbixx.h>
#include <sftscc.h>
#include <sfcndecs.h>
#include <scc.h>

extern XPCB port_tbl[MAXPORTS];

/* ------------------------------------------------ */
/* One of these routines for each RS232 port        */
/* Transmitter buffer empty interrupt               */
/* ------------------------------------------------ */
/* After successful transmission, this int occurs */
/* ISR to transmit next character                   */
/* ------------------------------------------------ */
void far tx_port0()          /*& Hardware transmitter empty ISR */
{
        int_ntry();         /*$ Save entry state */
        sti();              /*$ Re-enable interrupts */
        nseoi();     /*$ Issue non-specific EOI to 80186 */
        tx_char(&port_tbl[0]);/*$ Tx char & buff management */
        int_exit();         /*$ Restore entry state */
}
void far tx_port1()          /*& Hardware transmit ISR */
{
        int_ntry();         /*$ Save entry state */
        sti();              /*$ Re-enable interrupts */
        nseoi();     /*$ Issue non-specific EOI to 80186 */
        tx_char(&port_tbl[1]);/*$ Tx char & buff management */
        int_exit();         /*$ Restore entry state */
}
void far tx_port2()          /*& Hardware transmit ISR */
{
        int_ntry();         /*$ Save entry state */
        sti();              /*$ Re-enable interrupts */
        nseoi();         /*$ Issue non-specific EOI to 80186 */
        tx_char(&port_tbl[2]);/*$ Tx char & buff management */
        int_exit();         /*$ Restore entry state */
}
void far tx_port3()          /*& Hardware transmit ISR */
{
        int_ntry();         /*$ Save entry state */
        sti();              /*$ Re-enable interrupts */
        nseoi();     /*$ Issue non-specific EOI to 80186 */
        tx_char(&port_tbl[3]);/*$ Tx char & buff management */
```

```
        int_exit();            /*$ Restore entry state */
}
void far tx_port4()            /*& Hardware transmit ISR */
{
        int_ntry();            /*$ Save entry state */
        sti();                 /*$ Re-enable interrupts */
        nseoi();        /*$ Issue non-specific EOI to 80186 */
        tx_char(&port_tbl[4]);/*$ Tx char & buff management */
        int_exit();            /*$ Restore entry state */
}
void far tx_port5()            /*& Hardware transmit ISR */
{
        int_ntry();            /*$ Save entry state */
        sti();                 /*$ Re-enable interrupts */
        nseoi();        /*$ Issue non-specific EOI to 80186 */
        tx_char(&port_tbl[5]);/*$ Tx char & buff management */
        int_exit();            /*$ Restore entry state */
}
void far tx_port6()            /*& Hardware transmit ISR */
{
        int_ntry();            /*$ Save entry state */
        sti();                 /*$ Re-enable interrupts */
        nseoi();          /*$ Issue non-specific EOI to 80186 */
        tx_char(&port_tbl[6]);/*$ Tx char & buff management */
        int_exit();            /*$ Restore entry state */
}
void far tx_port7()            /*& Hardware transmit ISR */
{
        int_ntry();            /*$ Save entry state */
        sti();                 /*$ Re-enable interrupts */
        nseoi();        /*$ Issue non-specific EOI to 80186 */
        tx_char(&port_tbl[7]);/*$ Tx char & buff management */
        int_exit();            /*$ Restore entry state */
}
```

SOFTWARE ISR

```
/* MODULE PATH: \RS232\ISRSFT.C
   Software ISR for all port communication services
*/
/*
   About software interrupts & the IBM ARTIC Board
   specifically the IBM Microcode interface:

   IBM register usage restricts compatibility with BIOS calls
   (conventions programmers may be accustomed to).
   IE Registers SI, DS, & BX cannot be used for parameter
   passing. They are used by the Realtime Control Microcode
```

(RCM) during first-level interrupt handling. Register AH
should contain the requesting task number that is known
to the RCM.

This routine is shared by all ports requesting
communications services. This routine is physically
located in the COMM_TSK module only. Unique vector
numbers that all point to this routine are assigned
to each task using communications services.
*/

```c
#include <icadeclt.h>
                /* IBM RIC (Realtime Interface Coprocessor)
                   C language support header */
#include <jfbixx.h>
#include <sftscc.h>
#include <sfcndecs.h>
#include <scc.h>
#include <rxflags.h>

extern INT board_init;

/* -------------------------------------------- */
/* This routine is the primary software ISR for */
/* user access to communications functions      */
/* -------------------------------------------- */
/* Routine to direct software ISR requests       */
/* -------------------------------------------- */
/*
  Conventions for all requests:

  AH must contain the task number of the requesting task.
  AL must contain the desired service code (see sftscc.h).
  CX = segment of structure XSFTINT.
  DX = offset of structure XSFTINT.

        Further documentation is available elsewhere.
*/

void far sft_isr()         /*& DETERMINE routing of request */
{
struct intenv far *intxregs;
COMMPTRF cptr;
XPCBPTRF pcbxptr;
  intxregs = int_ntry();                  /*$ SAVE entry state */
  cptr = (COMMPTRF) ((ULONG)
    ((((ULONG) intxregs->DX) << 16) | ((UINT)intxregs->CX)));
  pcbxptr = cptr->chldstrc + cptr->portnum;
                /*$ First order of biz is INIT all ports */
  if ((cptr->taskno == COMM_TSK) && (!board_init))
```

```
            {
            (void) initallports(cptr);          /*$ INIT all ports    */
            cptr->retcode = 0;                   /*$ SET good retcode */
            board_init = 1;                      /*$ SET bd init done */
            }
      else
            {
            if (board_init)            /*$ If structure initialized */
                                       /*$ DO COMMAND for 1 port     */
                cptr->retcode = (UCHAR) proc1port(cptr);
                           /* Struct NOT inited, set bad code  */
            else    cptr->retcode = BADPORTNUM;
            }
    cptr->rxcode = pcbxptr->rx_errstat;/*$ RETURN avail info   */
    cptr->txcode = pcbxptr->tx_errstat;
    cptr->rettxcnt = pcbxptr->tx_remcnt;
    cptr->retrxcnt = pcbxptr->rx_curcnt;
    cptr->errtxcnt = pcbxptr->tx_numerr;
    cptr->errrxcnt = pcbxptr->rx_numerr;
    cptr->retreqst = pcbxptr->rx_flags;
    pcbxptr->sftflg |= 1;
                                /*$ If a COMM_TSK request exists   */
  if ((cptr->taskno != COMM_TSK)
   && (pcbxptr->rx_flags & ~FLGFORINTDIS))
      svcrsume(COMM_TSK);                        /*$ RESUME COMM_TSK */
  sfw_exit(0,cptr->vrbsftptr);
}
/* MODULE PATH: \RS232\SFTISR.C
   Software interrupt service routines for ports
*/
/*
   About software interrupts & the IBM ARTIC Board--
   specifically the IBM Microcode interface:

   IBM register usage restricts compatibility with BIOS calls
   (conventions programmers may be accustomed to).
   IE Registers SI, DS, & BX cannot be used for parameter
   passing. They are used by the Realtime Control Microcode
   (RCM) during first-level interrupt handling.
   Register AH should contain the requesting task number that
   is known to the RCM.
*/
#include <icadeclt.h>
           /* IBM RIC (Realtime Interface Coprocessor)
              C language support header */
#include <jfbixx.h>
#include <sftscc.h>
#include <sfcndecs.h>
#include <scc.h>
#include <rxflags.h>
```

```
#include <commprm.h>
#include <conio.h>

/*
  NOTE:
  The following constants used only for SCC init tables &
  are unique to this module -- offsets in SCC init tables
  for communications parameters.
*/

#define BAUD1OFF 14   /* low byte, baud time const */
#define BAUD2OFF 16   /* high byte, baud time const */
#define PRTY1OFF 4    /* parity */
#define STOP1OFF 4    /* stop bits */
#define DATA1OFF 6    /* rx data bits, receive disabled */
#define DATA2OFF 22   /* rx data bits, receive enabled */
#define DATA3OFF 8    /* tx data bits, transmit disabled */
#define DATA4OFF 24   /* tx data bits, transmit enabled */

/* ------------------------------------- */
/* GLOBAL DATA for this module           */
/* ------------------------------------- */
INT board_init = 0; /* flag for ARTIC init done */

/* ------------------------------------- */
/* STATIC DATA for this module           */
/* ------------------------------------- */
/* baud rates supported */
static UCHAR prm_baud[]=
   {
   /* contents of WR12 & WR13 */
   0x15,0x04,        /* 110 */
   0x7E,0x01,        /* 300 */
   0xBE,0x00,        /* 600 */
   0x5E,0x00,        /* 1200 */
   0x2E,0x00,        /* 2400 */
   0x16,0x00,        /* 4800 */
   0x0A,0x00,        /* 9600 */
   0x04,0x00         /* 19.2 */
   };

/* Stop bits supported */
static UCHAR prm_stop[]=
   {
   /* bits 2 & 3 of WR4 */
   0x04,     /* 1 */
   0x0C,     /* 2 */
   0x08,     /* 1.5 */
   };
```

```
/* Parity values supported */
static UCHAR prm_parity[]=
   {
   /* bits 0 & 1 of WR4 */
         0,     /* none */
         1,     /* odd  */
         3      /* even */
         };

/* rx data bits supported */
static UCHAR prm_rxdata[]=
         {
         /* bits 6 & 7 of WR3 */
         0x00,   /* 5 bits */
         0x80,   /* 6 bits */
         0x40,   /* 7 bits */
         0xc0    /* 8 bits */
         };

/* tx data bits supported */
static UCHAR prm_txdata[]=
         {
         /* bits 6 & 7 of WR5 */
         0x00,   /* 5 */
         0x20,   /* 6 */
         0x40,   /* 7 */
         0x60    /* 8 */
         };
/* ----------------------------------------------- */
/* This routine used during port init              */
/* ----------------------------------------------- */
/* Routine to clear receiver (4 bytes total)       */
/* ----------------------------------------------- */
void clr_rx4(XPCBPTRF pcbx)
               /*& Clear whatever is in receiver */
{
INT i;
     for (i = 0; i < 4; i++)
          inp(pcbx->datareg);/*$ read next character */
}
/* ----------------------------------------------- */
/* This routine is used by software receive ISRs   */
/* ----------------------------------------------- */
/* Routine to reset (clear) comm buffer(s)         */
/* ----------------------------------------------- */

void reset_tx(XPCBPTRF pcbx) /*& Reset comm buffer(s) */
{
INT i;
          pcbx->tx_usrptr = pcbx->txbstart;    /*$ init ptrs */
          for (i = 0; i < TXBUFFSIZ; i++)      /*$ clr tx buff*/
```

```
                        *(pcbx->tx_usrptr + i) = 0;
           pcbx->tx_usrptr = pcbx->txbstart;/*$init ptrs & data*/
           pcbx->tx_comptr = pcbx->txbstart;
           pcbx->tx_remcnt = 0;
           pcbx->tx_curcnt = 0;
           pcbx->tx_errstat = 0;
           pcbx->tx_numerr = 0;
}
/* --------------------------------------------- */
/* This routine is used by software receive ISRs  */
/* --------------------------------------------- */
/* Routine to reset (clear) rx comm buffer         */
/* --------------------------------------------- */

void reset_rx(XPCBPTRF pcbx) /*& Reset comm buffer(s) */
{
INT i;
           pcbx->rx_usrptr = pcbx->rxbstart; /*$ init ptrs   */
           for (i = 0; i < RXBUFFSIZ; i++)    /*$ clear rx buff */
             *(pcbx->rx_usrptr + i) = 0;
           pcbx->rx_usrptr = pcbx->rxbstart;/*$init ptrs & data*/
           pcbx->rx_comptr = pcbx->rxbstart;
           pcbx->rx_remcnt = RXBUFFSIZ;
           pcbx->rx_curcnt = 0;
           pcbx->rx_errstat = 0;
           pcbx->rx_numerr = 0;
}
/* --------------------------------------------- */
/* This routine is used by software init ISRs     */
/* --------------------------------------------- */
/* Routine to set communications parameters       */
/* --------------------------------------------- */

void put_comm(XPCBPTRF pcbxx)
/*& Put comm parm into SCC init table - only for COMM_TSK*/
{
if (pcbxx->cxparm[0] != 0xff)
   {
   pcbxx->scc_tbl[BAUD1OFF] = prm_baud[pcbxx->cxparm[0]];
   pcbxx->scc_tbl[BAUD2OFF] = prm_baud[pcbxx->cxparm[0] + 1];
   }
   if (pcbxx->cxparm[1] != 0xff)
   {
   pcbxx->scc_tbl[PRTY1OFF] &= ~0X03;
   pcbxx->scc_tbl[PRTY1OFF] |= prm_parity[pcbxx->cxparm[1]];
   }
   if (pcbxx->cxparm[2] != 0xff)
   {
   pcbxx->scc_tbl[STOP1OFF] &= ~0X0c;
   pcbxx->scc_tbl[STOP1OFF] |= prm_stop[pcbxx->cxparm[2]];
```

```
    }
    if (pcbxx->cxparm[3] != 0xff)
    {
    pcbxx->scc_tbl[DATA1OFF]  &=  ~0xc0;
    pcbxx->scc_tbl[DATA1OFF]  |=  prm_rxdata[pcbxx->cxparm[3]];
    pcbxx->scc_tbl[DATA2OFF]  &=  ~0xc0;
    pcbxx->scc_tbl[DATA2OFF]  |=  prm_rxdata[pcbxx->cxparm[3]];
    pcbxx->scc_tbl[DATA3OFF]  &=  ~0x60;
    pcbxx->scc_tbl[DATA3OFF]  |=  prm_txdata[pcbxx->cxparm[3]];
    pcbxx->scc_tbl[DATA4OFF]  &=  ~0x60;
    pcbxx->scc_tbl[DATA4OFF]  |=  prm_txdata[pcbxx->cxparm[3]];
    }
}
/* ------------------------------------------------ */
/* This routine is used by software init ISRs     */
/* ------------------------------------------------ */
/*   Routine to set communications parameters       */
/* ------------------------------------------------ */

void set_comm(COMMPTRF cptr)
                    /*& Set comm parm into PCB table */
{
INT i;
XPCBPTRF pcbxptr;
        pcbxptr = cptr->chldstrc + cptr->portnum;
        for (i = 0; i < NUMCOMMPARM; i++)
        {
        if (cptr->commparm[i] != 0xff)
              pcbxptr->cxparm[i] = cptr->commparm[i];
        }
}
/* ------------------------------------------------ */
/* This routine is used by software init ISRs     */
/* ------------------------------------------------ */
/* Routine to initialize a port                    */
/* ------------------------------------------------ */

int chan_init(COMMPTRF cptr)
      /*& Initialize a port used by COMM_TSK only */
{
XPCBPTRF pcbxptr;
 pcbxptr = cptr->chldstrc + cptr->portnum;
 if (!board_init)    /*$ if board not initialized */
 {
 /*$ fill-in RS232 request block */
  pcbxptr->IBMPRBPTR->TXVECT = (VECTOR) pcbxptr->tx_inth;
  pcbxptr->IBMPRBPTR->RXVECT = (VECTOR) pcbxptr->rx_inth;
  pcbxptr->IBMPRBPTR->SCVECT = (VECTOR) pcbxptr->er_inth;
  pcbxptr->IBMPRBPTR->EXVECT = (VECTOR) pcbxptr->st_inth;
  pcbxptr->IBMPRBPTR->TSKNUM = (UCHAR) cptr->taskno;
```

```
    pcbxptr->IBMPRBPTR->RS232NUM = cptr->portnum;
    /*$ allocate port to invoking task (acquire RRB) */
    pcbxptr->badport =
            (UCHAR) svcalloc((char *) pcbxptr->IBMPRBPTR);
    }
    if (!pcbxptr->badport)/*$ if NOT a BAD port */
    {
    /*$ fill-in necessary PCB info (port control block) */
    pcbxptr->ctrlreg = pcbxptr->IBMPRBPTR->SCCB;/*$ ctrl reg*/
    pcbxptr->datareg =
            pcbxptr->IBMPRBPTR->SCCB + 16;/*$ data reg addr */
    cptr->rxtxcode = DO2BUFF;/*$ code to clear both buffers */
    clr_rx4(pcbxptr);          /*$ clear hardware receiver */
    reset_tx(pcbxptr);         /*$ reset comm buffers */
    reset_rx(pcbxptr);         /*$ reset comm buffers */
    sccreg(pcbxptr->IBMPRBPTR->RS232NUM,
                    0,pcbxptr->scc_tbl);/*$ configure SCC */
    }
    return(pcbxptr->badport);
}
/* -------------------------------------------- */
/* This routine is used by COMM_TSK for init      */
/* -------------------------------------------- */
/* Routine to initialize all ports                */
/* -------------------------------------------- */

int initallports(COMMPTRF cptr)
    /*& Initialize ALL ports used by COMM_TSK only */
{
XPCBPTRF pcbxptr;
    pcbxptr = cptr->chldstrc;
    cptr->portnum = 0;/*$ ensure starting at first port */
    for (cptr->portnum = 0; cptr->portnum < MAXPORTS;
                                    (cptr->portnum)++)
            {
            pcbxptr = cptr->chldstrc + cptr->portnum;
            --(pcbxptr->scc_tbl[0]); /*$ decr tbl cnt to
                                    avoid interrupt enable */
            chan_init(cptr);          /*$ initialize a port */
            cptr->rxtxcode= DO2BUFF; /*$ code to clear both buffs*/
            clr_rx4(pcbxptr);         /*$ clear hardware receiver */
            reset_tx(pcbxptr);        /*$ reset comm buffers */
            reset_rx(pcbxptr);        /*$ reset comm buffers */
            ++(pcbxptr->scc_tbl[0]); /*$ restore table count */
            pcbxptr->rx_flags = 0;   /*$ zero all request flags */
            }
    cptr->portnum = 0;/*$ ensure ending with 1st port in tbl*/
    return(0);
}
```

```
/* ----------------------------------------------- */
/* This routine is used by software receive ISRs  */
/* ----------------------------------------------- */
/* Routine to receive characters fm internal buff */
/* ----------------------------------------------- */

int recv_it(COMMPTRF cptr)
                  /*& Place incoming data in buff */
{
UINT i;
XPCBPTRF pcbxptr;
UINT posneg;
                            /*$ get structure addr */
   pcbxptr = cptr->chldstrc + cptr->portnum;
   if (cptr->descnt >= 0)   /*$ desired count positive? */
      posneg = 0;           /*$ set switch flag to positive */
   else                     /*$ desired count is negative    */
      {
      posneg = 1;              /*$ set switch flag to negative */
                               /*$ make desired count positive */
      cptr->descnt = (0 - cptr->descnt);
      }
   switch(posneg)
   {
   case(0): /*$ positive incoming count */
                            /*$ enough char avail?        */
                            /*$ no, return avail char     */
                            /*$ yes, return desired amnt */
         if ((INT) pcbxptr->rx_curcnt < cptr->descnt)
               cptr->retcnt = pcbxptr->rx_curcnt;
         else cptr->retcnt = (UINT) cptr->descnt;
         for (i = 0; i < cptr->retcnt; i++)
               {                /*$ move data into application */
               *(cptr->dataptr) = *(pcbxptr->rx_usrptr);
               ++(pcbxptr->rx_remcnt);/*$ incr cnt not in use */
               --(pcbxptr->rx_curcnt);/*$ decr cnt available */
               ++(cptr->dataptr);     /*$incr destination addr*/
               ++(pcbxptr->rx_usrptr);/*$ incr source addr */
               if    ((ULONG)pcbxptr->rx_usrptr ==
                     (ULONG)(pcbxptr->rxbstart + RXBUFFSIZ))
                        pcbxptr->rx_usrptr = pcbxptr->rxbstart;
               }
      break;
   case(1):    /*$ negative incoming count */
               /*$ enough space? */
               /*$ no, not enough space, no process */
         if (cptr->descnt > (INT) pcbxptr->rx_remcnt)
               {
               cptr->retcode = NOBUFSPACE;
               cptr->retcnt = 0;
               }
```

```
        else
                {
                     /*$ yes,enough space*/
                     /*$ return char to buff */
                cptr->retcnt = (UINT) cptr->descnt;
           for (i = 0; i < cptr->retcnt; i++)
                    {
                --(pcbxptr->rx_usrptr);/*$decr source addr*/
                     /*$ check for buffer wrap */
                if ((ULONG)pcbxptr->rx_usrptr ==
                     (ULONG)(pcbxptr->rxbstart - 1))
                      pcbxptr->rx_usrptr += RXBUFFSIZ;
                *(pcbxptr->rx_usrptr) = *(cptr->dataptr);
                                      /*$ move data      */
                ++(pcbxptr->rx_curcnt);  /*$ incr cnt in use*/
                --(pcbxptr->rx_remcnt);  /*$ decr cnt notuse*/
                --(cptr->dataptr);       /*$ decr dest addr */
                }
            }
    break;
    default:
    break;
    }
    return(cptr->retcode);
}
/* --------------------------------------------- */
/* This routine is used by software transmit ISRs */
/* --------------------------------------------- */
/* Routine to transmit characters fm internal buff*/
/* --------------------------------------------- */

int tx_async(COMMPTRF cptr)
              /*& Place data in buff & begin tx */
{
INT i;
XPCBPTRF pcbxptr;
    pcbxptr = cptr->chldstrc + cptr->portnum;
                          /*$ enough buffer space? */
    if ((TXBUFFSIZ - (INT) pcbxptr->tx_remcnt) < cptr->descnt)
          {
          cptr->retcode = NOBUFSPACE;
          cptr->retcnt = 0;
          }
    else      /*$ move data from application into buffer    */
      {
                            /*$ return desired cnt     */
          cptr->retcnt = (UINT) cptr->descnt;
          for (i = 0; i < cptr->descnt; i++)
            {                    /*$ move data into buffer */
               *(pcbxptr->tx_usrptr) = *(cptr->dataptr);
```

```
                    ++(pcbxptr->tx_remcnt);/*$ incr cnt to xmit */
                    ++(cptr->dataptr);      /*$ incr source addr */
                    ++(pcbxptr->tx_usrptr);/*$ incr dest addr    */
                    if ((ULONG) pcbxptr->tx_usrptr ==
                        (ULONG)(pcbxptr->txbstart + TXBUFFSIZ))
                      pcbxptr->tx_usrptr = pcbxptr->txbstart;
                    } /* FOR end */
                    /*$ start tx if not already transmitting */
            i = inp(pcbxptr->ctrlreg); /*$ read reg 0 */
            if ((i & TXBUFMTY)
            && ((INT) pcbxptr->tx_remcnt == cptr->descnt))
                  /*$ previous tx done & these need send? */
              tx_1_char(pcbxptr);
            } /* else is enough buffer space end */
            return(cptr->retcode);
    }
    /* ------------------------------------------------ */
    /* This routine is used by software transmit ISRs */
    /* ------------------------------------------------ */
    /* Routine to process one port                    */
    /* ------------------------------------------------ */

INT proc1port(COMMPTRF cptr) /*& Process 1 port */
{
UCHAR tmpsw;
XPCBPTRF pcbxptr;
  pcbxptr = cptr->chldstrc + cptr->portnum;
  switch (cptr->operation)
  {
  case (RETNINFO):
        cptr->retcode = 0;/*$ return comm buffers info */
  break;
  case (SENDCHAR):
        cptr->retcode = (UCHAR) tx_async(cptr);
                  /*$ put char(s) to tx comm buffer */
  break;
  case (RECVCHAR):
        cptr->retcode = (UCHAR) recv_it(cptr);
                  /*$ get char(s) from rx comm buffer */
  break;
  case (RESETBUF):
        cptr->retcode = 0;
        switch(cptr->rxtxcode)
        {
        case(DO2BUFF):
              reset_tx(pcbxptr);         /*$ reset tx buffer */
              reset_rx(pcbxptr);         /*$ reset rx buffer */
        break;
        case(DOTXBUFF):
              reset_tx(pcbxptr);         /*$ reset tx buffer */
```

```
        break;
        case(DORXBUFF):
                reset_rx(pcbxptr);           /*$ reset rx buffer */
        break;
                default:
                cptr->retcode = (UCHAR) BADRXTXVAL;
                           /*$ set BAD return code */
        break;
        }
break;
case(SET_DTRX):                              /*$ set for receive */
        cptr->retcode = 0;
        if (cptr->taskno == COMM_TSK) tmpsw =
                        pcbxptr->cxparm[5];
        else                    tmpsw = cptr->commparm[5];
        switch(tmpsw)
        {
        case(HSHAKE0): /*$ no handshaking */
          pcbxptr->rx_flags &= ~FLGFORDTR;
        break;
        default:  /*$ bad handshake code */
                cptr->retcode = BADHSHAKEC;
        break;
        }/* switch end */
        break;
        case(SET_RTSX):   /*$ set for send */
                cptr->retcode = 0;
                if (cptr->taskno == COMM_TSK) tmpsw =
                        pcbxptr->cxparm[5];
                else            tmpsw = cptr->commparm[5];
                switch(tmpsw)
                {
                case(HSHAKE0): /*$ no handshake */
                        pcbxptr->rx_flags &= ~FLGFORRTS;
                break;
                default:   /*$ bad handshake code */
                        cptr->retcode = BADHSHAKEC;
                break;
                }/* switch end */
        break;
        case (RESETPRT):
                if (cptr->taskno == COMM_TSK)
                {
                pcbxptr = cptr->chldstrc + cptr->portnum;
                put_comm(pcbxptr);
                /*$ set new comm parm into init tbl fm PCB tbl */
                if (pcbxptr->rx_flags & FLGFORINTDIS)
                /*$ if init without interrupts requested */
                        --(pcbxptr->scc_tbl[0]);
                /*$ decr scctbl count to skip interrupt enable */
                cptr->retcode = (UCHAR) chan_init(cptr);
```

```
                        /*$ port re-init */
                        if (pcbxptr->rx_flags & FLGFORINTDIS)
                        /*$ if interrupts disabled */
                        {
                                cptr->rxtxcode = DO2BUFF;
                                /*$ set code to clear both buffers */
                                clr_rx4(pcbxptr); /*$ clear hardware rxvr*/
                                reset_tx(pcbxptr);/*$ reset comm buffers */
                                reset_rx(pcbxptr);/*$ reset comm buffers */
                                ++(pcbxptr->scc_tbl[0]);
                                /*$ increment scctbl count to original */
                                } /* if interrupts disabled end */
                        xmitcntl(cptr->portnum,1);/*$ enable transmit */
                        pcbxptr->rx_flags = 0;
                        }
                else
                {
                set_comm(cptr);
                /*$ new communications parm into PCB tbl */
                pcbxptr->rx_flags |= FLGFORRESET;
                /*$ flg reset request */
                /*$ check for init with interrupts disabled */
                if (cptr->cinitx) pcbxptr->rx_flags |= FLGFORINTDIS;
                else              pcbxptr->rx_flags &= ~FLGFORINTDIS;
                cptr->retcode = 0;          /*$ set good code */
                }
        break;
        default:
                cptr->retcode = (UCHAR) BADREQUEST;
        break;
        } /* switch end */
        return(cptr->retcode);
}
```

APPLICATION PROGRAMMER'S INTERFACE (API)

```
/* MODULE PATH: \RS232\INTERFCN.H
   Function declarations for INTERSFT.C
*/
/* =======================================================
   These functions provide a transparent user interface to
   communications via software ISR.
   =======================================================

ALL of these functions use the services of the COMM_TSK
module via a software interrupt vector which points to the
FAR interrupt handler sft_isr() which is physically
```

located in the COMM_TSK module. ALL port services provided
for the user are via this ISR.

Odd vector numbers from 0x21 thru 0x5d (spaced by 4) are
reserved for use by iterations of this module. This module
should only be linked with tasks that service ports
(IE application-specific tasks and the COMM_TSK).
*/

```
/* ================================================ */
COMMPTR get_cptronly(void);
/*& Return pointer to COMMINFO without init        */
/* ================================================ */
/*
```
This function will return the FAR address of the COMMINFO
structure which is used to communicate information to and
from the COMM_TSK module. This function is available in
the event that a user function needs to obtain this
address in a function other than the function that called
get_cptrinit(). This function can be safely used AFTER a
call has been made to get_cptrinit() which initializes the
structure and allocates the software services' VECTOR
REQUEST BLOCK.
*/

```
/* ====================================== */
COMMPTR get_cptrinit(struct cbptr *ptrcb);
/*& Init COMMINFO & return pointer        */
/* ====================================== */
/*
```
This function should be called BEFORE any other function
that utilizes the port. It initializes the COMMINFO
structure which is used to communicate with the COMM_TSK
module and returns a FAR pointer to this structure. It
also allocates a VECTOR REQUEST BLOCK AND a ONE-SHOT
SOFTWARE TIMER for use by the invoking task. All of this
is transparent to the user. The argument supplied by the
user is a pointer to an IBM-defined structure that contains
pointers to various resource information pertinent to this
task (see IBM sample code for details). After the initial
call, this function can be called at any time to re-initialize
parts of the COMMINFO structure (overwrite anything the
user has supplied); these subsequent calls will not
re-allocate resources.
*/

```
/* ==================================================== */
UINT resetport(UINT prmbaud, UINT prmparity,
               UINT prmstop,UINT prmdata, UINT prm232422,
               UINT prmhshake);
               /*& Reset port communications parameters */
```

```
/* ========================================================== */
/*
This function should be called AFTER get_ptrinit() and
BEFORE any other function that utilizes the port.  It
initializes the port assigned to this task using
information supplied by the user and information
transparent to the user (which is contained in the
COMMINFO sturcture). Valid arguments for the
communications parameters supplied by the user are:
```

prmbaud	prmparity	prmstop	prmdata
0 = 110	0 = none	0 = 1 bit	0 = 5 bits
2 = 300	1 = odd	1 = 2 bits	1 = 6 bits
4 = 600	2 = even	2 = 1.5 bits	2 = 7 bits
6 = 1200			3 = 8 bits
8 = 2400			
10 = 4800			
12 = 9600			
14 = 19200			

```
prm232422                       prmhshake
0 = RS232                       0 = none
1 = RS422 (not currently supported)
```

```
The ISR attempts to initialize the port with the data
supplied. Little validation of data is performed. It is
the user's responsibility to ensure correct parameters.
Invalid data produces unpredictable results.
*/
```

```
/* ================================================= */
UINT rxtxrequest(UCHAR requestcode,UCHAR far *dataddr,
              INT descnt);/*& Perform tx or rx     */
/* ================================================= */
/*
This function performs both transmit and receive functions
for an application task.  Before it is used, the task
should have issued a get_cptrinit() followed by a
resetport(). Valid arguments for the "requestcode" argument
are SENDCHAR (to transmit) and RECVCHAR (to receive). These
values are defined in SFTSCC.H which should be INCLUDEd in
the program.
Non-zero return codes indicate failure.
```

```
For the "dataddr" argument, the application program must
supply a FAR pointer to its data area.
```

NOTE:
(If you are not using the LARGE memory model to compile
the application task, you may need to cast the address to
a far pointer. You CAN cast a NEAR pointer to a FAR
pointer because the segment value is added and the address
integrity is maintained.)

The "descnt" argument is the desired count to transmit or
receive. It should be > 0 and <= TXBUFFSIZ or RXBUFFSIZ, as
appropriate. These values are defined in JFBIXX.H which
should be INCLUDEd in the program BEFORE SFTSCC.H.
(SFTSCC.H definitions are dependent on JFBIXX.)

If "descnt" contains a positive value:

If the requestcode is SENDCHAR, the "descnt" number of
characters will be placed in the transmit buffer and
transmission will begin. At entry, if there is not enough
buffer space for ALL characters, none will be transmitted.
A non-zero code is returned in the event of failure or
no characters being transmitted. The characters are
moved from the "dataddr" address specified to the
transmit buffer (the "dataddr" value is incremented
to obtain subsequent characters).

If the requestcode is RECVCHAR, the "descnt" number of
characters will be fetched from the receive buffer
into the starting address specified in "dataddr" (this
address is incremented for subsequent characters).
In the event that fewer characters are available than
the "descnt" number requested, all available characters
will be fetched and a good return code will be returned.
The user must check the global value "xxcntretn" to
determine the actual number of characters obtained.

If "descnt" contains a negative value:
If the requestcode is SENDCHAR, the operation will fail.
If the requestcode is RECVCHAR, the (0-descnt) number of
characters will be returned to the receive buffer
if the receive buffer has enough room for ALL characters.
In this case, the dataddr must point to the LAST character
being returned to the buffer. (This addr is decremented
to get subsequent characters.)
*/
/* ================================ */
UINT resetcombufs(UCHAR buffercode);
/*& Reset communications buffer(s)   */
/* ================================ */
/*
This function resets the communication buffer indicated

in "buffercode." A reset means zeroing all buffer
management areas and the buffers themselves. Pointers are
appropriately re-initialized also.

This function might be used prior to invoking resetport()
in the event of a persistent communications failure. In
other words, clear the buffers and counts and retry the
communications. The functions performed by this function
are also performed transparently when invoking resetport().

Valid entries for "buffercode" are defined in SFTSCC.H
and are:
      DOTXBUFF to reset the transmit buffer only
      DORXBUFF to reset the receive buffer only
      DO2BUFF to reset both transmit & receive buffers
*/
/* === */
UINT getcomminfo(void);/*& Fill COMMINFO & data for user */
/* === */
/*
This function fills the latest information available in the
communications area into seven global variables available
for inspection by the user. This information is
automatically supplied after EVERY call that uses the
COMM_TSK services (all the functions herein except for
"get_ptronly()" and "xxpause()").
This function allows obtaining the available information
without performing any other service.

The seven global variables available to the user are:

          xxcntretn = actual character count performed in
          this receive/transmit call
          txwaiting = count of characters in transmit buffer
          that are awaiting transmission.
          rxavailbl = count of characters in receive buffer
          that are available to user.
          txerrorch = count of errors in the transmit buffer
          since last reset.
          rxerrorch = count of errors in the receive buffer
          since last reset.
          txerrcode = error code(s) of current transmit errors
          (since last reset).
          rxerrcode = error code(s) of current receive errors
          (since last reset).
*/
/* ==================================== */
void getisradr(void);/*& Get adr of ISR */
/* ==================================== */

```c
/* MODULE PATH: \RS232\INTERSFT.C
   Software Interrupt Interface to Communications
*/
/*
  To ease the task-switching burden by the RCM & to
  enhance performance under RCM, this module assigns
  a unique vector to the software ISR for each task
  using this module's services. All vectors point to
  the same routine.  Nine vectors are reserved for this
  module for the software ISR.

  This module uses a one-shot software timer (oneshot.c).
  The software timer number reserved corresponds directly
  to the task number as known to the RCM.

  This module is designed to be supplied as object-code-
  only to users. It requires ONESHOT.OBJ also.

  Minimal error checking is performed. It is the user's
  responsibility to provide correct arguments to
  available routines.
*/
#include <icadeclt.h>
                /* IBM RIC (Realtime Interface Coprocessor)
                   C language support header */
#include <jfbixx.h>
#include <sftscc.h>
#include <sfcndecs.h>
#include <scc.h>
#include <dos.h>
#include <interfcn.h>/* Global fcn declaration this module */
#include <rxflags.h>
#include <oneshot.h>

static void retonevector(COMMPTR cptr,struct cbptr *ptrcb);

/*----------------------------*/
/* GLOBAL DATA for this module */
/*(Data known to user programs)*/
/*----------------------------*/
/* IBM-defined structure for VRB Vector Request Block
   one per task -- vector for communications services */
struct vrbstruct sftvrb =
        {
        0,0,1,COMMVECTOR,COMM_TSK,0,NULL,NULL,NULL,{0}
        };

/*
```

```
        These areas are updated with EACH call to the software
        ISR (always contains the latest info from the comm
        buffer management code).
*/

UINT xxcntretn;/* actual character count of operation */
UINT txwaiting;/* count awaiting transmission */
UINT rxavailbl;/* count available in receive buffer */
UINT txerrorch;/* count in error in transmit buffer */
UINT rxerrorch;/* count in error in receive buffer */
UINT txerrcode;/* error code in transmit buffer */
UINT rxerrcode;/* error code in receive buffer */

VECTOR cvecthold = NULL; /* buckets to hold needed addresses
                            - do not separate */
XPCBPTRF cvecth2ld = NULL;

/*----------------------------*/
/* STATIC DATA for this module */
/* (hidden from user)          */
/*----------------------------*/

/* Structure for comm interface */
static COMMINFO comminit =
        {
        COMM_TSK,NULL,{0xff},0,0,0,0,0,0,0,0,0,0,0,
        DO2BUFF,0,&sftvrb,0,1
        };

static union REGS xxregs;       /* regs for interrupts */

/* -------------------- */
/* Return needed vectors */
/* -------------------- */
static void retonevector(COMMPTR cptr,struct cbptr *ptrcb)
{
UINT far *tskseg;
struct thstruct far *tmp;
UINT segiwant;
VECTOR *xyz;
XPCBPTRF *zzz;
                /*$ GET task table pointer */
        tskseg = (UINT far *) ptrcb->IBPTR->TSKTABPTR;
                /*$ GET specific task in task table */
        tskseg += COMM_TSK;
                /*$ GET specific task segment */
        segiwant = *tskseg;
                /*$ GET specific task header addr */
        tmp = (struct thstruct far *)
                        ((((ULONG) segiwant) << 16) | 0);
```

```
                    /*$ GET offset of VECTHOLD from task header */
          segiwant = tmp->EXTOFF;
                    /*$ MAKE total addr of VECTHOLD */
          xyz = (VECTOR *) (((UCHAR *) tmp) + segiwant);
                 /*$ Contents of VECTHOLD becomes NEWVECT into VRB */
          cptr->vrbsftptr->NEWVECT = *xyz;
                    /*$ GET consecutive addr of VECTH2LD */
          zzz = (XPCBPTRF *)
                    (((UCHAR *) tmp) + segiwant + (sizeof(VECTOR)));
                    /*$ Contents of VECTH2LD becomes some
                                        desired struct addr */
          cptr->chldstrc = *zzz;
}
/*-----------------------------*/
/* static function declarations */
/*-----------------------------*/
static void docommrequest(UCHAR requestcode);
static void initcomminfo(COMMPTR cptr,struct cbptr *ptrcb);
static UINT waitforportreset(COMMPTR cptr);


/*-------------------------------------*/
/* Routine to perform user request     */
/*-------------------------------------*/
static void docommrequest(UCHAR requestcode)
{
COMMPTR  cptr;
COMMPTRF fcptr;
  cptr = &comminit;
  fcptr = (COMMPTRF) cptr;
  xxregs.x.ax = (cptr->taskno << 8);
        /*$ SET UP for interrupt */
  xxregs.x.dx = (UINT) (((((ULONG) fcptr)&0xffff0000l)>>16);
  xxregs.x.cx = (UINT) (((ULONG) fcptr) & 0x0000ffffl);
  cptr->operation = requestcode;
  cptr->retcode = 0;
  cptr->retcnt =  0;

  switch(requestcode)  /*$ VALIDATE request type */
    {
        case(SENDCHAR):
        case(RECVCHAR):
        case(RESETBUF):
        case(RETNINFO):
        case(RESETPRT):
        case(SET_DTRX):
        case(SET_RTSX):
                int86(cptr->vrbsftptr->VECTNUM,&xxregs,&xxregs);
                                    /*$ PERFORM request */
        break;
        default:
```

```
                              cptr->retcode = BADREQUEST; /* bad request code */
                break;
                } /* switch end */

        xxcntretn = cptr->retcnt;/*$ RETURN all available info */
        txwaiting = cptr->rettxcnt;
        rxavailbl = cptr->retrxcnt;
        txerrorch = cptr->errtxcnt;
        rxerrorch = cptr->errrxcnt;
        txerrcode = cptr->txcode;
        rxerrcode = cptr->rxcode;
    }
/*------------------------------------*/
/* Routine to init COMMINFO structure  */
/*------------------------------------*/
static void initcomminfo(COMMPTR cptr,struct cbptr *ptrcb)
/* arg0 = pointer COMMINFO structure */
/* arg1 = pointer to struct containing task pointers */
{
    cptr->retcode = 0;

    cptr->taskno = ptrcb->TCBPTR->TSKN;
    if (!cptr->cinitf) /*$ If COMMINFO init NOT done,
                            prevents second allocation */
            {
            if (cptr->taskno == COMM_TSK)
                    {
                    cptr->vrbsftptr->TSKNUM = COMM_TSK;
                    cptr->vrbsftptr->VECTNUM = COMMVECTOR;
                    cptr->vrbsftptr->NEWVECT = cvecthold;
                    cptr->chldstrc = cvecth2ld;
                    ptrcb->THEADPTR->EXTOFF=(UINT)&cvecthold;
                    cptr->portnum = 0;
                    }
            else
                    {
                    cptr->vrbsftptr->TSKNUM = (UCHAR) cptr->taskno;
                        /*$ GET vector number into VRB (calc) */
                    cptr->vrbsftptr->VECTNUM =(UCHAR)
                    (((cptr->taskno - FRSTSKNUM) * VSPACE)
                            + COMMVECTOR + VSPACE);
                    cptr->portnum=(UCHAR)(cptr->taskno - FRSTSKNUM);
                    retonevector(cptr,ptrcb);
                    }
                    /*$ SET taskno into TRB timer number */
            timrb.TIMNUM = (UCHAR) cptr->taskno;
                    /*$ SET taskno into TRB task number  */
            timrb.TSKNUM = (UCHAR) cptr->taskno;
                    /*$ ALLOCATE services vector RRB for RCM */
            svcalloc((char *) cptr->vrbsftptr);
```

```
                svcalloc((char *) &timrb);/*$ ALLOCATE software timer */
                cptr->cinitf = 1;           /*$ SET INIT DONE flag      */
                }
        cptr->commparm[0] = 0xff; /*$ SET comm parm for NO CHANGE */
        cptr->commparm[1] = 0xff;
        cptr->commparm[2] = 0xff;
        cptr->commparm[3] = 0xff;
        cptr->commparm[4] = 0;
        cptr->commparm[5] = 0;
        cptr->dataptr = NULL;   /*$ ZERO misc data areas */
        cptr->descnt = 0;
        cptr->rettxcnt = 0;
        cptr->retrxcnt = 0;
        cptr->errtxcnt = 0;
        cptr->errrxcnt = 0;
        cptr->txcode = 0;
        cptr->rxcode = 0;
        cptr->rxtxcode = DO2BUFF;/*$ SET to clear both buffers */
        docommrequest(RETNINFO);
}
/*-------------------------------------*/
/* Routine to wait til RESET in process */
/*-------------------------------------*/
static UINT waitforportreset(COMMPTR cptr)
{
        docommrequest(RESETPRT);/*$ ASK COMMTSK to reset port */
        if (!cptr->retcode)      /*$ If request was OK        */
             {
               docommrequest(RETNINFO);/*$ ENSURE request DONE  */
               if (cptr->retreqst & FLGFORRESET)
                     {
                                     /*$If request NOT done  */
                     posti((UCHAR)cptr->taskno,0x20);
                     svcasap();      /*$ GIVE a little time  */
                                     /*$ ENSURE request done */
                     docommrequest(RETNINFO);
                     }
                              /*$ If not DONE, set BAD code */
             if (cptr->retreqst & FLGFORRESET)
                              cptr->retcode = RESETIMOUT;
             }
     return(cptr->retcode);
}
/*-------------------------------*/
/* GLOBAL ROUTINES for this module */
/* (Available to user)          */
/* See INTERFCN.H for details    */
/*-------------------------------*/
```

```
/*-------------------------------------------*/
/* Routine to return COMMINFO structure addr */
/*-------------------------------------------*/
COMMPTR get_cptronly(void)
 /*& RETURN pointer to COMMINFO without INIT */
{
COMMPTR cptr;
        cptr = &comminit;
        return(cptr);
}
/*-------------------------------------------*/
/* Routine to return COMMINFO structure addr */
/* and to initialize all structure info      */
/*-------------------------------------------*/
COMMPTR get_cptrinit(struct cbptr *ptrcb)
        /*& INIT COMMINFO & return pointer */
{
COMMPTR cptr;
        cptr = &comminit;
        initcomminfo(cptr,ptrcb);
        return(cptr);
}
/*-----------------------------------*/
/* Routine to init communications parm */
/*-----------------------------------*/
UINT resetport(UINT prmbaud, UINT prmparity,
               UINT prmstop, UINT prmdata,
               UINT prm232422, UINT prmhshake)
               /*& RESET communications parameters for port */
{
COMMPTR cptr;
        cptr = &comminit;
        cptr->retcode = 0;
        switch(cptr->taskno)
        {
        case(COMM_TSK):
                cptr->commparm[0] = (UCHAR) 0xff;
                cptr->commparm[1] = (UCHAR) 0xff;
                cptr->commparm[2] = (UCHAR) 0xff;
                cptr->commparm[3] = (UCHAR) 0xff;
                cptr->commparm[4] = (UCHAR) 0;/* rs232 */
                cptr->commparm[5] = (UCHAR) 0;/* no handshake */
                docommrequest(RESETPRT);
        break;
        default:
          if (((prmbaud < 15)  &&
            (!(prmbaud % 2)) ) || (prmbaud == (UCHAR) 0xff))
                cptr->commparm[0] = (UCHAR) prmbaud;
          else
                {
```

```
                        cptr->commparm[0] = (UCHAR) 0xff;
                        cptr->retcode = BADCOMMPRM;
                        }
                if ((prmparity < 3) || (prmparity==(UCHAR) 0xff))
                     cptr->commparm[1] = (UCHAR) prmparity;
                else
                        {
                        cptr->commparm[1] = (UCHAR) 0xff;
                        cptr->retcode = BADCOMMPRM;
                        }
                if ((prmstop < 3) || (prmstop == (UCHAR) 0xff))
                        cptr->commparm[2] = (UCHAR) prmstop;
                else
                        {
                        cptr->commparm[2] = (UCHAR) 0xff;
                        cptr->retcode = BADCOMMPRM;
                        }
                if ((prmdata < 4) || (prmdata == (UCHAR) 0xff))
                        cptr->commparm[3] = (UCHAR) prmdata;
                else
                        {
                        cptr->commparm[3] = (UCHAR) 0xff;
                        cptr->retcode = BADCOMMPRM;
                        }
                        cptr->commparm[4] = (UCHAR) prm232422;
                        cptr->commparm[5] = (UCHAR) prmhshake;
                if (!cptr->retcode)
                        cptr->retcode = (UCHAR) waitforportreset(cptr);
            break;
            }/* switch end */
            return(cptr->retcode);

}

/*----------------------------------------------------------*/
/* Routine to perform transmit or rx requests by user */
/*----------------------------------------------------------*/
UINT rxtxrequest(UCHAR requestcode, UCHAR far *dataaddr,
                 INT descnt)/*& PERFORM tx or rx */
{
COMMPTR cptr;
   cptr = &comminit;
   cptr->retcode = 0;
   cptr->dataptr = dataaddr;/*$ SET data addr in user pgm    */
   cptr->descnt = descnt;  /*$ SET user desired count       */

   switch(requestcode)/*$ VALIDATE counts and requestcode   */
           {
           case(SENDCHAR):
```

```
                    if ((descnt < 1) || (descnt > TXBUFFSIZ))
                        cptr->retcode = BADXXCOUNT;/* bad cnt tx   */
            break;
            case(RECVCHAR):
                if((descnt < -RXBUFFSIZ) || (descnt > RXBUFFSIZ))
                        cptr->retcode = BADXXCOUNT;/* bad count rx   */
            break;
            default:
                cptr->retcode = BADREQUEST;/* bad request code   */
            break;
            } /* switch end */
                                        /*$ PERFORM user request   */
        if (!cptr->retcode) docommrequest(requestcode);

        return(cptr->retcode);
    }
    /*----------------------------------------------------------*/
    /* Routine to perform communications buffer reset request*/
    /*----------------------------------------------------------*/
    UINT resetcombufs(UCHAR buffercode)
                        /*& RESET communications buffer(s) */
    {
    COMMPTR cptr;
            cptr = &comminit;
            cptr->rxtxcode = buffercode;   /*$ SET buffer code */
            docommrequest(RESETBUF); /*$ PERFORM user request */
            return(cptr->retcode);
    }
    /*------------------------------------------------*/
    /* Routine to get comm buffer information only   */
    /*------------------------------------------------*/
    UINT getcomminfo(void)/*& FILL COMMINFO and data for user */
    {
    COMMPTR cptr;
            cptr = &comminit;
            docommrequest(RETNINFO);/*$ PERFORM user request */
            return(cptr->retcode);
    }
```

ONE-SHOT SOFTWARE TIMER

```
    /* MODULE PATH \RS232\ONESHOT.H
       Externs for modules using ONESHOT.C (timer)
    */
    void far timeret(void); /* ISR for timer return */

    /* IBM-defined structure for TRB
       Timer Request Block -- one per task
    */
```

```
extern struct trbstruct timrb;

/* ==================================== */
void xxpause(UINT duration,UCHAR taskn);
/*& pause in increments of 5ms */
/* ==================================== */
/*
This function is defined in ONESHOT.C.
This fcn should be used AFTER the call to get_cptrinit().
This fcn will pause for the specified "duration" # of 5ms
intervals (IE duration = 1 means pause 5ms,
duration = 2 means pause 10ms, etc).
Fcn uses "one-shot" software timer transparent to the user.
The resources required for timer usage are allocated by
get_cptrinit(). */

/* ONESHOT.C -- One-shot software timer */
/*
   This module is necessary when using INTERSFT.C
   (the API for the COMM_TSK).
   This module provides a one-shot software timer
   for pausing in increments of 5ms.
   This module is designed to be supplied as object-code-
   only to users.
*/
#include <icadeclt.h>
                /* IBM RIC (Realtime Interface Coprocessor)
                        C language support header */
#include <jfbixx.h>
#include <sftscc.h>
#include <interfcn.h>/* global fcns this module */

void far timeret(void); /* ISR fcn declaration */

/*----------------------------*/
/* GLOBAL DATA for this module */
/*----------------------------*/

/* IBM-defined structure for TRB
   Timer Request Block -- one per task */
struct trbstruct timrb =
        {
        0,0,7,COMM_TSK,COMM_TSK,0
        };

/*-------------------------------------*/
/* Routine to pause for awhile         */
/* duration is increments of 5ms       */
/*-------------------------------------*/
void xxpause(UINT duration,UCHAR taskno)
```

```
{
                            /*$ SET timer to pause per specs */
        svctimer(taskno,duration,timeret);
        /*$ While waiting, GIVE another task a chance */
        svcsspnd(taskno);
}


/*-------------------------------*/
/* Routine for timer return      */
/*-------------------------------*/

void far timeret(void)
{
        int_ntry();                 /*$ SAVE machine state     */
        resumei(timrb.TSKNUM);      /*$ PUT task on dispatch que */
        int_exit();                 /*$ RESTORE machine state */
}
```

MAKE FILE FOR MSC 5.1

```
# MODULE PATH: \RS232\CTSK.MAK
# (Makefile for COMM_TSK under MSC 5.1)
# All modules are compiled with PACKED structures
# on 1-byte boundaries
# (this is an IBM requirement for most request blocks
# and resource blocks).
# The following modules are compiled without
# optimization or stack checking
# (they contain ISRs that cannot use stack checking
# or optimizations).
# Assumes ARTIC directory exists.

cc=cl /AL /c /Od /G1 /I\msc\include
                        /I\RS232 /I\artic\h /Zp /W3 /Gs

C:\RS232\ISRRX.obj:   C:\RS232\ISRRX.c   C:\RS232\JFBIXX.h
    $(cc) $*.c

C:\RS232\ISRTX.obj:   C:\RS232\ISRTX.c   C:\RS232\JFBIXX.h
    $(cc) $*.c

C:\RS232\ISRSP.obj:   C:\RS232\ISRSP.c   C:\RS232\JFBIXX.h
    $(cc) $*.c

C:\RS232\ISREX.obj:   C:\RS232\ISREX.c   C:\RS232\JFBIXX.h
    $(cc) $*.c

C:\RS232\ISRSFT.obj:  C:\RS232\ISRSFT.c  C:\RS232\JFBIXX.h
```

```
        $(cc) $*.c


# The following modules are compiled with default
# optimization & stack checking.

cc=cl /AL /c /G1 /I\msc\include /I\RS232 /I\artic\h /Zp /W3

C:\RS232\ONESHOT.obj:  C:\RS232\ONESHOT.c   C:\RS232\JFBIXX.h
        $(cc) $*.c

C:\RS232\COMMDAT.obj:  C:\RS232\COMMDAT.c   C:\RS232\JFBIXX.h
        $(cc) $*.c

C:\RS232\SCCINIT.obj:  C:\RS232\SCCINIT.c   C:\RS232\JFBIXX.h
        $(cc) $*.c

C:\RS232\HDWISR.obj:   C:\RS232\HDWISR.c    C:\RS232\JFBIXX.h
        $(cc) $*.c

C:\RS232\SFTISR.obj:   C:\RS232\SFTISR.c    C:\RS232\JFBIXX.h
        $(cc) $*.c

C:\RS232\INTERSFT.obj  C:\RS232\INTERSFT.c  C:\RS232\JFBIXX.h
        $(cc) $*.c

# COMMTSK is created here by name

C:\RS232\COMMTSK.exe:  C:\artic\obj\icaheadc.obj\
                C:\RS232\SCCINIT.obj\
                C:\RS232\ISRSFT.obj\
                C:\RS232\ONESHOT.obj\
                C:\RS232\COMMDAT.obj\
                C:\RS232\SFTISR.obj\
                C:\RS232\INTERSFT.obj\
                C:\RS232\HDWISR.obj\
                C:\RS232\ISREX.obj\
                C:\RS232\ISRSP.obj\
                C:\RS232\ISRTX.obj\
                C:\RS232\ISRRX.obj
                \msc\bin\Link /NOD/M (at)C:\RS232\CTSK.LNK

# MODULE PATH: \RS232\CTSK.LNK
C:\ARTIC\OBJ\ICAHEADC.obj+
C:\RS232\SCCINIT.obj+
C:\RS232\COMMDAT.obj+
C:\RS232\ISRSFT.obj+
C:\RS232\ONESHOT.obj+
C:\RS232\SFTISR.obj+
C:\RS232\INTERSFT.obj+
```

```
C:\RS232\HDWISR.obj+
C:\RS232\ISREX.obj+
C:\RS232\ISRSP.obj+
C:\RS232\ISRTX.obj+
C:\RS232\ISRRX.obj
C:\RS232\COMMTSK
/map
C:\ARTIC\LIB\icatskl+
C:\ARTIC\LIB\icams51+
C:\MSC\LIB\llibce
```

APPENDIX G

Zilog 8530 SCC Driver in Intel Assembly

The purpose of this appendix is to provide an Intel assembly example of communications code that makes effective use of ISRs in both inter-process and background communications. This example is directly comparable to the C code in Appendix F.

The code contained in this appendix was originally written as a communications driver for an STD bus box that used a Pro-Log Corporation (Monterey, CA) 7863 Multimaster CPU/Communications board that contained an Intel 8088 CPU and a single Zilog 8530 SCC. The code is intended to be bound together with other modules in creating an embedded system for the target hardware; however it can be compiled as a separate object module. It is readily adaptable to other boards and environments that use Zilog 8530 SCCs whether or not the system is embedded. A number of companies are currently manufacturing lines of communications boards that use Zilog 8530 SCCs, and the code contained herein is readily adaptable to those boards. Only channel A of the two 8530 channels is used in the example code; however, a channel B configuration is shown, but commented out.

USER DOCUMENTATION

```
;MODULE PATH: \ASM232\P7863.DOC
;
;The code can be compiled and converted to a .BIN format after
;binding with other modules as appropriate. Using an EPROM
;burner that accepts the .BIN format, the code can be placed
;into EPROM.
```

```
;
;Read ISRHDR.ASM & IMHDR.ASM respectively. These two text files
;contain more-than-adequate documentation for use of the driver
;by anyone familiar with Intel assembly language and the 7863
;board.
;
;The driver can be modified for specific applications:
;
; 1. It is supplied with the data segment at 7bf0 absolute.
;    To modify the data segment location, change the 'data
;    segment at 7bfh' statement in the 1st line of DATASEG.ASM.
;    (The program location is determined by 'segment fix-ups' of
;    the EXE2BIN program.)
;
; 2. Issuing the software interrupt type 14h with ah=0 (SCC
;    INIT) automatically sets hardware interrupts.  The driver
;    sets hardware interrupts into the vector table beginning at
;    interrupt type 0e0h (0000:(4*e0h)) and uses 84 consecutive
;    bytes.  If you want to change the beginning location of the
;    hardware interrupts, change only the 'INT_VECT EQU 0e0h'
;    statement of EQU7863.ASM.  (It is the user program's
;    responsibility to set the software interrupt type to the
;    offset/segment of ISR_MAIN (same segment that is set in
;    EXE2BIN, offset 0).  Interrupt type 14h is used for the
;    software interrupt for IBM compatibility (0000:(4*14h)).
;
; 3. After making the above changes as desired, put all *.ASM
;    files in the same directory and assemble, link, and use
;    EXE2BIN. The resulting .BIN file is ROMable code.
;
; 4. The driver supports multiple ports in polled mode if the
;    user expands the 'ncom_prt' table of DATASEG.ASM. If
;    multiple ports are in use, dx MUST contain the correct port
;    number (0..n -- corresponding to ncom_prt table) for ALL
;    software interrupt requests.  (Port zero is used for invalid
;    numbers and valid incorrect numbers will give unpredictable
;    results.)
;
; 5. The 'get status' (ah=3) interrupt returns ALL status
;    bits and many will not apply in polled mode.  AH should be
;    'AND-ED' with 01h to remove undesired bits -- AL 'AND-ED'
;    with 05h.  AL bit 0 and AL bit 2 give 'receive char
;    available' and 'transmit buffer empty' respectively.
;
;    'Normal use' in interrupt mode would look something like
;    this:
;
;    SET SOFTWARE INTERRUPT (0000:(type*4)) to
;    (DRIVER SEGMENT:0000).
;
```

```
;      INITIALIZATION (see IMHDR.ASM):
;      Issue ah=5 interrupt with al=1 to select interrupt mode.
;      Issue ah=0 interrupt with al=E3h for 9600baud, no parity, 1
;          stop, 8 bits/ch.
;      This will automatically set hardware interrupts at
;                  (0000:(INT_VECT*4)) for 84 bytes.
;
;      SEND/RECEIVE: Using ah=1 and ah=2 respectively
;                  (see IMHDR.ASM).
;
;
;Allow 2K in ROM for your driver (it currently takes 1930
;bytes in .BIN format).  Allow 600 bytes in RAM for the data
;area
;(address as specified in SEGMENT AT ???? statement in
;DATASEG.ASM). The data area requires 547 bytes minimum at
;present (including 2 256-byte buffers for receive/transmit).
;


; MODULE PATH: \ASM232\ISRHDR.ASM
;;;;;;;;;;;;;;;;;;;;;;;;;;;;;;;;;;;;;;;;;;;;;;;;;;;;;;;;;;;;;;;
; INTERRUPT SERVICE ROUTINES for Prolog 7863 CPU/COMM
; board RS232 COMM I/O
;
;  These routines provide a user interface for RS232
;  communications IO for the above board.  The interface
;  is compatible with IBM BIOS interrupt 14h with some
;  exceptions:
;
; 1. error codes do not have identical meanings.
;
; 2. al is not preserved on a send char (ah = 1) request.
;
; 3. When operating in interrupt mode (sending or
;    receiving), the status returned in ah pertains to all
;    characters in the internal buffer and may not pertain
;    to the specific character(s) in process.  Any character
;    in error in the internal buffer will cause an error
;    return in ah.  The error status is reset when the buffer
;    is empty or after an ah=3 status request.
;
; 4. RS232_BASE & RS232_TIM_OUT data areas are not used.
;
; 5. Registers ax, dx, & cx are modified by the main routine.
;    (IBM BIOS modifies only ax.)
;
; 6. Call (ah = 4) is added to provide character count of
;    the internal receive and transmit buffers.
;
```

```
; 7. Call (ah = 5) is added to provide switching between
;    polled & interrupt-driven modes of operation.
;
;;;;;;;;;;;;;;;;;;;;;;;;;;;;;;;;;;;;;;;;;;;;;;;;;;;;;;;;;;;;;;
; BASIC OPERATION:
;
; 1. The (ah = 5) routine sets a 'mode flag' in memory and
;    requires a valid flag value in al at entry.
;    It always initializes the SCC with the default values
;    and with interrupts disabled.  It is mandatory that this
;    request be followed by an init (ah = 0) request for the
;    following:
;
;   a) Any request for interrupt mode (interrupts are
;      enabled by ah = 0).
;   b) Any polled mode request if other than the default
;      comm parameters (ah = 5 always sets default comm parm).
;
; 2. The (ah = 0) init request requires the same parameters
;    in al as IBM BIOS; however, the operation mode flag
;    previously set is used to determine polled or interrupt
;    mode during initialization. If the first call to this
;    routine has not been preceded by an (ah=5) mode request,
;    a default mode of POLLED is used with the communications
;    parameters contained in al, PROVIDED THAT MEMORY GARBAGE
;    IN THE OP-MODE LOCATION DOES NOT EQUAL THE INTERRUPT
;    DRIVEN VALUE. In other words the initial mode of
;    operation may be unpredictable if an ah = 5 request
;    is not the first request of interrupt 14h.
;
; 3. Polled mode simply gets/puts one character to/from the
;    appropriate data port.
;
; 4. In interrupt mode, send and receive Interrupt Service
;    Routines (I_A_XMT and I_A_REC respectively) read/write
;    to/from two internal 255-byte buffers.  For this reason,
;    error codes returned during character get/put to/from
;    these buffers may not pertain to the specific
;    character(s) in transit.  One character in error in the
;    given buffer will set the buffer error code.
;
; 6. INTERRUPT SERVICE ROUTINES PROVIDED:
;
;    ISR_MAIN = SOFTWARE Primary ISR (IBM 14h compatible).
;    I_A_REC  = HARDWARE Receiver ISR.
;    I_A_XMT  = HARDWARE Transmitter ISR.
;    ISR_SP_A = HARDWARE Receiver error ISR.
;    DMMY_A   = HARDWARE Dummy channel 'a' ISR.
;    DMMY_B   = HARDWARE Dummy channel 'b' ISR.
```

HEADERS

```
;MODULE PATH: \ASM232\EQUBIOS.ASM
;;;;;;;::::::::::::::::::::::::::::::::::::::::::::::::::;;;;
; EQUATES for IBM BIOS int 14h
;;;;;;;::::::::::::::::::::::::::::::::::::::::::::::::::;;;;
;
; masks for baud rate requests in al (ah=0)
;
BAUD110    EQU   000h         ;0000 0000   110 baud request
BAUD150    EQU   020h         ;0010 0000   150 baud request
BAUD300    EQU   040h         ;0100 0000   300 baud request
BAUD600    EQU   060h         ;0110 0000   600 baud request
BAUD1200   EQU   080h         ;1000 0000   1200 baud request
BAUD2400   EQU   0A0h         ;1010 0000   2400 baud request
BAUD4800   EQU   0C0h         ;1100 0000   4800 baud request
BAUD9600   EQU   0E0h         ;1110 0000   9600 baud request
;
; masks for parity requests in al (ah=0)
;
PARNONE    EQU   000h         ;0000 0000   no parity
PARODDD    EQU   008h         ;0000 1000   odd parity
PAREVEN    EQU   018h         ;0001 1000   even parity
;
; masks for stop bits in al (ah=0)
;
STOPONE    EQU   000h         ;0000 0000   one stop bit
STOPTWO    EQU   004h         ;0000 0100   two stop bits
;
; masks for word length in al (ah=0)
;
WORD7      EQU   002h         ;0000 0010   7 bits
WORD8      EQU   003h         ;0000 0011   8 bits
;
; masks for CPU port
;
CPUPORT1   EQU   000h         ;0000 0000   COM1
CPUPORT2   EQU   001h         ;0000 0001   COM2
;
; masks for AH = ?? ISR requests
;
RESETALL   EQU   000h ;0000 0000   reset SCC
SENDCHAR   EQU   001h ;0000 0001   send character(s)
RECVCHAR   EQU   002h ;0000 0010   recv character(s)
GETSTATS   EQU   003h ;0000 0011   get status in ah
GETCOUNT   EQU   004h ;0000 0100   get buffer counts
SLCTMODE   EQU   005h ;0000 0101   select opmode POLLED/INT_DR
```

```
; MODULE PATH: \ASM232\EQU7863.ASM
;;;;;;:::::::::::::::::::::::::::::::::::::::::::::::::::::
; EQUATES for Pro-Log 7863 Multimaster 8088 CPU/Comm card.
;
; conventions -- all immediate data = capital letters
;                storage locations  = small   letters
;;;;;;:::::::::::::::::::::::::::::::::::::::::::::::::::::
;
INT_VECT  EQU 0e0h ;begin hdwr interrupt vector locations
;
;;;;;;:::::::::::::::::::::::::::::::::::::::::::::::::::::
; zilog 8530 SCC I/O PORT EQUATES
;;;;;;:::::::::::::::::::::::::::::::::::::::::::::::::::::
;
; output functions 16 bit
;
B422CTRL  EQU 0bffch     ;ch B RS-422 control
B422XMIT  EQU 0bffdh     ;ch B RS-422 xmt data
A232CTRL  EQU 0bffeh     ;ch A RS-232 control
A232XMIT  EQU 0bfffh     ;ch A RS-232 xmt data
;
; input functions 16 bit
;
B422STAT  EQU B422CTRL   ;ch B RS-422 status
B422RECV  EQU B422XMIT   ;ch B RS-422 rec data
A232STAT  EQU A232CTRL   ;ch A RS-232 status
A232RECV  EQU A232XMIT   ;ch A RS-232 rec data
;
; opmodes
;
POLLED    EQU 0          ;polled mode
INT_DR    EQU 1          ;interrupt-driven mode
;
; misc equates
;
MINUS     EQU -1         ;zero
ZRO       EQU 0          ;zero
ONE       EQU 1          ;one
MAXCHAR   EQU 255        ;internal rx & tx buffer sizes
TXBUFEMT  EQU 04h        ;tx buffer empty
TXIPBIT   EQU 10h        ;tx interrupt pending bit of RR3
TIMEOUT   EQU 080h       ;time out errs
IBUFOVRN  EQU TIMEOUT    ;internal buffer overflow
TIMECNT   EQU 10         ;time out loop count (polled mode)
;
;;;;;;:::::::::::::::::::::::::::::::::::::::::::::::::::::
; 8530 SCC CONTROL REGISTER EQUATES
; (all except WR0 require 2 bytes to be programmed)
;
; NOTE: Each SCC Channel has 16 Write registers
```

```
;                    10 for control
;                     2 for synch char generation
;                     2 for baud rate generation
;                     2 shared by both channels
;                         1 = interrupt vector
;                         1 = master interrupt control
;;;;;;::::::::::::::::::::::::::::::::::::::::::::::::::::::::::
;
WR0          EQU  00  ;CRC init, mode init, register pointers
WR1          EQU  01  ;Tx/rx interrupt and data transfer mode
WR2          EQU  02  ;Intrrpt vect (accessed either chan)
WR3          EQU  03  ;Receive parameters and control
WR4          EQU  04  ;Tx/rx miscellaneous parm & modes
WR5          EQU  05  ;Transmit parm and control
WR6          EQU  06  ;Synch char or SDLC address field
WR7          EQU  07  ;Synch char or SDLC flag
WR8          EQU  08  ;Transmit buffer
WR9          EQU  09  ;Master interrupt ctrl & reset (both chan)
WRA          EQU  10  ;Misc tx/rx control bits
WRB          EQU  11  ;Clock mode control
WRC          EQU  12  ;Lower byte of baud rate gen time const
WRD          EQU  13  ;Upper byte of baud rate gen time const
WRE          EQU  14  ;Misc control bits
WRF          EQU  15  ;External/status interrupt control
;
;;;;;;::::::::::::::::::::::::::::::::::::::::::::::::::::::::::
; 8530 SCC STATUS REGISTER EQUATES
;  (All except RR0 require 2 byte read - page 3-28)
;
; NOTE: Each 8530 SCC Channel has 8 Read registers
;                     4 for status
;                     2 for baud rate generation
;                     1 for interrupt vector
;                     1 for receive buffer
; Channel A has additional reg for reading interrupt
; pending bits of both channels (RR3).
;;;;;;::::::::::::::::::::::::::::::::::::::::::::::::::::::::::
;
RR0          EQU  00  ;Tx/rx buffer status and external status
RR1          EQU  01  ;Special Receive condition status
RR2          EQU  02  ;Interrupt vector (modified only chan B)
RR3          EQU  03  ;Interrupt pending bits (channel A only)
RR8          EQU  08  ;Receive buffer
RRA          EQU  10  ;Misc status
RRC          EQU  12  ;Lower byte of baud rate gen time const
RRD          EQU  13  ;Upper byte of baud rate gen time const
RRF          EQU  15  ;External/status interrupt info
;
;;;;;;::::::::::::::::::::::::::::::::::::::::::::::::::::::::::
; 8530 SCC WRITE REGISTER INITIALIZATION VALUE EQUATES
```

```
;
; NOTE: Initialization of the SCC is a 3-step process
;    1) op modes (i.e. bits/char, parity, vect, time const)
;    2) hdwr enable (i.e. xmitter, rxvr, baud rate generator)
;    3) interrupts enabled
;    Below sequence approximates initialization order.
;;;;;;::::::::::::::::::::::::::::::::::::::::::::::::::::::::
;
;   master interrupt control (shared both channels)
;   no modification of interrupt allowed in WR9 bits below
WR9INIT1   EQU 0C0H ;1100 0000 hdwr init master int disable
WR9INIA1   EQU 080H ;1000 0000 chan A reset mast int disable
WR9INIB1   EQU 040H ;0100 0000 chan B reset mast int disable
WR9MSKIE   EQU 009H ;0000 1001 mask to enable-vect stat(lo)
WR9MSKIS   EQU 001H ;0000 0001 mask vect inc stat/stat lo
;
;   tx/rx misc parm & mode
;   after init, stop bit mask disables sync
WR4INIA1   EQU 040H ;0100 0000 *16 clk,8bit sync,
                    ;   sync enable,no parity
WR4MSKS1   EQU 004H ;0000 0100 mask 1 stop bit, disable sync
WR4MSKS2   EQU 00CH ;0000 1100 mask 2 stop bit, disable sync
WR4MSKPE   EQU 003H ;0000 0011 mask for even parity
WR4MSKPO   EQU 001H ;0000 0001 mask for odd parity
WR4DEFA1   EQU 044H ;0100 0100 *16 clk, 1 stop, no parity
;
;    Interrupt vector (either channel)
;    variable interrupt not used
WR2INIA1   EQU INT_VECT ;0000 variable intrrpt vect
;
;   rx parm & control
;   no auto enable/hunt/CRC/addr search/no synch char inhibit
WR3IN7A1   EQU 040H ;0100 0000 receive 7 bits, rx disabled
WR3IN8A1   EQU 0C0H ;1100 0000 receive 8 bits, rx disabled
WR3MSKER   EQU 001H ;0000 0001 mask to enable receive
WR3MSKAU   EQU 020H ;0010 0000 mask to enable auto
WR3MSKCR   EQU 008H ;0000 1000 mask to enable CRC
WR3MSKER   EQU 001H ;0000 0001 mask to enable receive
WR3DEFA1   EQU 0C1H ;1100 0001 8 bits, enable (default)
;
;   tx parm & control
;   no send break/SDLC/CRC/DTR
WR5IN7A1   EQU 020H ;0010 0000 transmt 7 bits, tx disabled
WR5IN8A1   EQU 060H ;0110 0000 transmt 8 bits, tx disabled
WR5MSKED   EQU 080H ;1000 0000 mask to enable DTR
WR5MSKER   EQU 008H ;0000 1000 mask to enable transmit
WR5MSKEC   EQU 001H ;0000 0001 mask to enable CRC
WR5MSKRS   EQU 002H ;0000 0010 mask to enable RTS
WR5MSKCR   EQU 004H ;0000 0100 mask enable CRC 16 polynomial
WR5DEFA1   EQU 0EAH ;1110 1010 8 bits, DTR,RTS, enable
```

```
;   program sync char
;   not used
WR6INIA1  EQU 000H        ;0000 0000 not used
;
;   program sync char
;   not used
WR7INIA1  EQU 000H        ;0000 0000 not used
;
;   misc controls
;   not used
WRAINIA1  EQU 000H        ;0000 0000 not used
;
;   clock controls
;   not supported
WRBINIA1  EQU 056H        ;0101 0110 not used
;
;   lower byte BRG time const
WRCINIA1  EQU 0000H       ;0000 0000
;   upper byte BRG time const
WRDINIA1  EQU 0000H       ;0000 0000
WRCMSK00  EQU 0572H       ; 110 baud    TC mask
WRCMSK01  EQU 03FEH       ; 150 baud    TC mask
WRCMSK02  EQU 01FEH       ; 300 baud    TC mask
WRCMSK03  EQU 00FEH       ; 600 baud    TC mask
WRCMSK04  EQU 007EH       ; 1200 baud   TC mask
WRCMSK05  EQU 0040H       ; 2400 baud   TC mask
WRCMSK06  EQU 001EH       ; 4800 baud   TC mask
WRCMSK07  EQU 000EH       ; 9600 baud   TC mask
;
;   misc control (must init set BRG enable to zro)
WREINIA1  EQU 0002H       ;0000 0010 br clock= Pclk
WREMSKBR  EQU 0001H       ;0000 0001 mask to enable BR GEN
WREINIA2  EQU 0003H       ;0000 0011 mask inc both above
;
;   various reset conditions/crc init/ reg pointers
;WROINIA1  EQU 0080H ;1000 0000 reset tx CRC
;WROMSKRC  EQU 0040H ;0100 0000 msk reset rx crc chker
;WROMSKC0  EQU 0000H ;0000 0000 mask command 0 no-op
;WROMSKC1  EQU 0008H ;0000 1000 msk command 1 point high
;WROMSKC2  EQU 0010H ;0001 0000 msk cmmd 2 reset ext\stat
;WROMSKC3  EQU 0018H ;0001 1000 msk cmmd 3 reset SDLC mode
WROMSKC4  EQU 0020H  ;0010 0000 msk cmmd 4 on nxt rx ch
WROMSKC5  EQU 0028H  ;0010 1000 msk cmmd 5 reset tx pending
WROMSKC6  EQU 0030H  ;0011 0000 msk cmmd 6 parity err reset
WROMSKC7  EQU 0038H  ;0011 1000 msk cmmd 7 reset highest IUS
WRORESTX  EQU 00C0H  ;1100 0000 reset tx underrun
;   external status/interrupt control
WRFINIA1  EQU 0000H  ;0000 0000 disable external stat
;   interrupt conditions
WR1INIA1  EQU 0012H  ;0001 0010 rx on ch/enable tx int
```

```
    ;WR1INIB1   EQU 0000H ;0000 0000 dis rx/tx int
    ;
    ; Read register equates
    ;
    RRORXCHR   EQU 001h       ;0000 0001 rx char available
    RROOVRRN   EQU TXBUFEMT   ;0000 0100 tx buff empty,causes int
    RROCTSMK   EQU 020h       ;0010 0000 cts
    RROTXUNR   EQU 040h       ;0100 0000 tx underrun
    RROMASK2   EQU 060h       ;0000 0000 cts/tx underrun, no apply
    RROMASK1   EQU 0FFh       ;1111 1111 return all flags
    ;
    RR1PARER   EQU 010h        ;0001 0000 parity error
    RR1OVRRN   EQU 020h        ;0010 0000 overrun err
    RR1FRAME   EQU 040h        ;0100 0000 frame  error
    RR1MSKRX   EQU 070h        ;0111 0000 all above errors
    RR1UNKWN   EQU 080h        ;1000 0000 unknown err /timeout
    RR1MSKCL   EQU 071h        ;0111 0001 abv errs plus all sent
```

COMMUNICATIONS DATA

```
    ; MODULE PATH: \ASM232\DATASEG.ASM
    data segment at 7bfh              ; abs 7bf0h
    ;
    ;;;;;;;;;;;;;;;;;;;;;;;;;;;;;;;;;;;;;;;;;;;;;;;;;;;;;;;;;;;;;;;
    ; Miscellaneous data area
    ;;;;;;;;;;;;;;;;;;;;;;;;;;;;;;;;;;;;;;;;;;;;;;;;;;;;;;;;;;;;;;;
    ;
    ;;;;;;;;;;;;;;;;;;;;;;;;;;;;;;;;;;;;;;;;;;;;;;;;;;;;;;;;;;;;;;;
    ; Channel A data area
    ;;;;;;;;;;;;;;;;;;;;;;;;;;;;;;;;;;;;;;;;;;;;;;;;;;;;;;;;;;;;;;;
    tx_remcnt      dw 0 ;tx internal buff byte cnt not in use
    tx_curcnt      dw 0 ;tx byte count (cnt actually xmitted)
    tx_off_curbuf  dw offset ib_tx ;internal tx buff, chan a
    tx_off_urdbuf  dw ? ;offset of next user put in tx buff
    tx_errstat     db 0 ;channel a error status (transmit)
    tx_flag1       db 0 ;buff ovrn flag
                   db 0 ;dummy
    ;
    rx_flag2       db 0 ;internal buff ovrn flag
    rx_errchar     db 0 ;# char in error
    rx_errstat     db 0 ;channel a error status (receive)
    rx_curcnt      dw 0 ;receive byte count (cnt actually rx)
    rx_off_urdbuf  dw offset ib_rx ;next user read in rx buff
    rx_off_curbuf  dw offset ib_rx ;rx internal buffer, chan a
    rx_remcnt      dw 0 ;rx internal buff byte cnt not in use
    rx_flag        db ZRO ;char request flag
    ;
    op_mode        db    MINUS    ;default mode = need ah=5
    cur_ctrl       dw    A232CTRL ;curr control reg
```

```
cur_recv          dw    A232RECV ;curr rx data reg
cur_xmit          dw    A232XMIT ;curr tx data reg
cur_init          dw    offset init_a ;offset init tbl for port
cur_sccoff        dw ? ;curr offset in scc_tbl for cur_comprt
cur_comprt        db 0 ;curr comm port (0-n)
;
; Internal comm buffers
;
ib_tx             db    MAXCHAR dup(?)   ;tx internal buff
ib_tx_en          db    -1
ib_rx             db    MAXCHAR dup(?)   ;rx internal buff
ib_rx_en          db    -1
;
INIT_1    equ $                     ;start all tables
; all tables should follow without interruption
;   TABLE B HAS BEEN COMMENTED OUT for this application
;;;;;;;;;;;;;;;;;;;;;;;;;;;;;;;;;;;;;;;;;;;;;;;;;;;;;;;;;;;;;;;
; Table for initializing SCC channel B
;
; Consists of REG# followed by init value
; Channel B is not supported by this software
; values disable channel B
;;;;;;;;;;;;;;;;;;;;;;;;;;;;;;;;;;;;;;;;;;;;;;;;;;;;;;;;;;;;;;;
;BTBLOFF   equ $
;init_b    db    BTBLENG
;          db    WR9
;          db    WR9INIT1 ;reset both channel  (hdwr int)
;          db    WR9
;          db    WR9INIB1 ;reset chan b (disabl interrpts)
;          db    WR3
;          db    0        ;rcv 5 bits, rcv disable
;          db    WR5
;          db    0        ;tx  5 bits, tx  disable
;          db    WRF
;          db    WRFINIA1 ;disable extrn stat int
;          db    WR1
;          db    WR1INIB1 ;disable tx/rx int
;BTBLEND   equ $
;;
;BTBLEN1   equ BTBLEND-BTBLOFF
;BTBLENG   equ BTBLEN1-1
;;;;;;;;;;;;;;;;;;;;;;;;;;;;;;;;;;;;;;;;;;;;;;;;;;;;;;;;;;;;;;;;;
; Table for initializing SCC channel A
;
; Consists of REG# followed by init value
; Init values w/labels changed by interrupt init request
;;;;;;;;;;;;;;;;;;;;;;;;;;;;;;;;;;;;;;;;;;;;;;;;;;;;;;;;;;;;;;;;
ATBLOFF   equ $
init_a    db    ATBLENG
          db    WR9
```

```
                db   WR9INIT1  ;reset channel a & b
                db   WR4
parity          db   WR4DEFA1  ;*16 clk, 1stop, no parity(default)
                db   WR2
                db   WR2INIA1  ;interrupt vector
                db   WR3
rec_bits        db   WR3IN8A1  ;rcv 8 bits, rcv disable (default)
                db   WR5
xmt_bits        db   WR5IN8A1  ;tx  8 bits, tx  disable (default)
                db   WR9
                db   WR9MSKIS  ;vector includes stat/lo
                db   WRA
                db   WRAINIA1  ;misc ctrl  not used
                db   WRB
                db   WRBINIA1  ;clk  ctrl  not supported ??
                db   WRC
lo_time         db   WRCMSK07  ;low time const  (9600 default)
                db   WRD
hi_time         db   0         ;high time const  (9600 default)
                db   WRE
                db   WREINIA1  ;br clk =  pclk
                db   WRF
                db   WRFINIA1  ;disable extrn stat int
                db   WR3
rx_enabl        db   WR3DEFA1  ;rx enable,8bits (default)
                db   WR5
tx_enabl        db   WR5DEFA1  ;tx enable,8bits,dtr,rts (default)
                db   WRE
                db   WREINIA2  ;enable BR GEN
                db   WR0
                db   WR0MSKC4  ;enable on next char
                db   WR0
                db   WR0MSKC6  ;err reset
                db   WR0
                db   WR0RESTX  ;reset tx underrun
                db   WR1
                db   WR1INIA1  ;enable both tx/rx interrupts
ATBLEND  equ $
ATBLEN1  equ ATBLEND-ATBLOFF
ATBLENG  equ ATBLEN1-1
;;;;;;;;;;;;;;;;;;;;;;;;;;;;;;;;;;;;;;;;;;;;;;;;;;;;;;;;;;;;;
; Table for selecting time constants for given baud rate
; (positionally dependent in increasing baud rate)
; conforms to al values required by IBM BIOS init request
;;;;;;;;;;;;;;;;;;;;;;;;;;;;;;;;;;;;;;;;;;;;;;;;;;;;;;;;;;;;;
tim_cont dw WRCMSK00     ;110 baud
         dw WRCMSK01     ;150 baud
         dw WRCMSK02     ;300 baud
         dw WRCMSK03     ;600 baud
         dw WRCMSK04     ;1200baud
```

```
            dw WRCMSK05      ;2400baud
            dw WRCMSK06      ;4800baud
            dw WRCMSK07      ;9600baud
;;;;;;;;;;;;;;;;;;;;;;;;;;;;;;;;;;;;;;;;;;;;;;;;;;;;;;;;;;;;;;;;;;;
; Table for all SCC init   (CHANNEL B IS COMMENTED OUT)
;        (in desired init sequence)
;;;;;;;;;;;;;;;;;;;;;;;;;;;;;;;;;;;;;;;;;;;;;;;;;;;;;;;;;;;;;;;;;;;
scc_tbl    dw SCBLENG
;
SCBLOFF    equ $            ;start of table
;fst_scc   dw B422CTRL,B422XMIT,offset init_b
scc_2      dw A232CTRL,A232XMIT,offset init_a
SCNDSCC    equ $               ;start of second entry
                               ;(calculate entry length)
SCBLEND    equ $            ;end of last entry
;
SCELENG    equ SCNDSCC-SCBLOFF  ;entry length
SCBLEN1    equ SCBLEND-SCBLOFF  ;table length
SCBLENG    equ SCBLEN1/SCELENG  ;number SCCs in table
;;;;;;;;;;;;;;;;;;;;;;;;;;;;;;;;;;;;;;;;;;;;;;;;;;;;;;;;;;;;;;;;;;;
; Table for setting SCC vectors (in specified sequence)
;;;;;;;;;;;;;;;;;;;;;;;;;;;;;;;;;;;;;;;;;;;;;;;;;;;;;;;;;;;;;;;;;;;
vect_tbl   dw VTBLENG
;
VTBLOFF    equ $
fst_entry  dw offset dmmy_b ;all chan b routines are dmmys
           dw seg dmmy_b
VSECOND    equ $
           dw offset dmmy_b
           dw seg dmmy_b
           dw offset dmmy_b
           dw seg dmmy_b
           dw offset dmmy_b
           dw seg dmmy_b
           dw offset i_a_xmt    ;tx int
           dw seg i_a_xmt
           dw offset dmmy_a     ;extrn/stat int
           dw seg dmmy_a
           dw offset i_a_rec    ;rx int
           dw seg i_a_rec
           dw offset isr_sp_a   ;special rx int
           dw seg isr_sp_a
VTBLEND    equ $
VTBLEN1    equ VTBLEND-VTBLOFF  ;total table length
VTBLEN2    equ VSECOND-VTBLOFF  ;amount processed each pass
VTBLENG    equ VTBLEN1/VTBLEN2  ;processing loop cnt
;;;;;;;;;;;;;;;;;;;;;;;;;;;;;;;;;;;;;;;;;;;;;;;;;;;;;;;;;;;;;;;;;;;
; Table for correlating com port value to scc_tbl
;   port# (0-n) is offset in this tbl
;   points to offset in scc_tbl        ;.
```

```
;;;;;;;;;;;;;;;;;;;;;;;;;;;;;;;;;;;;;;;;;;;;;;;;;;;;;;;;;
ncom_prt   db NCBLENG
;
NCBLOFF    equ $
fst_cp     dw offset scc_2
NCBSCND    equ $                ;second entry addr (cal entry len)
NCBLEND    equ $
;
NCBLEN1    equ NCBSCND-NCBLOFF       ;entry length
NCBLEN2    equ NCBLEND-NCBLOFF       ;table length
NCBLENG    equ NCBLEN2/NCBLEN1       ;# com ports
;
data       ends
```

ISR PROCESSING

```
; MODULE PATH: \ASM232\IMHDR.ASM

;;;;;;;;;;;;;;;;;;;;;;;;;;;;;;;;;;;;;;;;;;;;;;;;;;;;;;;;;;;;
; INTERRUPT SERVICE ROUTINE for Prolog 7863 CPU/COMM board
;
; Interface compatible with IBM BIOS int 14h with some mods
;
; Note: Timeout codes of interrupt mode may indicate
;        buffer overflow.
;
;   If ah = 0 = RESETALL:
;   (If this request is not preceded by an ah=5 request,
;     first time only, op_mode results can be unpredictable.)
;
;                   al: bits 7,6,5 = baud rate
;                       000 = 110
;                       001 = 150
;                       010 = 300
;                       011 = 600
;                       100 = 1200
;                       101 = 2400
;                       110 = 4800
;                       111 = 9600
;                   al: bits 4,3   = parity
;                       00 = none
;                       01 = odd
;                       10 = even
;                   al: bits 2     = stop bits
;                       0 = 1 stop bit
;                       1 = 2 stop bits
;                   al: bits 1,0   = length
;                       10 = 7 bits/char
;                       11 = 8 bits/char
```

```
;
;   dx must = port number (0,n)
;   operation mode (polled or interrupt) is determined by
;   last ah=5 request if no ah=5 request has been made, the
;   default opmode is POLLED.
;
;   At exit, the SCC has been re-initialize according to
;   specified parm in al, and last ah=5 request (if any).
;
;
; If ah = 1 = SENDCHAR:
;     If cx < 2, a single character will be sent
;         al must contain the character to send
;         At exit: ah contains buffer error status as follows:
;                 1000 0000  bit 7 = timeout
;     If cx > 1, a block will be sent
;         es:si must point to the first char to send
;         cx must contain the block count
;         At exit:
;         The data is in the tx internal buffer and
;             the transmission should be in process.
;         At exit: ah contains buffer error status as follows:
;                 1000 0000  bit 7 = timeout
;
; If ah = 2 = RECVCHAR:
;     If cx =1 or 0, one character from the internal buffer is
;         returned in al.
;     At exit, al contains the character received.
;         ah = buffer status code (non zro = possible error).
;                 1111 0000  bit 7 = timeout
;                            bit 6 = frame eror
;                            bit 5 = rx ovverrun
;                            bit 4 = parity error
;         cx = number of characters returned.
;         dx = number of characters available in rx buffer.
;     If cx > 1 , a block of cx (specified) length is returned
;           from the rx internal buffer to the user buffer
;           specified by es:di.
;     If there are fewer characters available in the
;         internal buffer than the requested count, the
;         count that is available will be returned to the
;         user program, and the only error indication will
;         be the returned count in cx.
;       es:di must point to the receive buffer
;       (user ensure buffer size OK)
;       cx must contain the block count
;       At exit:
;           ax = 0 means everything ok.
;           al = number of characters in error in internal buff.
;           ah = buffer status code (non zro = possible error).
```

```
;                       1111 0000  bit 7 = timeout
;                                  bit 6 = frame eror
;                                  bit 5 = rx ovverrun
;                                  bit 4 = parity error
;        cx = number of characters returned.
;        dx = number of characters available in rx buffer
;                              following this call.
;     UNGETS (ah = 2, cx is negative).
;     If cx = -1, the char in al is returned to the internal
;           buffer.
;     If cx < 0  , the negative number specified is returned
;           to the rx internal buffer from the user buffer
;           specified by es:di. (es:di must point to the last
;           character of the string to be returned.)
;           cx must contain the negative count to be un_gotten
;           If there are fewer spaces available in the
;           internal buffer than the requested count, no
;           characters will be returned to the internal buffer,
;           cx = 0 on return and ah will have bit 7 set.
;     At exit:
;           ax = 0 means everything ok.
;           al = # of characters in error in internal buff.
;           ah = buffer status code (non zro = possible error).
;               1111 0000  bit 7 = timeout
;                          bit 6 = frame eror
;                          bit 5 = rx ovverrun
;                          bit 4 = parity error
;        cx = number of characters returned to internal buff.
;        dx = number of characters available in rx buffer
;           following this call.
;
;           If ah = 3 = GETSTATS:
;                   At exit (polled mode) al = RR0 status
;                   1111 0000  bit 7 = break/abort
;                              bit 6 = tx undderrun
;                              bit 5 = CTS
;                              bit 4 = sync/hunt
;                              bit 3 = DCD
;                              bit 2 = tx buff empty
;                              bit 1 = BR gen 0 cnt
;                              bit 0 = rx char avail
;                      ah = RR1 status bits
;                   1111 0000  bit 7 = timeout
;                              bit 6 = frame eror
;                              bit 5 = rx ovverrun
;                              bit 4 = parity error
;                              bit 0 = all sent
;               At exit (interrupt mode)
;               al = rx buffer status code
;                          (non zro = possible error)
```

```
;                              1111 0000  bit 7 = timeout
;                                         bit 6 = frame eror
;                                         bit 5 = rx ovverrun
;                                         bit 4 = parity error
;                      ah = tx buffer status code
;                                  (non zro = possible error)
;                         1000 0000  bit 7 = timeout
;
;          If ah = 4 = GETCOUNT
;                 (Interrupt mode internal buffer counts):
;              At exit:
;                   ax = number of bytes in rx buff
;                   dx = number of bytes in tx buff
;
;          If ah = 5 = SLCTMODE:
;              Mode select. Sets mode in mem & inits SCC with
;              interrupts disabled and default parm.
;
;                   At entry,  al = 0 POLLED or 1 INT_DR
;                              dx = port (0,n)
;
;                   At exit:  nothing returned
;
;
; At exit :  ax,cx,dx  modified
;


; MODULE PATH: \ASM232\IMAIN.ASM
Title PROLOG_7863_ISR_FOR_RS232_COMM_IO
;
;INCLUDE ISRHDR.ASM
;INCLUDE EQU7863.ASM
;INCLUDE EQUBIOS.ASM
;INCLUDE DATASEG.ASM
;.XLIST
INCLUDE ISRHDR.ASM
INCLUDE EQU7863.ASM
INCLUDE EQUBIOS.ASM
INCLUDE DATASEG.ASM
;.LIST
code segment public
     assume cs:code,ds:data
;.XLIST
INCLUDE IMHDR.ASM
;.LIST
isr_main        proc    far
;
    sti                          ;enable interrupts
```

```
        push ds                 ;save old ds
        push bx
        push es
        push di
        push si
        pushf
;
        push ax                 ;ensure data segment
        mov ax,seg data
        push ax
        pop ds
        pop ax
;
        cmp ah,SLCTMODE         ;mode change request?
        je get_opmode           ;request is mode change
;
        cmp byte ptr op_mode,POLLED  ;are we in polled mode
        jne go_onreq            ;if not, normal process
        cmp dl,cur_comprt       ;we are in polled, same port?
        je go_onreq             ;same port, go on to request
        call getscc_parm        ;get new port data
;
go_onreq:
        cmp ah,SENDCHAR ;AH IS1
        jz send_it      ;request is to send
        cmp ah,RECVCHAR ;AH IS2
        jz recv_it      ;request is to receive
        cmp ah,GETSTATS ;AH IS3
        jz get_stats    ;request is for SCC status
        cmp ah,GETCOUNT ;AH IS4
        jz get_bcnts    ;request is for internal buffer counts
        cmp ah,RESETALL ;AH IS0
        jz get_ini      ;request is for SCC init
;
        jmp short exit_mi ;invalid request
;
send_it:
        cmp byte ptr op_mode,POLLED
        jne tx_id
        call psender            ;tx polled
        jmp short exit_mi       ;rx complete, exit
tx_id:
        cmp cx,2                ;tx int driven
        jge xmt_it              ; >=2, use it
        mov cx,1                ;ensure 1
xmt_it:
        call xmt_asyc           ;tx int driven
        jmp short exit_mi       ;send complete, exit
recv_it:
        cmp byte ptr op_mode,POLLED
```

```
        jne rx_id
        call prec_ver                  ;rx polled
        jmp short exit_mi              ;rx complete, exit
rx_id:
        call rec_ver                   ;rx int driven
        jmp short exit_mi              ;rx complete, exit
get_stats:
        call get_stus
        jmp short exit_mi              ;got status, exit
get_bcnts:
        call get_bstats
        jmp short exit_mi              ;got status, exit
get_opmode:
        call get_om
        jmp short exit_mi              ;mode changed, exit
get_ini:
        call init_main
;
exit_mi:        popf
                pop si
                pop di
                pop es
                pop bx
                pop ds
;
                iret
;
isr_main        endp

;:::::::::::::::::::::::::::::::::::::::::::::::::::::::::::::::;;;;;
; Transmit buffer empty INTERRUPT SERVICE ROUTINE, chan A.
; Nxt char of mssg is moved to transmit buffer, byte count,
; nxt addr are adjusted.  If last char has been sent,
; transmitter interrupt is reset.
;
;   At entry: NA
;
;   At exit: xmit byte count decremented & stored
;            # buffer spaces available incremented & stored
;            xmit buf pointer incremented & stored
;                       (buff wrapped if appro)
;            next byte sent or transmit interrupt reset
;            highest IUS reset
;            Nothing destroyed.
;:::::::::::::::::::::::::::::::::::::::::::::::::::::::::::::::;;;;;
i_a_xmt         proc far
;
                sti                            ;enable interrupts
                push ds                        ;save old ds
                push ax
```

```
                    push dx
                    push di
                    push si
                    push es
                    pushf
;
                    push ax                 ; save ax in
                    mov ax,seg data         ;ensure data seg
                    push ax
                    pop ds
                    pop ax                  ;restore incoming ax
;
                    push ds                 ;ensure es = ds
                    pop es
;
                    mov si,offset tx_off_curbuf ;curr buff offset
                    mov di,offset tx_curcnt    ;curr buff count
                    mov bx,offset tx_remcnt    ;avail buffer cnt
;
                    call xmt_char               ;send char
;
                    call reset_ius              ;reset highest IUS
;
                    popf
                    pop es
                    pop si
                    pop di
                    pop dx
                    pop ax
                    pop ds
;
                    iret
;
i_a_xmt         endp
;:::::::::::::::::::::::::::::::::::::::::::::::::::::::::::::::
; Receive async tx char INTERRUPT SERVICE ROUTINE, chan A.
;   Errors of framing,rx overrun,parity genenerate sp int.
;
;   At entry: NA
;
;   At exit: character stored in buffer.
;           next storage addr incremented
;                       (buffer wrap if appro)
;           number of characters received incremented
;           number of avail buffer spaces decremented
;           highest IUS reset
;           nothing destroyed.
;:::::::::::::::::::::::::::::::::::::::::::::::::::::::::::::;;;;;
i_a_rec         proc far
;
```

```
                sti                          ;enable interrupts
                push ds                      ;save old ds
                push ax
                push bx
                push dx
                push di
                push si
                push es
                pushf
;
                push ax                      ;ensure data segment
                mov ax,seg data
                push ax
                pop ds
                pop ax
;
                push ds                      ;segment curr buff
                pop es                       ;get seg to es
;
                mov ax,offset ib_rx_en ;last buffer addr +1
                dec ax                       ;last buffer addr
;
                mov di,offset rx_off_curbuf ;ptr curr offset
                mov si,[di]                  ;curr offset to si
;
                inc word ptr [di]            ;inc offset
                cmp si,ax                    ;tim to wrap buff?
                jnz no_wrap                  ;no wrap
                sub word ptr [di],MAXCHAR    ;yes, wrap buffer
;
no_wrap:        inc ax                       ;exceed last addr
                cmp si,ax                    ;addr exceeded?
                jb  no_excess                ;no, not exceeded
                sub si,MAXCHAR               ;yes, fix addr
;
no_excess:      mov di,offset rx_curcnt      ;current buff cnt
                mov bx,offset rx_remcnt      ;remaing buff cnt
;
                call get_1_ch                ;read char fm port
                                             ;stat in ah
                or rx_errstat,ah             ;set status
;
                dec  word ptr [bx]     ;dec # char allowed
                cmp word ptr [bx],ZRO  ;more allowed in buffer?
                jnb rx_dmov            ;more allowed, move data
                or byte ptr rx_errstat,IBUFOVRN
                                 ;set overrun error,no more allow
                inc byte ptr rx_errchar ;inc # char in error
;
rx_dmov:        mov es:[si],al               ;data to buffer
```

```
                        inc   word ptr [di]         ;inc # char rx
        ;
                        call reset_ius              ;reset highest ius
        ;
                        popf
                        pop es
                        pop si
                        pop di
                        pop dx
                        pop bx
                        pop ax
                        pop ds
        ;
                        iret
        ;
i_a_rec         endp
;::::::::::::::::::::::::::::::::::::::::::::::::::::::::::::;;;;;
; The SCC generates a special receive vectored interrupt
;  which calls this INTERRUPT SERVICE ROUTINE in the event
;  of framing/rx overrun errors. The error code is placed
;  in storage and the error code is reset.
;
; At entry:  NA
;
; At exit :  RR1 status is stored at rx_errstat
;            number char in error is incremented
;            number char rx is incremented
;::::::::::::::::::::::::::::::::::::::::::::::::::::::::::::;;;;;
;
isr_sp_a        proc far
        ;
                        sti
                        push ax
                        push dx
        ;
                          push ax                   ;ensure data segment
                          mov ax,seg data
                          push ax
                          pop ds
                          pop ax
        ;
                        mov dx,cur_ctrl             ;addr current ctrl port
                        mov al,RR1                  ;read register one
                        out dx,al                   ;point to RR1
                        in  al,dx                   ;read RR1
                        push ax                     ;save errcode
        ;
                        and al,RR1PARER             ;parity error?
                        cmp al,RR1PARER
                        jnz over_run
```

```
                or   rx_errstat,al      ;yes, parity error.
                jmp short set_it
;
over_run:       pop ax
                push ax
                and al,RR1OVRRN         ;overrun error?
                cmp al,RR1OVRRN
                jnz fr_err
                or   rx_errstat,al      ;yes, parity error.
                jmp short set_it
;
fr_err:         pop ax
                push ax
                and al,RR1FRAME         ;FRAME error?
                cmp al,RR1FRAME
                jnz unk_err
                or   rx_errstat,al      ;yes, parity error.
                jmp short set_it
;
unk_err:        pop ax
                mov al,RR1UNKWN
                or   rx_errstat,al      ;unknown error
                jmp short err_rxset
;
set_it:         pop ax
;
err_rxset:      inc byte ptr rx_errchar ;inc err count
                call err_reset          ;reset ctrl reg err & ius
;
                pop dx
                pop ax
                iret
isr_sp_a        endp
;::::::::::::::::::::::::::::::::::::::::::::::::::::::::::::::;;;;;
; Dummy interrupt service routine for channel B.
;
;   Nothing destroyed.
;
dmmy_b          proc far
;
                sti                     ;reenable interrupts
                push ax
                push dx
                pushf
;
                mov dx,B422CTRL         ;channel B port addr
                mov ax,WROMSKC7         ;highest IUS reset
                out dx,al               ;write reset
;
                popf
```

```
                         pop dx
                         pop ax
        ;
                         iret
        ;
        dmmy_b           endp
        ;::::::::::::::::::::::::::::::::::::::::::::::::::::::;;;;;
        ; Dummy interrupt service routine for channel A.
        ;
        ;   Nothing destroyed.
        ;
        dmmy_a           proc far
        ;
                         sti                 ;reenable interrupts
                         push ds
                         push ax
                         push dx
                         pushf
        ;
                         push ax             ;ensure data segment
                         mov ax,seg data
                         push ax
                         pop ds
                         pop ax
        ;
                         call reset_ius      ;highest IUS reset
        ;
                         popf
                         pop dx
                         pop ax
                         pop ds
        ;
                         iret
        ;
        dmmy_a           endp
        ;::::::::::::::::::::::::::::::::::::::::::::::::::::::;;;;;
        ; Routine to reset highest interrupt under service
        ; (destroys flags)
        ;
        reset_ius        proc
                         push dx
                         push ax
                         mov dx,cur_ctrl     ;channel A ctrl addr
                         mov ax,WROMSKC7     ;highest IUS reset
                         out dx,al           ;write reset
                         pop ax
                         pop dx
                         ret
        reset_ius        endp
        ;
```

```
;INCLUDE  ISRINIT.ASM
;INCLUDE  ISRTXRX.ASM
;INCLUDE  ISRMIS1.ASM
;INCLUDE  ISRMAIN.ASM
INCLUDE  ISRINIT.ASM
INCLUDE  ISRTXRX.ASM
INCLUDE  ISRMIS1.ASM
INCLUDE  ISRMAIN.ASM
;
code            ends
                end
```

OTHER PROCESSING ROUTINES

```
; MODULE PATH: \ASM232\ISRMAIN.ASM
;;;;;;;;;;;;;;;;;;;;;;;;;;;;;;;;;;;;;;;;;;;;;;;;;;;;;;;;;;;;;;;;
; Routine to receive data
;
; At entry: registers as in ISR request
; If ax = 2 = RECVCHAR:
;    If cx =1 or 0, one character from the internal buffer
;                   is returned in al.
;       At exit, al contains the character received.
;          ah = buffer status code (non zro = possible error).
;          cx = number of characters returned.
;          dx = number of characters available in rx buffer.
;    If cx > 1 , a block of cx (specified) length will be
;                   returned from the rx internal buffer to
;                   the user buffer specified by es:di.
;          If there are fewer characters available in the
;          internal buffer than the requested count, the
;          count that is available will be returned to the
;          user program, and the only error indication will
;          be the returned count in cx.
;          es:di must point to the receive buffer
;          (user ensure buffer size OK)
;          cx must contain the block count
;          At exit:
;          ax = 0 means everything ok.
;          al = # of characters in error in internal buff.
;          ah = buffer status code (non zro = possible error).
;          cx = number of characters returned.
;          dx = number of characters available in rx buffer
;               following this call.
;    UNGETS:
;    If cx = -1, the char in al will be returned to the
;                   internal buffer.
;    If cx < 0, the negative number specified is returned
;       to the rx internal buffer from the user buffer
```

```
;         specified by es:di. (es:di must point to the last
;         character of the string to be returned.)
;         cx must contain the negative count to be un_gotten
;         If there are fewer spaces available in the
;         internal buffer than the requested count, no
;         characters will be returned to the internal buffer,
;         cx = 0 on return and ah will have bit 7 set.
;         At exit:
;          ax = 0 means everything ok.
;          al = # of characters in error in internal buff.
;          ah = buffer status code (non zro = possible error).
;          cx = number of characters returned to internal buff.
;          dx = number of characters available in rx buffer
;               following this call.
;
; At exit :   ax,bx,cx,dx   modified
;
rec_ver         proc
;
                mov byte ptr rx_flag,ZRO
;
                cmp cx,ZRO                 ;is cx MINUS?
                jl  u_get                  ;yes, is unget
;
                cmp cx,ONE                 ;is cx <= 1 ?
                jle recv_char              ;yes, is recv char
;
                jmp short recv_blk         ;is rx block request


;
recv_char:      mov  cx,ONE     ;ensure count is one (not zro)
                mov byte ptr rx_flag,ONE
                jmp short recv_blk
;
u_get:          call unget_req             ;unget request
                jmp short exit_rv
;
recv_blk:       call chk_cnt       ;check counts available
                cmp cx,ZRO         ;if count = 0, exit
                jle exit_nochar    ;return nulls
;
                push bx            ;bx has err status/count
                push cx            ;cx has count to move
;
                mov bx,offset rx_curcnt  ;addr curr cnt to bx
                mov si,rx_off_urdbuf     ;set nxt read addr

nxt_char_get:   mov al,[si]              ;data to al
                inc si                   ;incrment data addr
                cmp si,offset ib_rx_en
```

```
                    jnz mov_adr
                    sub si,MAXCHAR
;
mov_adr:            mov rx_off_urdbuf,si     ;set nxt read addr
                    dec word ptr [bx]        ;decr curr cnt
                    inc word ptr rx_remcnt   ;inc avail cnt
;
                    cmp byte ptr rx_flag,ONE ;is char get?
                    je no_buff               ;yes, no buffer move
                    mov es:[di],al           ;data to buffer
                    inc di                   ;incr user buffer
no_buff:            loop nxt_char_get
;
                    pop cx                   ;get count moved
                    pop dx                   ;get errcodes/stat
;
                    push ax                  ;save char in al
                    push dx                  ;save errcodes/stat
                    mov dx,[bx]              ;new cnt avail, buff
                    pop ax                   ;errcodes/stat
                    pop bx                   ;char in bl if get
;
                    cmp byte ptr rx_flag,ONE ;is char get?
                    jne exit_rv
                    mov al,bl                ;set char for get
                    jmp short exit_rv
;
exit_nochar:        xor ax,ax                ;errcodes = 0
                    push ax
                    push ax
                    pop dx                   ;# avail = 0
                    pop cx                   ;# returned = 0
                    or ah,TIMEOUT            ;set timeout code
;
exit_rv:            ret
rec_ver             endp
;;;;;;;;;;;;;;;;;;;;;;;;;;;;;;;;;;;;;;;;;;;;;;;;;;;;;;;;;;;;;;;
; Routine to check requested char count against what is
; avail in buffer. If there are less char in the internal
; rx buffer, the routine modifies the count to be returned
; to the main pgm.
;
; At entry:  cx = cnt requested
; At exit :  cx = new cnt, bx = buff errstat
;
;;;;;;;;;;;;;;;;;;;;;;;;;;;;;;;;;;;;;;;;;;;;;;;;;;;;;;;;;;;;;;;
chk_cnt             proc
;
                    push ax
;
```

```
                        mov ax,rx_curcnt  ;get avail cnt in buff
                        cmp ax,cx         ;comp avail to requested cnt
                        jge exit_ccx
;
                        mov cx,ax         ;set new count
                        mov bh,rx_errstat ;get errstat
                        mov bl,rx_errchar ;get # char in error
;
exit_ccx:       pop ax
                ret
chk_cnt         endp
;;;;;;;;;;;;;;;;;;;;;;;;;;;;;;;;;;;;;;;;;;;;;;;;;;;;;;;;;;;;
; Routine to check count to unget cnt against avail buffer
; space. If there is less space in the internal rx buffer,
; the routine modifies the unget count to 0 and ungets
; nothing.
;
; At entry:  cx = cnt requested  (minus)
; At exit :  cx = new cnt (positive), bx = buff errstat
;
;;;;;;;;;;;;;;;;;;;;;;;;;;;;;;;;;;;;;;;;;;;;;;;;;;;;;;;;;;;;
chk_ucnt        proc
;
                push ax
;
                xor ax,ax         ;make number positive
                sub ax,cx
                mov cx,ax
;
                mov ax,rx_remcnt  ;get avail cnt in buff
                cmp ax,cx         ;comp avail to requested cnt
                jge exit_uccx
;
                xor cx,cx         ;set new count
                mov bh,rx_errstat ;get errstat
                mov bl,rx_errchar ;get # char in error
;
exit_uccx:      pop ax
                ret
chk_ucnt        endp
;;;;;;;;;;;;;;;;;;;;;;;;;;;;;;;;;;;;;;;;;;;;;;;;;;;;;;;;;;;;
; Routine to send data polled mode
;
; At entry: al = char to send
; At exit : al = 0, ah = RRO status
;;;;;;;;;;;;;;;;;;;;;;;;;;;;;;;;;;;;;;;;;;;;;;;;;;;;;;;;;;;;
psender         proc
;
                push cx
                push dx
```

```
;
                mov cx,TIMECNT
                mov dx,cur_ctrl            ;cont reg
                push ax                    ;save char in
;
chkformt:       in al,dx
                and ax,TXBUFEMT
                cmp ax,TXBUFEMT
                je send_out
                loop chkformt
                pop ax                     ;get char
                                           ;(relieve stack)

                xor ax,ax
                mov ah,TIMEOUT
                jmp short xit1
;
send_out:       pop ax                     ;get char
                call send_1_char
                and ah,0                   ;all status
                                           ;meaningless
;
xit1:           pop dx
                pop cx
                ret
;
psender         endp
;;;;;;;;;;;;;;;;;;;;;;;;;;;;;;;;;;;;;;;;;;;;;;;;;;;;;;;;;;;;;;
; Routine to write 1 char to port
; At entry: al = char to send
; At exit : al = 0, ah = RRO status
;;;;;;;;;;;;;;;;;;;;;;;;;;;;;;;;;;;;;;;;;;;;;;;;;;;;;;;;;;;;;;
send_1_char     proc                       ;char in al
                push dx
                mov dx,cur_xmit            ;curr data reg
                out dx,al                  ;send char
                mov dx,cur_ctrl
                in al,dx
                and al,RROTXUNR            ;xmitter underrun
                mov ah,al
                xor al,al
                pop dx
                ret
send_1_char     endp
;;;;;;;;;;;;;;;;;;;;;;;;;;;;;;;;;;;;;;;;;;;;;;;;;;;;;;;;;;;;;;
; Routine to receive data polled mode
;
; At entry:      NA
; At exit :      char in al, status in ah
;;;;;;;;;;;;;;;;;;;;;;;;;;;;;;;;;;;;;;;;;;;;;;;;;;;;;;;;;;;;;;
prec_ver        proc
```

```
;
                push cx
                push dx
;
                mov cx,TIMECNT
                mov dx,cur_ctrl            ;curr ctrl reg
;
chkforch:       in  al,dx                  ;get stat
                and al,RRORXCHR
                cmp al,RRORXCHR            ;char avail?
                je get_rxch                ;char avail
                loop chkforch              ;no char avail
;
                xor ax,ax                  ;no char avail
                mov ah,TIMEOUT
                jmp short exit_pver
;
get_rxch:       call get_1_ch  ;return RRO/char in ax
                and ah,0       ;all status meaningless
;
exit_pver:      pop dx
                pop cx
                ret
prec_ver        endp
;;;;;;;;;;;;;;;;;;;;;;;;;;;;;;;;;;;;;;;;;;;;;;;;;;;;;;;;;;;;
; Routine to receive one character from data port
; At entry: none
; At exit: al = char received
;          flags destroyed
;
get_1_ch        proc
;
                push dx
;
                xor ax,ax
                mov dx,cur_recv            ;curr data reg
                in  al,dx
;
                pop dx
                ret
;
get_1_ch        endp
;;;;;;;;;;;;;;;;;;;;;;;;;;;;;;;;;;;;;;;;;;;;;;;;;;;;;;;;;;;;
;Routine to process unget requests -- partial ungets are
; not allowed. If there is not enough buffer space to
; return the count, no characters are returned to
; the internal buffer from the user program.
;    UNGETS:
; If cx = -1, the char in al is returned to the internal
;                         buffer.
```

```
; If cx < 0, the negative number specified is returned
;    to the rx internal buffer from the user buffer
;    specified by es:di. (es:di must point to the last
;    character of the string to be returned.)
;    cx must contain the negative count to be un_gotten
;    If there are fewer spaces available in the
;    internal buffer than the requested count, no
;    characters will be returned to the internal buffer,
;    cx = 0 on return and ah will have bit 7 set.
;    At exit:
;       ax = 0 means everything ok.
;       al = # of characters in error in internal buff.
;       ah = buffer status code (non zro = possible error).
;       cx = positive # of chars returned to internal buff
;       dx = number of characters available in rx buffer
;              following this call.
;
; At exit :  ax,bx,cx,dx  modified
;

unget_req        proc
;
                 cmp cx,MINUS              ;is cx = -1 ?
                 jne blk_uget             ;no, is a block unget
                 mov byte ptr rx_flag,ONE ;yes,set flag
;
blk_uget:        call chk_ucnt            ;check counts available
                 cmp cx,ZRO               ;if count = 0, exit
                 je exit_uochar           ;return nulls
;
                 push bx                  ;bx has err status/count
                 push cx                  ;cx has count to move
;
                 mov bx,offset rx_curcnt  ;addr curr cnt to bx
                 mov si,rx_off_urdbuf     ;set nxt read addr
;
nxt_char_put:    dec si                   ;dec buff addr
                 cmp si,(offset ib_rx)-1  ;chk buff bgn ovrn
                 jnz chk_ch               ;chk for char mov
                 add si,MAXCHAR           ;incr to buff end
;
chk_ch:          cmp byte ptr rx_flag,ONE ;is char get?
                 je mov_al                ;yes, mov char fm al
                 mov al,es:[di]           ;no, data to al, not mov
;
mov_al:          mov [si],al              ;data to internal buff
                 dec di                   ;dec data addr
;
                 mov rx_off_urdbuf,si     ;set nxt read addr
                 inc word ptr [bx]        ;inc buff curr count
                 dec word ptr rx_remcnt   ;dec avail cnt
```

```
                      loop nxt_char_put
        ;
                      pop cx                        ;get count moved
                      pop ax                        ;get errcodes/stat
                      mov dx,[bx]               ;new cnt avail in buff
                      jmp short exit_ug
        ;
        exit_uochar:  xor ax,ax                     ;errcodes = 0
                      push ax
                      push ax
                      pop dx                     ;# avail = 0
                      pop cx                     ;# returned = 0
                      or ah,TIMEOUT             ;set timeout code
        ;
        exit_ug:      ret
        unget_req     endp




        ; MODULE PATH: \ASM232\ISRINIT.ASM
        ;:::::::::::::::::::::::::::::::::::::::::::::::::::::::::::
        ; Routine to initialize SSC channel X using table
        ; formats above (init_a)
        ;
        ; At entry, table a must contain desired values
        ;           dx contains port
        ;           si contains table offset
        ;
        ; At exit,  SCC initialized to values in table init_a.
        ;           si,flags   destroyed
        ;
        i_chan        proc
                      push ax
                      push cx
        ;
            lods byte ptr INIT_1 ;tbl length to al, si points to next
                      xor cx,cx            ;clear cx
                      mov cl,al            ;tbl length to cl
        ;
        iloopa:
            lods byte ptr INIT_1  ;nxt tbl element to al, increment si
                      out dx,al        ;write tbl element to port
                      loop iloopa      ;loop till end of tbl
        ;
                      pop cx
                      pop ax
                      ret
        i_chan        endp

        ;:::::::::::::::::::::::::::::::::::::::::::::::::::::::::::::;;;
```

```
; Routine to get pointer to curr scc_tbl entry
;
; At entry, cur_comprt = desired value (0-n)
;           (assumes 2byte entries in cptbl)
;
;
; At exit,  cur_sccoff = offset in scc_tbl of desired
;                               values, FLAGS destroyed
;
;
get_scc         proc
                push ax
                push bx
;
                xor ax,ax           ;clear ax
                mov al,cur_comprt   ;current 0-n value
                shl ax,1            ;multiply by 2
                mov bx, offset fst_cp ;1st com port offset
                add bx,ax           ;offset in comm port tbl
                mov ax,[bx]         ;offset in scc_tbl
                mov cur_sccoff,ax   ;offset to storage
;
                pop bx
                pop ax
                ret
get_scc         endp
;:::::::::::::::::::::::::::::::::::::::::::::::::::::::::::::::
; Routine to get corresponding time constants from table
; for given baud rate
;
; At entry, ah = 0 (init request)
;           al = init parm per IBM BIOS
;             note: hi nibble of al contains baud bits
;             each supported baud increases from 0 by 2
;               (IBIOS.EQU masks for baud rate requests)
;
;
; At exit,  time counts have been inserted in init_a table
;       (both lo & hi) for baud rate requested by init request.
;       FLAGS destroyed.
;
;
get_tim_cont    proc
;
                push cx
                push bx
                push ax
;
                and ax,BAUD9600     ;isolate baud bits
                mov cl,4            ;baud bits in high nibble
                shr ax,cl           ;move baud bits to lo nibble
;
                mov bx,offset tim_cont ;offset of tbl
                add bx,ax           ;offset in tbl for tim_cont
```

```
                mov ax,[bx]        ;tim constant to ax
        ;
                mov byte ptr lo_time,al   ;set lo time const
                mov byte ptr hi_time,ah   ;set hi time const
        ;
                pop ax
                pop bx
                pop cx
                ret
get_tim_cont    endp
;::::::::::::::::::::::::::::::::::::::::::::::::::::::::::::::::::::
; Routine to get corresponding parity mask
;
; At entry, ah = 0 (init request)
;           al = init parm per IBM BIOS
;       note: hi & lo nibble of al contain parity bits
;
; At exit,  parity mask has been inserted in parity
;           for parity requested by init request.
;           FLAGS destroyed.
;
get_parity      proc
        ;
                push cx
                push ax
        ;
                mov byte ptr parity,WR4INIA1 ;no parity,no stop
                and ax,PAREVEN   ;isolate parity bits
                mov cl,3
        ;
                shr ax,cl    ;parity msk is shifted request bits
                or  byte ptr parity,al    ;add parity to msk
        ;
                pop ax
                pop cx
        ;
                ret
        ;
get_parity      endp
;::::::::::::::::::::::::::::::::::::::::::::::::::::::::::::::::::::;
; Routine to get corresponding stop bit mask
;    (must follow parity routine)
;
; At entry, ah = 0 (init request)
;           al = init parm per IBM BIOS
;                note:  lo nibble of al contain stop bits
;
; At exit,  stop bit mask has been inserted at parity label
; for #stop bits requested by init request. FLAGS destroyed.
;
```

```
get_stop        proc
                push ax
;
                and ax,STOPTWO          ;isolate stop bits
                cmp ax,STOPTWO
                jz two_stop
;
                or  byte ptr parity,WR4MSKS1 ;one stop
                jmp exitgs
;
two_stop:       or  byte ptr parity,WR4MSKS2 ;two stop
;
exitgs:         pop ax
                ret
get_stop        endp
;:::::::::::::::::::::::::::::::::::::::::::::::::::::::::::::::
; Routine to get corresponding #bits/char
;
; At entry, ah = 0 (init request)
;           al = init parm per IBM BIOS
;                note:  lo nibble of al contain # bits
;
; At exit,  # bit/char mask has been inserity in WR3/WR5
;           of init_a tbl for # bits/char requested by init
;           request. flags destroyed.
get_nbits       proc
                push bx
                push ax
;
                and ax,WORD8            ;isolate #bits  bits
                cmp ax,WORD8
                jz bits8
;
                mov ax,WR3IN7A1                 ;7bits/char
                mov bx,WR5IN7A1
                jmp movmsk
;
bits8:
                mov ax,WR3IN8A1                 ;8bits/char
                mov bx,WR5IN8A1
;
movmsk:         mov byte ptr rec_bits,al
                or  ax,WR3MSKER                 ;# bits, enable
                mov byte ptr rx_enabl,al
;
                mov byte ptr xmt_bits,bl
                or  bx,WR5MSKER    ;# bits, enable
                or  bx,WR5MSKED    ;# bits, enable, DTR
                or  bx,WR5MSKRS    ;# bits, enable, DTR, RTS
                mov byte ptr tx_enabl,bl
```

```
                ;
                        pop ax
                        pop bx
                        ret
get_nbits       endp
;::::::::::::::::::::::::::::::::::::::::::::::::::::::::::::;;
; Routine to generate interrupt vector table for servicing
; SCC interrupts (put vectors into RAM at a location between
; 0 - 3ff depending on interrupt type number -- currently
; programmed start vector is FOH).
;
;   At exit: vector table is in RAM
;   FLAGS    destroyed.
;
gen_itbl        proc
                ;
                        push ax
                        push bx
                        push cx
                        push di
                        push es
                ;
                        xor ax,ax               ;ax = 0
                        mov es,ax               ;es = 0
                        mov ax,INT_VECT         ;al = int type number
                ;
                        clc                     ;zro carry flg
                        rcl ax,1                ;rotate left thru carry
                        rcl ax,1                ;multiply by 4
                        mov di,ax               ;vector table addr to di
                ;
                        mov cx,VTBLENG          ;number of entries in tbl
                        mov bx,offset fst_entry
                ;
set_vect:               mov ax,[bx]
                        mov word ptr es:[di],ax  ;offset to vect tbl
                        add di,2                 ; inc to segment
                        add bx,2                 ; inc top nxt entry
                        mov ax,[bx]
                        mov word ptr es:[di],ax  ;seg to vector tbl
                        add di,6                 ;inc to nxt vector
                        add bx,2                 ;inc to nxt entry
                        loop set_vect
                ;
                        pop es
                        pop di
                        pop cx
                        pop bx
                        pop ax
                ;
```

```
            ret
;
gen_itbl        endp
;::::::::::::::::::::::::::::::::::::::::::::::::::::::::::::::::
; Routine to initialize all storage.
;
mostmem_init    proc
                push ax
;   INIT TIME CONST TBL
                mov word ptr tim_cont,WRCMSK00
                mov word ptr tim_cont+2,WRCMSK01
                mov word ptr tim_cont+4,WRCMSK02
                mov word ptr tim_cont+6,WRCMSK03
                mov word ptr tim_cont+8,WRCMSK04
                mov word ptr tim_cont+10,WRCMSK05
                mov word ptr tim_cont+12,WRCMSK06
                mov word ptr tim_cont+14,WRCMSK07
; INIT CHAN A TABLE
                mov byte ptr init_a,ATBLENG
                mov byte ptr init_a+1,WR9
                mov byte ptr init_a+2,WR9INIT1
                mov byte ptr init_a+3,WR4
                mov byte ptr init_a+4,WR4DEFA1
                mov byte ptr init_a+5,WR2
                mov byte ptr init_a+6,WR2INIA1
                mov byte ptr init_a+7,WR3
                mov byte ptr init_a+8,WR3IN8A1
                mov byte ptr init_a+9,WR5
                mov byte ptr init_a+10,WR5IN8A1
                mov byte ptr init_a+11,WR9
                mov byte ptr init_a+12,WR9MSKIS
                mov byte ptr init_a+13,WRA
                mov byte ptr init_a+14,WRAINIA1
                mov byte ptr init_a+15,WRB
                mov byte ptr init_a+16,WRBINIA1
                mov byte ptr init_a+17,WRC
                mov byte ptr init_a+18,WRCMSK07
                mov byte ptr init_a+19,WRD
                mov byte ptr init_a+20,ZRO
                mov byte ptr init_a+21,WRE
                mov byte ptr init_a+22,WREINIA1
                mov byte ptr init_a+23,WRF
                mov byte ptr init_a+24,WRFINIA1
                mov byte ptr init_a+25,WR3
                mov byte ptr init_a+26,WR3DEFA1
                mov byte ptr init_a+27,WR5
                mov byte ptr init_a+28,WR5DEFA1
                mov byte ptr init_a+29,WRE
                mov byte ptr init_a+30,WREINIA2
                mov byte ptr init_a+31,WR0
```

```
                mov byte ptr init_a+32,WROMSKC4
                mov byte ptr init_a+33,WR0
                mov byte ptr init_a+34,WROMSKC6
                mov byte ptr init_a+35,WR0
                mov byte ptr init_a+36,WRORESTX
                mov byte ptr init_a+37,WR1
                mov byte ptr init_a+38,WR1INIA1
;   INIT CHAN B TABLE
;               mov byte ptr init_b,BTBLENG
;               mov byte ptr init_b+1,WR9
;               mov byte ptr init_b+2,WR9INIT1
;               mov byte ptr init_b+3,WR9
;               mov byte ptr init_b+4,WR9INIB1
;               mov byte ptr init_b+5,WR3
;               mov byte ptr init_b+6,ZR0
;               mov byte ptr init_b+7,WR5
;               mov byte ptr init_b+8,ZR0
;               mov byte ptr init_b+9,WRF
;               mov byte ptr init_b+10,WRFINIA1
;               mov byte ptr init_b+11,WR1
;               mov byte ptr init_b+12,WR1INIB1
;   INIT SCC_TBL
                mov word ptr scc_tbl,SCBLENG
                mov word ptr scc_tbl+2,A232CTRL
                mov word ptr scc_tbl+4,A232XMIT
                mov word ptr scc_tbl+6,offset init_a
;   OLD SCC_TBL
;               mov word ptr scc_tbl+2,B422CTRL
;               mov word ptr scc_tbl+4,B422XMIT
;               mov word ptr scc_tbl+6,offset init_b
;               mov word ptr scc_tbl+8,A232CTRL
;               mov word ptr scc_tbl+10,A232XMIT
;               mov word ptr scc_tbl+12,offset init_a
;   INIT VECTOR TABLE
                mov word ptr fst_entry,offset dmmy_b
                mov word ptr fst_entry+2,seg dmmy_b
                mov word ptr fst_entry+4,offset dmmy_b
                mov word ptr fst_entry+6,seg dmmy_b
                mov word ptr fst_entry+8,offset dmmy_b
                mov word ptr fst_entry+10,seg dmmy_b
                mov word ptr fst_entry+12,offset dmmy_b
                mov word ptr fst_entry+14,seg dmmy_b
                mov word ptr fst_entry+16,offset i_a_xmt
                mov word ptr fst_entry+18,seg i_a_xmt
                mov word ptr fst_entry+20,offset dmmy_a
                mov word ptr fst_entry+22,seg dmmy_a
                mov word ptr fst_entry+24,offset i_a_rec
                mov word ptr fst_entry+26,seg i_a_rec
                mov word ptr fst_entry+28,offset isr_sp_a
                mov word ptr fst_entry+30,seg isr_sp_a
```

```
;   COMM PORT TABLE
                mov byte ptr ncom_prt,NCBLENG
                mov word ptr fst_cp,offset scc_2
;
                pop ax
                ret
mostmem_init    endp
;:::::::::::::::::::::::::::::::::::::::::::::::::::::::::::::::::
; Routine to initialize tx memory area.  Nothing destroyed
;
tx_mem_init     proc
                push ax
;
                xor ax,ax               ;clear ax
                mov tx_curcnt,ax
                mov tx_errstat,al
                mov tx_flag1,al
                mov word ptr tx_remcnt,MAXCHAR
                mov word ptr tx_off_curbuf,offset ib_tx
                mov word ptr tx_off_urdbuf,offset ib_tx
;
                pop ax
                ret
tx_mem_init     endp
;:::::::::::::::::::::::::::::::::::::::::::::::::::::::::::::::::;
; Routine to initialize rx memory area. Nothing destroyed.
;
rx_mem_init     proc
                push ax
;
                xor ax,ax               ;clear ax
                mov rx_curcnt,ax
                mov rx_flag,al
                mov rx_flag2,al
                mov rx_errstat,al
                mov rx_errchar,al
                mov word ptr rx_remcnt,MAXCHAR
                mov word ptr rx_off_curbuf,offset ib_rx
                mov word ptr rx_off_urdbuf,offset ib_rx
;
                pop ax
                ret
rx_mem_init     endp
;:::::::::::::::::::::::::::::::::::::::::::::::::::::::::::::::::
; Routine to initialize all storage.
;
mem_init        proc
                call mostmem_init
                call tx_mem_init
                call rx_mem_init
```

```
                        ret
        mem_init        endp
;;;;;;;;;;;;;;;;;;;;;;;;;;;;;;;;;;;;;;;;;;;;;;;;;;;;;;;;;;;;;;;
; Routine to get SCC status
;
; At entry: registers as in ISR request
;                   At exit  ax =  status
;;;;;;;;;;;;;;;;;;;;;;;;;;;;;;;;;;;;;;;;;;;;;;;;;;;;;;;;;;;;;;
        get_stus        proc
;
                        push bx
;
                        cmp byte ptr op_mode,POLLED
                        je is_polled
;
                        mov ah,tx_errstat               ;interrupt mode
                        mov al,rx_errstat
                        mov byte ptr tx_errstat,ZRO
                        mov byte ptr rx_errstat,ZRO
                        mov byte ptr rx_errchar,ZRO
                        jmp short exit_gsx
;
        is_polled:      mov dx,cur_ctrl
                        in  al,dx       ;get RR0 status in al
                        and ax,RR0MASK1 ;zro ah, isolate al bits
                        push ax         ;save RR0 stat in al
                        mov ax,RR1      ; point to RR1
                        out dx,al
                        in  al,dx       ;get RR1 status in al
                        and ax,RR1MSKCL ;err + send all bits
                        pop bx          ;RR0 stat in bx
                        mov ah,al       ;RR1 in ah
                        mov al,bl       ;RR0 in al
;
        exit_gsx:       pop bx
;
                        ret
;
        get_stus        endp
;;;;;;;;;;;;;;;;;;;;;;;;;;;;;;;;;;;;;;;;;;;;;;;;;;;;;;;;;;;;;;;
; Routine to get internal buffer status
;
; At entry: registers as in ISR request
;
;                   At exit:
;                       ax = number of bytes in rx buff
;                       dx = number of bytes in tx buff
;
;;;;;;;;;;;;;;;;;;;;;;;;;;;;;;;;;;;;;;;;;;;;;;;;;;;;;;;;;;;;;;;
        get_bstats      proc
```

```
;
                       mov ax,rx_curcnt         ;al = curr cnt
                       mov dx,tx_curcnt         ;dl = curr cnt
;
                       ret
;
get_bstats       endp
;;;;;;;;;;;;;;;;;;;;;;;;;;;;;;;;;;;;;;;;;;;;;;;;;;;;;;;;;;;;;;
; Routine to change op mode (polled or int driven)
;
; At entry: registers as in ISR request
;                ah = 5
;                al = mode (0,1)
;                dx = port (0,n)
; At exit:   mode selected,scc parm in storage
;
;;;;;;;;;;;;;;;;;;;;;;;;;;;;;;;;;;;;;;;;;;;;;;;;;;;;;;;;;;;;;
get_om           proc
;
                       cmp al,ZRO
                       je mov_mode
                       cmp al,ONE
                       je mov_mode
                       jmp short exit_gom
;                                            ;yes,force hdwr init
mov_mode:              mov op_mode,al
                       call mem_init        ;memory init
                       call getscc_parm     ;init scc parm
                       call gen_itbl        ;generate int table
                       mov dx,cur_ctrl      ;ctrl port addr for chan
                       mov si,cur_init      ;init tbl offset for chan
                       call i_chan          ;init this channel
                       call flush_rx        ;flush rx port
;
exit_gom:              ret
;
get_om           endp
;;;;;;;;;;;;;;;;;;;;;;;;;;;;;;;;;;;;;;;;;;;;;;;;;;;;;;;;;;;;;
; Routine to get SCC parm
;
; At entry: dx = currnt port (0-n)
;
;                    At exit:  parm in storage
;
;;;;;;;;;;;;;;;;;;;;;;;;;;;;;;;;;;;;;;;;;;;;;;;;;;;;;;;;;;;;;
getscc_parm      proc
;
                       push ax
                       push bx
;
```

```
                mov al,ncom_prt         ;num of ports in table
                dec al                  ;max offset in table
                cmp dl,al
                jg use_zro              ;if invalid, use zro
                cmp dl,ZRO
                jg use_this             ;if invalid, use zro
;
use_zro:        xor dx,dx
use_this:       mov cur_comprt,dl       ;curr comm port (0,n)
                call get_scc            ;scc offset in scc_tbl
                mov bx,cur_sccoff       ;scc_tbl offset to bx
;
                mov ax,[bx]             ;store table parm
                mov cur_ctrl,ax
                mov ax,[bx+2]
                mov cur_xmit,ax
                mov cur_recv,ax
                mov ax,[bx+4]
                mov cur_init,ax
;
                pop bx
                pop ax
                ret
;
getscc_parm     endp
;;;;;;;;;;;;;;;;;;;;;;;;;;;;;;;;;;;;;;;;;;;;;;;;;;;;;;;;;;;;;;;;
; Routine to initialize SCC
;
; At entry: registers as in ISR request
;
;                   At exit:  init completed, dx destroyed
;
;;;;;;;;;;;;;;;;;;;;;;;;;;;;;;;;;;;;;;;;;;;;;;;;;;;;;;;;;;;;;;;;
init_main       proc
;
                push ax
;
        cmp byte ptr op_mode,INT_DR     ;interrupt driven?
        je nxt_stp                      ;yes,keep going
        mov byte ptr op_mode,POLLED     ;no, use polled
;
nxt_stp: call mem_init                  ;memory init
        call getscc_parm                ;get ctrl port,etc
        call get_parity                 ;get parity to tbl
        call get_tim_cont               ;get tim const to tbl
        call get_stop                   ;get stop bits to tbl
        call get_nbits                  ;get #bits/ch to tbl
        call gen_itbl                   ;put interrupts in ram
        mov dx,cur_ctrl                 ;ctrl port addr, chan
        mov si,cur_init                 ;init tbl offset, chan
```

```
            call i_chan                    ;init this channel
            call flush_rx                  ;flush rx port
;
            cmp byte ptr op_mode,POLLED
            jz exit_imx
            mov ax,WR9MSKIE   ;enable interrupts, int mode
            call mast_en
;
exit_imx:       pop ax
;
                ret
;
init_main       endp



; MODULE PATH \ASM232\ISRMIS1.ASM
;;;;;;;;;;;;;;;;;;;;;;;;;;;;;;;;;;;;;;;;;;;;;;;;;;;;;;;;;;;;;;;;
; Routine to wait for tx buffer empty
;
; At entry:   cur_stat contains current status  port addr
; At exit :   transmitter empty, flags destroyed
;
tx_empty        proc
;
                push ax
                push dx
;
                mov dx,cur_ctrl    ;curr ctrl register
tx_not_mt:      in al,dx           ;RR0 read
                and al,TXBUFEMT    ;isolate tx buff empty bits
                cmp al,TXBUFEMT    ;tx buffer empty?
                jnz tx_not_mt      ;no, not empty yet
;
                pop dx
                pop ax
                ret
;
tx_empty        endp
;;;;;;;;;;;;;;;;;;;;;;;;;;;;;;;;;;;;;;;;;;;;;;;;;;;;;;
; Routine to check the space in the tx buffer.
;
chk_tx_space       proc
                   mov byte ptr tx_flag1,ZRO
                   cmp cx,tx_remcnt
                   jle  exit_cts
                   mov byte ptr tx_flag1,ONE
exit_cts:       ret
chk_tx_space    endp
;
```

```
;;;;;;;;;;;;;;;;;;;;;;;;;;;;;;;;;;;;;;;;;;;;;;;;;;;;;;;;;;;;;;
; Routine to move a blk of TX data to the internal buffer
; from the user pgm.
;
; At entry:  cx = number of bytes to move
;            es:si = address of first byte to move (user pgm)
;                di = destination offset (internal buff)
;
; At exit :
;            data moved if all ok
;            tx_curcnt is incremented
;            tx_remcnt is decremented
;            tx_off_urdbuf is updated
;
move_data       proc
;
                push cx                ;save count
                cmp cx,ONE             ;char tx?
                jz is_c                ;yes, no buff move
;
nxt_move:       mov  al,es:[si]        ;data to internal buffer
is_c:           mov  [di],al           ;data to internal buffer
                inc di                 ;inc addr
                cmp di,offset ib_tx_en    ;buff end?
                jnz new_ptr            ;no
                sub di,MAXCHAR         ;yes,wrap
new_ptr:        mov word ptr tx_off_urdbuf,di ;in cur buf addr
;
                inc si                 ;inc adr
                inc word ptr tx_curcnt ;inc cur cnt
                dec word ptr tx_remcnt ;dec rem cnt
                loop nxt_move          ;move nxt byte
;
                pop cx
                ret
;
move_data       endp
;;;;;;;;;;;;;;;;;;;;;;;;;;;;;;;;;;;;;;;;;;;;;;;;;;;;;;;;;;;;;;
; Routine to transmit a block of data.
; Number of bytes and addr of data are placed in storage.
; First byte is sent (thereafter, transmitter interrupt
; will send additional bytes and increment count). After
; last byte is sent, transmitter interrupt is reset,
; and tx_errstat contains completion code.
;
; At entry:  cx = number of bytes to be sent
;            es:si = address of first byte to send
;
; At exit :  Data has been moved to the internal
; buffer/tx underway.
```

```
;
xmt_asyc        proc
;
     push bx
     push di
;
     cmp word ptr tx_curcnt,ZRO  ;current buffer count
     jne no_wait_tx              ;no, continue
;
     call tx_empty           ;yes, cnt = 0,wait for tx empty
;
no_wait_tx:
     call chk_tx_space           ;cnt > 0, enough buff space?
     cmp tx_flag1,ZRO            ;enough buff space?
     jne not_enough             ;no, not enough
;
     mov di,tx_off_urdbuf       ;set up for move
     call move_data             ;move data to internal
;
     push ax                    ;save registers
     push dx
     mov dx,cur_ctrl            ;set ctrl reg
     mov ax,RR3                 ;point to RR3
     out dx,al                  ;point to RR3
     in al,dx                   ;get RR3 status
     and al,TXIPBIT             ;isolate Tx int pending bit
     cmp al,TXIPBIT             ;is interrupt pending ?
     pop dx                     ;restore registers
     pop ax
     je exit_xa                 ;int is pending, exit
     cmp word ptr tx_curcnt,ZRO ;int not pending, is cnt 0?
     je exit_xa                 ;cnt is zero, exit
     jmp short start_int        ;no IP, cnt > 0, start int
;
not_enough:    or tx_errstat,IBUFOVRN
               jmp short exit_xa
;
start_int:     push ds
               pop es
               mov di,offset tx_curcnt
               mov si,offset tx_off_curbuf
               mov bx,offset tx_remcnt
               call xmt_char
;
exit_xa:       xor ax,ax
               or ah,tx_errstat
               pop di
               pop bx
               ret
;
```

```
        xmt_asyc        endp
;;;;;;;;;;;;;;;;;;;;;;;;;;;;;;;;;;;;;;;;;;;;;;;;;;;;;;;;;;;;;;
; This routine writes wr1 to disable/enable the receiver.
; interrupt.
;
; At entry:  ax = code
;                 (WR9INIMSKIE enables, WR9MSKIS disables)
;
; At exit :  WR9 is written with the code contained in ax
;            flags destroyed
mast_en         proc
;
                push ax
                push dx
;
                push ax
;
                mov dx,cur_ctrl         ;addr current ctrl port
                mov al,WR9              ;writ register 9
                out dx,al               ;point to WR9
                pop ax                  ;code to dis/enable rx/tx
                out dx,al               ;dis/enable interrupts
;
                pop dx
                pop ax
                ret
;
mast_en         endp
;;;;;;;;;;;;;;;;;;;;;;;;;;;;;;;;;;;;;;;;;;;;;;;;;;;;;;;;;
; This routine flushes the receiver data port.
;
; At entry:  NA
;
; At exit :  rx data port has been read 4 times ,
;   flags destroyed
;
flush_rx        proc
;
                push ax
                push dx
                push cx
;
                mov cx,4
                mov dx,cur_recv         ;addr current ctrl port
flush_agn:      in al,dx                ;read data port
                loop flush_agn          ;loop agin
;
                pop cx
                pop dx
                pop ax
```

```
            ret
;
flush_rx        endp
;
;;;;;;;;;;;;;;;;;;;;;;;;;;;;;;;;;;;;;;;;;;;;;;;;;;;;;;;;;;;;;
; This routine resets err in WRO and resets highest IUS.
;
; At entry:  none
;
; At exit :  WRO has been written for err reset
;            WRO has been written for rest highest IUS
;            flags destroyed
;
err_reset       proc
;
                push ax
                push dx
;
                mov dx,cur_ctrl         ;addr current ctrl port
                mov al,WROMSKC6         ;error reset
                out dx,al              ;reset err
                call reset_ius         ;reset highest ius
;
                pop dx
                pop ax
                ret
;
err_reset       endp


; MODULE PATH: \ASM232\ISRTXRX.ASM
;:::::::::::::::::::::::::::::::::::::::::::::::::::::::::::::::
;Routine to tx a character (used by transmitter interrupts)
;
;   At entry: si = points to offset of nxt char to be sent
;             es = segment of buffer with next char to send
;             di = offset num char remaining to send
;             bx = offset num char allowed in buff
;
;   At exit: char count, nxt char adjusted
;            ax,dx,di,flags destroyed
;:::::::::::::::::::::::::::::::::::::::::::::::::::::::::::::::
xmt_char        proc
;
        xor ax,ax                      ;zero to ax
        cmp ax,[di]                    ;last char?
        jz was_last                    ;yes it was last
        dec word ptr [di]              ;decrement count (not last)
        inc word ptr [bx]              ;increment count (allowed)
```

```
;
        mov ax,offset ib_tx_en          ;last addr +1
        dec ax                          ;last addr
        mov di,[si]                     ;offset of data to di
        inc word ptr [si]               ;inc data addr
        cmp di,ax                       ;last addr?
        jnz new_point                   ;no, not last addr
        sub word ptr [si],MAXCHAR       ;yes, wrap buffer
new_point:
        inc ax                          ;inc to last addr +1
        cmp di,ax                       ;addr exceeded?
        jb movd                         ;no, not exceeded
        sub di,MAXCHAR                  ;yes, fix addr
movd:   mov al,es:[di]                   ;data to al
;
        call send_1_char                ;xmit data/ret stat, ah
        or tx_errstat,ah                ;data out
        jmp short exit_xc               ;exit
;
was_last:
        mov dx,cur_ctrl                 ;control port addr
        mov ax,WROMSKC5                 ;reset tx int pending
        out dx,al                       ;reset
;
exit_xc:        ret
;
xmt_char        endp
```

Appendix H

Diskette Organization

Chapter/ Appendix	Diskette Path	Description
2	\TEXT\PORTS1.C	Memory-mapped port I/O routines
2	\TEXT\PORTS2.C	Intel-specific I/O routines
2	\TEXT\PORTS3.C	16-bit I/O routines
2	\TEXT\PORTS4.C	Higher-level multitasking I/O
2	\TEXT\PORTS5.C	16-bit Multitasking read routine
2	\TEXT\PORTS6.C	16-Bit read with port validation
2	\TEXT\PORT7.C	Port data tables and flags
3	\TEXT\INTELSU.ASM	Intel start-up example
3	\TEXT\MOTOSU.ASM	Motorola start-up example
4	\TEXT\ISRSHLL.ASM	Intel ISR shell example
4	\TEXT\IDMMY.C	Motorola dummy ISR example
4	\TEXT\TIMR.ASM	Hypothetical timer routines
A	\CP\NEWDAT.H	Redefined data types
A	\CP\CP.H	Control panel header
A	\CP\CPDAT.C	Control panel data tables
A	\CP\IO.C	Control panel port I/O C routines
A	\CP\CP.C	CP C processing routines
A	\CP\CPMAIN.C	Module for compiling CP code
B	\CPTEST\CPSIM.C	Main routine for CP simulator
B	\CPTEST\CPTIO.C	C I/O routines for simulator
B	\CPTEST\CPTMAIN.C	For compiling CP simulator code
B	\CPTEST\TESTCP.EXE	Executable for CP simulator
C	\X1553\ADAPTER.H	1553 adapter header
C	\X1553\ADPTABLS.H	1553 adapter table definitions
C	\X1553\MSGTBLS.H	1553 message table definitions
C	\X1553\ADPTROM.C	1553 adapter data tables
C	\X1553\ADPTINIT.C	1553 adapter initialization in C
C	\X1553\TEST.C	1553 adapter self-tests in C

Chapter/Appendix	Diskette Path	Description
C	\X1553\SNDBLOCK.C	1553 block message send in C
C	\X1553\TESTMAIN.C	Module for compiling adapter code
D	\MTA\M1553.H	1553 message header
D	\MTA\ADR1553.H	1553 address definitions
D	\MTA\ADPTDEFS.C	1553 adapter defined in tables
D	\MTA\M1553DAT.C	1553 messages defined in tables
D	\MTA\INTERRPT.C	32Hz ISR for example
D	\MTA\ISREOM.C	EOM ISR for 1553 adapter
D	\MTA\CMDMAIN.C	Module for compiling example
F	\RS232\SCC.H	8530 SCC header
F	\RS232\SFTSCC.H	8530 SCC implementation header
F	\RS232\JFBIXX.H	Miscellaneous header
F	\RS232\SFCNSDEC.H	Miscellaneous function declarations
F	\RS232\INTERFCN.H	API function declarations
F	\RS232\RXFLAGS.H	Miscellaneous communications flags
F	\RS232\ONESHOT.H	Header for one-shot timer
F	\RS232\COMMPRM.H	Communication parameter header
F	\RS232\ONESHOT.C	One-shot timer C routines
F	\RS232\COMMDAT.C	Communications data tables
F	\RS232\SCCINIT.C	SCC initialization routines
F	\RS232\HDWISR.C	Routines shared by Hardware ISRs
F	\RS232\INTERSFT.C	Routines shared by Software ISRs
F	\RS232\ISRSFT.C	Software ISR interface to hardware
F	\RS232\SFTISR.C	Software ISR routines
F	\RS232\ISRSP.C	Special receive ISRs for hardware
F	\RS232\ISREX.C	External/status ISRs for hardware
F	\RS232\ISRTX.C	Hardware transmitter ISRs
F	\RS232\ISRRX.C	Hardware receiver ISRs
F	\RS232\CTSK.LNK	Link file for MAKE use
F	\RS232\CTSK.MAK	MAKE file for MSC 5.1
G	\ASM232\IMHDR.ASM	Main documentation header
G	\ASM232\ISRHDR.ASM	ISR documentation header
G	\ASM232\IMAIN.ASM	Main processing routines
G	\ASM232\ISRMAIN.ASM	Main ISR processing routines
G	\ASM232\ISRINIT.ASM	SCC init routines
G	\ASM232\ISRMIS1.ASM	Miscellaneous ISR routines
G	\ASM232\ISRRXTX.ASM	ISR transmit/receive routines
G	\ASM232\DATASEG.ASM	Communications data structures
G	\ASM232\EQU7863.ASM	Equates for 7863 board
G	\ASM232\EQUBIOS.ASM	Equates for BIOS compatibility
G	\ASM232\7863.DOC	Additional user documentation

INDEX